내신
중학영어듣기 2
모의고사 20회

DARAKWON

저자 약력

서재교 EBS 수능변형문제 시리즈(모자이크), 맨처음 수능영어 독해모의고사(다락원) 외 집필
현) 대전 스카이피아 원장, 모자이크 EBS 변형문제 출제위원

이소영 EBS 변형문제(모자이크), 천기누설 EBS 고난도 변형문제(비투비) 외 집필
De La Salle University 교육 심리학과 졸

이연홍 맨처음 수능영어 독해모의고사(다락원), EBS 우수문항 고난도 변형문제(모자이크) 외 집필
현) 창원 명장학원 원장, 모자이크 EBS 변형문제 출제위원
경북대 졸

김소원 체크체크(천재교육), EBS 변형문제(모자이크) 외 집필

이건희 맨처음 수능영어[기본·완성·실력·독해모의고사], 내공[영문법·구문·단어·듣기](다락원)
체크체크, 싱크로드, 열공(천재교육), Grammar In(비상), EBS 변형문제(모자이크) 외 집필
인스타그램 http://instagram.com/gunee27

내공 **중학영어듣기 ②**
모의고사 20회

지은이 서재교, 이소영, 이연홍, 김소원, 이건희
펴낸이 정규도
펴낸곳 (주)다락원

초판 1쇄 발행 2019년 9월 30일
초판 6쇄 발행 2023년 10월 20일

편집 정지인, 서민정, 이동호
디자인 윤지영, 박선영, 엘림
삽화 양현숙
영문 감수 Michael A. Putlack

다락원 경기도 파주시 문발로 211
내용문의 (02)736-2031 내선 501
구입문의 (02)736-2031 내선 250~252
Fax (02)732-2037
출판등록 1977년 9월 16일 제 406-2008-000007호

ISBN 978-89-277-0852-0 54740
     978-89-277-0850-6 54740 (set)

http://www.darakwon.co.kr
다락원 홈페이지를 방문하시면 상세한 출판 정보와 함께 동영상
강좌, MP3 자료 등 다양한 어학 정보를 얻으실 수 있습니다.

내공
중학영어듣기 ②
모의고사 20회

DARAKWON

Structures & Features
이 책의 구성과 특징

실전 모의고사 20회

최근 시·도 교육청 영어듣기능력평가를 분석·반영하여 실전에 대비할 수 있도록
구성하였습니다. 실제 시험과 유사한 모의고사를 20회 풀어보게 하였으며, 매회
영국식 발음을 5문항씩 제공하여 다양한 발음에 노출되도록 합니다.

Listen and Check

모의고사를 다시 한 번 들은 후 들은
내용을 한 번 더 확인해 봅니다.

Dictation Test

모의고사 전 지문의 받아쓰기를 통해 다시 한번 내용을 확인하고 중요 표현들과 연음을 학습할 수 있습니다. 발음과 표현 팁을 통해 심층 학습을 할 수 있습니다.

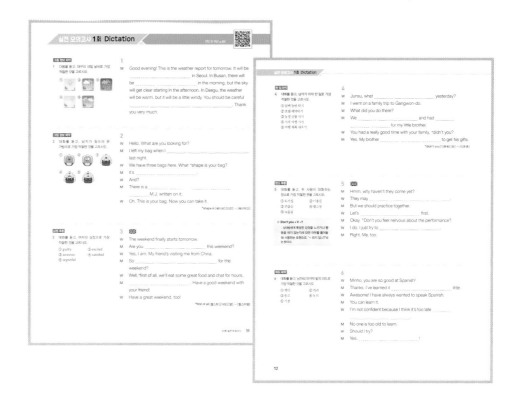

Vocabulary Test

모의고사에 나온 단어를 듣고 영어 단어와 한글 뜻을 같이 써 보면서 어휘를 학습합니다. 또한, 모의고사에 나온 문장들을 다시 듣고 빈칸을 채우며 중요 표현을 복습합니다.

온라인 부가 자료 제공

www.darakwon.co.kr

미국식 발음 100%로 녹음된 파일과 영국식 발음 100%로 녹음된 파일 2종 MP3 파일을 제공합니다. 또한, 0.8배속/1.0배속/1.2배속 MP3 파일을 제공하여 실력에 따라 듣기 속도를 다르게 하여 학습할 수 있습니다.

모의고사에 나온 단어와 표현을 정리한 휴대용 미니 암기장으로 언제 어디서든 학습이 가능합니다.

Contents

목차

실전 모의고사 1회 8

실전 모의고사 2회 18

실전 모의고사 3회 28

실전 모의고사 4회 38

실전 모의고사 5회 48

실전 모의고사 6회 58

실전 모의고사 7회 68

실전 모의고사 8회 78

실전 모의고사 9회 88

실전 모의고사 10회 98

실전 모의고사 11회 108

실전 모의고사 12회 118

실전 모의고사 13회 128

실전 모의고사 14회 138

실전 모의고사 15회 148

실전 모의고사 16회 158

실전 모의고사 17회 168

실전 모의고사 18회 178

실전 모의고사 19회 188

실전 모의고사 20회 198

Vocabulary Test 210

실전 모의고사

1 다음을 듣고, 대구의 내일 날씨로 가장 적절한 것을 고르시오.

①   ②   ③

④   ⑤

2 대화를 듣고, 남자가 찾으러 온 가방으로 가장 적절한 것을 고르시오.

①   ②   ③

④   ⑤

3 대화를 듣고, 여자의 심정으로 가장 적절한 것을 고르시오.
① guilty ② excited ③ anxious
④ satisfied ⑤ regretful

4 대화를 듣고, 남자가 어제 한 일로 가장 적절한 것을 고르시오.
① 암벽 등반 하기 ② 호텔 예약하기
③ 동생 선물 사기 ④ 가족 여행 가기
⑤ 여행 계획 세우기

5 대화를 듣고, 두 사람이 대화하는 장소로 가장 적절한 곳을 고르시오.
① 독서실 ② 미용실 ③ 연습실
④ 헬스장 ⑤ 녹음실

6 대화를 듣고, 남자의 마지막 말의 의도로 가장 적절한 것을 고르시오.
① 제안 ② 격려 ③ 충고
④ 동의 ⑤ 거절

7 대화를 듣고, 여자가 가지려고 하는 취미 활동을 고르시오.
① 독서하기 ② 운동하기
③ 요리하기 ④ 옷 만들기
⑤ 사진 찍기

8 대화를 듣고, 여자가 대화 직후에 할 일로 가장 적절한 것을 고르시오.
① 운전하기 ② 전화하기
③ 점심 먹기 ④ 목적지 정하기
⑤ 인터넷 검색하기

9 대화를 듣고, 남자가 관람한 연극에 대해 언급하지 않은 것을 고르시오.
① 배우의 특징 ② 연극의 장르
③ 연극의 주제 ④ 관람한 장소
⑤ 연극에 대한 소감

10 대화를 듣고, 여자가 하는 말의 내용으로 가장 적절한 것을 고르시오.
① 경영 세미나 ② 행사 유의 사항
③ 교우 관계 문제점 ④ 스포츠 경기 홍보
⑤ 이상적인 회사 생활

11 대화를 듣고, 토론 클럽에 대한 내용으로 일치하지 않는 것을 고르시오.
① 멤버는 총 8명이다.
② 많은 노력이 필요하다.
③ 멤버들은 함께 공부해야만 한다.
④ 두 개의 팀으로 나누어 진행된다.
⑤ 주제에 관해 자세히 공부해야 한다.

12 대화를 듣고, 여자가 아르바이트를 하는 목적으로 가장 적절한 것을 고르시오.
① 친구를 도와주기 위해서
② 월세를 지불하기 위해서
③ 부모님 선물을 사기 위해서
④ 해외로 여행을 떠나기 위해서
⑤ 가지고 싶은 물건을 사기 위해서

13 대화를 듣고, 여자가 지불해야 할 금액으로 가장 적절한 것을 고르시오.
① $12　　　② $13　　　③ $14
④ $15　　　⑤ $16

14 대화를 듣고, 두 사람의 관계로 가장 적절한 것을 고르시오.
① 점원 — 손님
② 부모 — 자식
③ 상담사 — 고객
④ 선생님 — 학생
⑤ 심사위원 — 참가자

15 대화를 듣고, 남자가 여자에게 요청한 일로 가장 적절한 것을 고르시오.
① 필기해 주기
② 병문안 가기
③ 공책 빌려주기
④ 물건 돌려주기
⑤ 학교 공지 알려 주기

16 대화를 듣고, 남자가 친구 집에 가지 못한 이유로 가장 적절한 것을 고르시오.
① 휴대폰이 꺼져서
② 강아지가 아파서
③ 잠이 들어버려서
④ 가고 싶지 않아서
⑤ 약속을 깜빡 잊어서

17 다음 그림의 상황에 가장 적절한 대화를 고르시오.

① ② ③ ④ ⑤

18 대화를 듣고, 남자가 실험에 관해 언급하지 않은 것을 고르시오.
① 실험 대상
② 실험 기간
③ 실험 장소
④ 식물의 원산지
⑤ 기대되는 실험 결과

[19–20] 대화를 듣고, 여자의 마지막 말에 이어질 남자의 말로 가장 적절한 것을 고르시오.

19 Man: _____
① It will be easy for us.
② Sure, I can do that for you.
③ You should tell me the truth.
④ Drawing is not as fun as painting.
⑤ I suggest you wake up much earlier.

20 Man: _____
① We need to go there during lunch break.
② It is the plain waffle with ice cream on it.
③ Well, we shouldn't go to that coffee shop.
④ I like it here because the decorations are nice.
⑤ I recommend you try the vanilla latte the next time.

Listen and Check

● 대화를 다시 듣고, 알맞은 것을 고르시오.

1 It will be bright and sunny in Busan.
☐ True ☐ False

2 Where did the man leave his bag?
☐ bus ☐ subway

3 Does the woman have plans for the weekend?
☐ Yes ☐ No

4 How long did the man go on a trip?
☐ one day ☐ two days

5 The man and the woman are practicing for the performance.
☐ True ☐ False

6 What does the woman want to do?
☐ go to Spain ☐ learn Spanish

7 Does the man know what the woman likes to do?
☐ Yes ☐ No

8 The man and the woman decided to have dinner at an Italian restaurant.
☐ True ☐ False

9 What is the play the man watched about?
☐ friendship ☐ love

10 How many rules did the woman mention?
☐ three ☐ four

11 Should participants study a topic before they have a debate?
☐ Yes ☐ No

12 The woman saves money to go abroad for vacation.
☐ True ☐ False

13 Is one postcard more expensive than one sticker set?
☐ Yes ☐ No

14 Where did the man memorize the words?
☐ at home ☐ at school

15 The woman readily lent her notebooks to the man.
☐ True ☐ False

16 Did the man and the woman promise to meet yesterday?
☐ Yes ☐ No

17 The woman can buy the cake.
☐ True ☐ False

18 When can the man know the results of his experiment?
☐ in three weeks ☐ in three months

19 Will the man drive the woman to class?
☐ Yes ☐ No

20 It's the first time the man goes to the café.
☐ True ☐ False

그림 정보 파악

1 다음을 듣고, 대구의 내일 날씨로 가장 적절한 것을 고르시오.

① ② ③
④ ⑤

1

M Good evening! This is the weather report for tomorrow. It will be _____ _____ _____ in Seoul. In Busan, there will be _____ _____ _____ in the morning, but the sky will get clear starting in the afternoon. In Daegu, the weather will be warm, but it will be a little windy. You should be careful _____ _____ _____ _____ _____. Thank you very much.

그림 정보 파악

2 대화를 듣고, 남자가 찾으러 온 가방으로 가장 적절한 것을 고르시오.

① ② ③
④ ⑤

2

W Hello. What are you looking for?

M I left my bag when I _____ _____ _____ last night.

W We have three bags here. What *shape is your bag?

M It's _____ _____ _____.

W And?

M There is a _____ _____ _____ _____ _____ M.J. written on it.

W Oh. This is your bag. Now you can take it.

*shape is [쉐이프] [이즈] → [쉐이피즈]

심정 추론

3 대화를 듣고, 여자의 심정으로 가장 적절한 것을 고르시오.

① guilty ② excited
③ anxious ④ satisfied
⑤ regretful

3

W The weekend finally starts tomorrow.

M Are you _____ _____ _____ this weekend?

W Yes, I am. My friend's visiting me from China.

M So _____ _____ _____ _____ for the weekend?

W Well, *first of all, we'll eat some great food and chat for hours.

M _____ _____ _____. Have a good weekend with your friend!

W Have a great weekend, too!

*first of all [펄스트] [어브] [얼] → [펄스터벌]

한 일 파악

4 대화를 듣고, 남자가 어제 한 일로 가장
적절한 것을 고르시오.

① 암벽 등반 하기
② 호텔 예약하기
③ 동생 선물 사기
④ 가족 여행 가기
⑤ 여행 계획 세우기

4

W Junsu, what _____ _____ _____ yesterday?

M I went on a family trip to Gangwon-do.

W What did you do there?

M We _____ _____ _____ and had _____
_____ _____ for my little brother.

W You had a really good time with your family, didn't you?

M Yes. My brother _____ _____ _____ to get his gifts.

장소 추론

5 대화를 듣고, 두 사람이 대화하는
장소로 가장 적절한 곳을 고르시오.

① 독서실   ② 미용실
③ 연습실   ④ 헬스장
⑤ 녹음실

🖤 **Don't you + V ~?**
: 상대방에게 특정한 감정을 느끼거나 행
동을 하지 않는지에 대한 여부를 물어볼
때 사용하는 표현으로, '~ 하지 않니?'라
는 뜻이다.

5

M Hmm, why haven't they come yet?

W They may _____ _____ _____ _____.

M But we should practice together.

W Let's _____ _____ _____ first.

M Okay. ♡Don't you feel nervous about the performance?

W I do. I just try to _____ _____ _____.

M Right. Me, too.

의도 파악

6 대화를 듣고, 남자의 마지막 말의 의도로
가장 적절한 것을 고르시오.

① 제안   ② 격려
③ 충고   ④ 동의
⑤ 거절

6

W Minho, you are so good at Spanish!

M Thanks. I've learned it _____ _____ _____ little.

W Awesome! I have always wanted to speak Spanish.

M You can learn it.

W I'm not confident because I think it's too late _____
_____ _____ _____.

M No one is too old to learn.

W Should I try?

M Yes. _____ _____ _____!

특정 정보 파악

7 대화를 듣고, 여자가 가지려고 하는 취미 활동을 고르시오.

① 독서하기
② 운동하기
③ 요리하기
④ 옷 만들기
⑤ 사진 찍기

7

W   Do you _____ _____ _____?

M   I do. I like playing football.

W   I see. What hobby do you think is _____ _____ _____?

M   Well, you like _____ _____, don't you?

W   That's right.

M   Then _____ _____ sewing clothes?

W   Sounds interesting! I'll try that.

할 일 파악

8 대화를 듣고, 여자가 대화 직후에 할 일로 가장 적절한 것을 고르시오.

① 운전하기
② 진화하기
③ 점심 먹기
④ 목적지 정하기
⑤ 인터넷 검색하기

8

M   It will be lunchtime soon. I'm hungry.

W   Is there _____ _____ _____ to eat?

M   Why don't we go to _____ _____ _____?

W   Is there a place you know?

M   It's easy to search *for a place _____ _____ _____.

W   Let me _____ _____ _____ _____.

*for a [폴] [어] → [포러]

언급 유무 파악

9 대화를 듣고, 남자가 관람한 연극에 대해 언급하지 <u>않은</u> 것을 고르시오.

① 배우의 특징
② 연극의 장르
③ 연극의 주제
④ 관람한 장소
⑤ 연극에 대한 소감

9

M   The play I saw yesterday was really touching.

W   What was the genre?

M   It was a drama. It was about the love _____ _____ _____ _____.

W   Were the actor and actress actually that old?

M   Yes, they were. It made me _____ _____ _____ the play.

W   Maybe I should _____ _____ _____.

화제·주제 파악

10 대화를 듣고, 여자가 하는 말의
내용으로 가장 적절한 것을 고르시오.

① 경영 세미나
② 행사 유의 사항
③ 교우 관계 문제점
④ 스포츠 경기 홍보
⑤ 이상적인 회사 생활

♥ **Pay attention, please.**

: 사람들에게 집중해 줄 것을 부탁할 때
사용하는 표현으로, '주목해 주세요.'라는
뜻이다. 'please'는 정중히 말할 때 덧붙
여 쓰지만, 그렇지 않을 때에는 빼고 사용
하기도 한다.

10

W ♥Pay attention, please. There are _____ _____
_____ for a fun and safe company track meet. First,
you should _____ _____ to the host's instructions.
You should also remember this is a social gathering, not a
competition. Finally, please _____ _____ your area
before you leave. I hope everyone _____ _____
_____ through this event.

내용 불일치 파악

11 대화를 듣고, 토론 클럽에 대한
내용으로 일치하지 <u>않는</u> 것을
고르시오.

① 멤버는 총 8명이다.
② 많은 노력이 필요하다.
③ 멤버들은 함께 공부해야만 한다.
④ 두 개의 팀으로 나누어 진행된다.
⑤ 주제에 관해 자세히 공부해야 한다.

11

M Julia, how is your debate club going on?
W It's _____ _____.
M How do you do it?
W First, we divide eight people into two teams.
M Okay.
W Then, they study a topic and _____ _____ _____
_____ _____.
M That requires _____ _____ _____ _____.
W Yes, it is. But it's worthwhile.

목적 파악

12 대화를 듣고, 여자가 아르바이트를
하는 목적으로 가장 적절한 것을
고르시오.

① 친구를 도와주기 위해서
② 월세를 지불하기 위해서
③ 부모님 선물을 사기 위해서
④ 해외로 여행을 떠나기 위해서
⑤ 가지고 싶은 물건을 사기 위해서

12 🇬🇧

M Stella, you look tired these days.
W I'm _____ _____ _____ _____.
M Why?
W I'm _____ _____ _____ _____ Spain during
summer vacation.
M Oh, really? That sounds cool!
W So I'm _____ _____ _____ _____.
M Don't push yourself too hard.
W I won't.

숫자 정보 파악

13 대화를 듣고, 여자가 지불해야 할 금액으로 가장 적절한 것을 고르시오.

① $12 ② $13
③ $14 ④ $15
⑤ $16

13

W How much is this postcard with the _____ _____?

M One costs four dollars, and a *set of three is ten dollars.

W How about _____ _____ _____?

M _____ _____ _____ _____ is two dollars.

W Then I'll buy one set of postcards and two sticker sets.

M Okay. The total is 14 dollars.

W Can I use a two-dollar _____ _____?

M Sure, you can.

*set of [셋] [어브] → [세더브]

관계 추론

14 대화를 듣고, 두 사람의 관계로 가장 적절한 것을 고르시오.

① 점원 — 손님
② 부모 — 자식
③ 상담사 — 고객
④ 선생님 — 학생
⑤ 심사위원 — 참가자

14

W James, did you memorize all the words?

M I did that _____ _____ _____ at school, Ms. Smith.

W Can I expect _____ _____ _____ this time? The test results will be sent to your parent.

M Oh, no. I'm not so sure about the results.

W You should _____ _____ until you can remember all the meanings.

M I'll _____ _____ _____ on the test.

요청한 일 파악

15 대화를 듣고, 남자가 여자에게 요청한 일로 가장 적절한 것을 고르시오.

① 필기해 주기
② 병문안 가기
③ 공책 빌려주기
④ 물건 돌려주기
⑤ 학교 공지 알려 주기

♥ **by the way**
: 대화의 주제를 전환할 때 사용하는 표현으로, '그건 그렇고~', '그나저나~'라는 뜻이다.
= anyway

15

M Jenny, you came to school yesterday, right?

W Yes. I _____ _____ _____ _____. How do you feel now?

M I got so much better. ♥By the way, did you _____ _____ in class?

W I did. I wrote down everything.

M Then may I _____ _____ _____?

W Sure. Just don't forget to return them.

16 대화를 듣고, 남자가 친구 집에 가지 <u>못한</u> 이유로 가장 적절한 것을 고르시오.

① 휴대폰이 꺼져서
② 강아지가 아파서
③ 잠이 들어버려서
④ 가고 싶지 않아서
⑤ 약속을 깜빡 잊어서

16

W Hey, Jacob. Why _____ _____ _____ yesterday?

M I'm sorry, but I had to _____ _____ _____ to the vet.

W I see. But please _____ _____ _____ even if it's late at night.

M Of course. I will let you know from now on.

W All right. _____ _____ _____ now?

M He looks fine after he took some medicine.

W I'm glad to hear that.

17 다음 그림의 상황에 가장 적절한 대화를 고르시오.

① ② ③ ④ ⑤

17

① W What would you like to drink?
   M I want to drink _____ _____.
② W How do you go to school?
   M I _____ _____ _____.
③ W Excuse me. Do you have this cake?
   M No. Somebody _____ _____ _____ earlier.
④ W Is there a problem?
   M I _____ _____ _____ _____.
⑤ W Do you want it to go, or will you eat here?
   M _____ _____ _____.

18 대화를 듣고, 남자가 실험에 관해 언급하지 <u>않은</u> 것을 고르시오.

① 실험 대상
② 실험 기간
③ 실험 장소
④ 식물의 원산지
⑤ 기대되는 실험 결과

18

W What are you doing for the science fair?

M I'm going to _____ _____ _____ with plants.

W With plants?

M Yes. Some studies show that _____ _____ _____ with positive words from people than ones that people don't talk to.

W That's interesting. Where are you _____ _____ _____ your experiment?

M At my house.

W _____ _____ do you have to watch them?

M Three months will do.

[19~20] 대화를 듣고, 여자의 마지막 말에 이어질 남자의 말로 가장 적절한 것을 고르시오.

19 Man: _____
① It will be easy for us.
② Sure, I can do that for you.
③ You should tell me the truth.
④ Drawing is not as fun as painting.
⑤ I suggest you wake up much earlier.

19

W   Oh, no. I'm late again.

M   _____ _____ _____?

W   For my art class!

M   You can _____ _____ now and go.

W   I should hurry. Can you _____ _____ _____ _____?

M   Sorry, but I have to leave now.

W   Then can you _____ _____ _____ later?

M   Sure, I can do that for you.

20 Man: _____
① We need to go there during lunch break.
② It is the plain waffle with ice cream on it.
③ Well, we shouldn't go to that coffee shop.
④ I like it here because the decorations are nice.
⑤ I recommend you try the vanilla latte the next time.

20 🇬🇧

W   Kevin, _____ _____ _____ to a café later?

M   Okay. Which one shall we go to?

W   How about the one right next to the office?

M   Okay. _____ _____ I frequently go in the morning.

W   Really? Have you tried the desserts there?

M   Yes, _____ _____ _____ _____.

W   Which of them _____ _____ _____?

M   It is the plain waffle with ice cream on it.

1 다음을 듣고, 모레의 날씨로 가장 적절한 것을 고르시오.

①

②

③

④

⑤

2 대화를 듣고, 남자가 구입할 물건으로 가장 적절한 것을 고르시오.

①

②

③

④

⑤

3 대화를 듣고, 남자의 심정으로 가장 적절한 것을 고르시오.
① proud   ② relaxed
③ shocked   ④ interested
⑤ embarrassed

4 대화를 듣고, 여자가 겨울 방학에 한 일로 가장 적절한 것을 고르시오.
① 해외여행   ② 등산하기
③ 스키 타기   ④ 봉사 활동
⑤ 바다 여행

5 대화를 듣고, 두 사람이 대화하는 장소로 가장 적절한 곳을 고르시오.
① 서점   ② 역사 박물관
③ 여행 안내소   ④ 여행사 사무실
⑤ UNESCO 본사

6 대화를 듣고, 남자의 마지막 말의 의도로 가장 적절한 것을 고르시오.
① 사과   ② 비난   ③ 부정
④ 감사   ⑤ 인정

7 대화를 듣고, 여자가 초대하지 않을 사람을 고르시오.
① Roy   ② Jim   ③ Paul
④ Daisy   ⑤ Samuel

8 대화를 듣고, 남자가 대화 직후에 할 일로 가장 적절한 것을 고르시오.
① 길 건너기   ② 버스에서 내리기
③ 자동차 운전하기   ④ 경찰에 신고하기
⑤ 친구에게 전화하기

9 대화를 듣고, 여자가 학교 축제에 관해 언급하지 않은 것을 고르시오.
① 백일장   ② 뮤지컬
③ 무료 음식   ④ 댄스 공연
⑤ 노래 콘테스트

10 다음을 듣고, 남자가 하는 말의 내용으로 가장 적절한 것을 고르시오.
① 시장이 열리는 원리
② 자선 행사의 주의 사항
③ 불우 어린이 돕기 행사
④ 재활용을 하는 이유
⑤ 에너지를 보존하는 방법

11 다음을 듣고, 건강 상담 웹사이트에 대한 내용과 일치하지 않는 것을 고르시오.
① 상담 비용은 무료이다.
② 온라인에 접속해야 한다.
③ 유명한 의사들과 상담이 가능하다.
④ 웹주소는 www.anyhealth.com이다.
⑤ 검색창에 병원 위치를 입력할 수 있다.

12 대화를 듣고, 여자가 전화를 건 목적으로 가장 적절한 것을 고르시오.
① 사고 소식을 알리기 위해서
② 메시지를 받고 싶지 않아서
③ 인원 점검을 확인하기 위해서
④ 가족의 행사를 공지하기 위해서
⑤ 안전사고에 대해 경고하기 위해서

13 대화를 듣고, 두 사람이 만날 시각을 고르시오.
① 9시　　　　　　 ② 9시 30분
③ 10시　　　　　　 ④ 10시 13분
⑤ 10시 30분

14 대화를 듣고, 두 사람의 관계로 가장 적절한 것을 고르시오.
① 상점 주인 — 직원
② 은행 직원 — 고객
③ 우체국 직원 — 고객
④ 비행기 승무원 — 승객
⑤ 관제탑 직원 — 기술자

15 대화를 듣고, 남자가 여자에게 부탁한 일로 가장 적절한 것을 고르시오.
① 숙제를 대신 해주기
② 도서관 자리 맡기
③ 책을 반납하기
④ 도서관에서 책 대출하기
⑤ 식사에 친구를 초대하기

16 대화를 듣고, 여자가 꽃을 산 이유로 가장 적절한 것을 고르시오.
① 친구를 문병하기 위해
② 집 거실을 장식하기 위해
③ 아는 사람을 조문하기 위해
④ 부모님의 개업을 축하하기 위해
⑤ 부모님의 결혼기념일을 축하하기 위해

17 다음 그림의 상황에 가장 적절한 대화를 고르시오.

①　　　 ②　　　 ③　　　 ④　　　 ⑤

18 다음을 듣고, 여자가 Green Papa's에 대해 언급하지 <u>않은</u> 것을 고르시오.
① 음식의 맛
② 친환경 음식
③ 재료의 우수성
④ 재료를 사온 장소
⑤ 유기농 재배의 유무

[19-20] 대화를 듣고, 남자의 마지막 말에 이어질 여자의 말로 가장 적절한 것을 고르시오.

19 Woman: _____
① Thanks for helping me.
② You had better come here.
③ I would say you were right.
④ I was not happy to be here.
⑤ The next time, I will say it to you.

20 Woman: _____
① You can't miss it.
② At the end of the hall.
③ Thanks for advising me.
④ Professor Lee is not in his office.
⑤ You can use my phone anytime.

Listen and Check

정답 및 해설 *p.011*

● 대화를 다시 듣고, 알맞은 것을 고르시오.

1 There will be clear skies tomorrow.
- [ ] True
- [ ] False

2 What did the man buy last week?
- [ ] gloves
- [ ] boots

3 Which middle school is the woman from?
- [ ] Sejong Middle School
- [ ] Wonju Middle School

4 Who is in the picture with the woman?
- [ ] her friends
- [ ] her family

5 Will the man go to Italy in June?
- [ ] Yes
- [ ] No

6 Someone stole the man's wallet but not his money.
- [ ] True
- [ ] False

7 Should Daisy take care of her grandfather?
- [ ] Yes
- [ ] No

8 Where did the man want to go?
- [ ] the mall
- [ ] the street

9 There was a dance contest at the woman's school festival.
- [ ] True
- [ ] False

10 Students should bring money to buy items.
- [ ] True
- [ ] False

11 A person has to pay money to use the services.
- [ ] Yes
- [ ] No

12 Who is Maggie Evans?
- [ ] April's mother
- [ ] April's grandmother

13 The man has been to Tyson's Center before.
- [ ] Yes
- [ ] No

14 The man decided to send the package by plane before he visited the post office.
- [ ] True
- [ ] False

15 The woman will check out a book for the man.
- [ ] True
- [ ] False

16 The woman bought the flowers because of her parents' wedding anniversary.
- [ ] True
- [ ] False

17 The man saw the woman for the first time.
- [ ] True
- [ ] False

18 Can a person order hamburgers at Green Papa's?
- [ ] Yes
- [ ] No

19 The place was beautiful, but the elephants were smaller than the man had expected.
- [ ] Yes
- [ ] No

20 Which floor is Professor Lee's office on?
- [ ] the first floor
- [ ] the third floor

그림 정보 파악

1 다음을 듣고, 모레의 날씨로 가장 적절한 것을 고르시오.

① ② ③

④ ⑤

1

W Hello, everyone. This is Helen Johnson with today's weather report. Yesterday, we had a _____ _____ _____ with blue skies. But it started getting cloudy this morning, and we will have heavy rain _____ _____ _____. These conditions will continue _____ _____ _____. We can expect _____ _____ starting from the day after tomorrow.

그림 정보 파악

2 대화를 듣고, 남자가 구입할 물건으로 가장 적절한 것을 고르시오.

① ② ③

④ ⑤

2

W Hello. What can I do for you?

M I'm looking for _____ _____ to wear in winter.

W How about a pair of boots?

M I _____ _____ _____ _____ last week.

W Then how about a hat or a pair of gloves?

M Good idea. But I am not used to wearing hats. So I will take _____ _____.

W Okay. Let me show some _____ _____ _____ _____ to you. Come this way.

심정 추론

3 대화를 듣고, 남자의 심정으로 가장 적절한 것을 고르시오.

① proud
② relaxed
③ shocked
④ interested
⑤ embarrassed

3

M Hi, Cathy. _____ _____ _____ _____?

W I am sorry. _____ _____ _____ _____?

M Oh, it's me, David, your classmate.

W Excuse me, but I don't know you *at all.

M Really? You are from Sejong Middle School, right?

W No. I am from Wonju Middle School.

M I am so sorry. _____ _____ _____ _____ _____ _____ _____.

*at all [엣] [올] → [에덜]

4 대화를 듣고, 여자가 겨울 방학에 한 일로 가장 적절한 것을 고르시오.

① 해외여행
② 등산하기
③ 스키 타기
④ 봉사 활동
⑤ 바다 여행

4

M Do you know what? I saw your picture on your blog.

W What picture did you see? I posted several pictures _____ _____ _____.

M It was you and your friends on a mountain. You were _____ _____ _____ _____ in the snow.

W I know what picture you are talking about. I went skiing with my friends.

M Oh, _____ _____ _____ _____ _____?

W Yes. I'm a winter lover and enjoy skiing and snowboarding every winter.

5 대화를 듣고, 두 사람이 대화하는 장소로 가장 적절한 곳을 고르시오.

① 서점
② 역사 박물관
③ 여행 안내소
④ 여행사 사무실
⑤ UNESCO 본사

♥ **feel free to + V**
: 어떤 행동을 거리낌 없이 할 때 쓰는 표현이며 '자유롭게 ~하다'는 의미이다.

5

W Good morning. What can I do for you, sir?

M I am planning to tour some Italian cities during my summer vacation.

W All right. We have _____ _____ _____ _____. Please ♥feel free to take a look at our brochure.

M Let me see. I like this UNESCO Heritage package.

W That's _____ _____ _____. Do you _____ _____ _____ _____ _____?

M Yes, please. I'd like to book a vacation for two in July.

6 대화를 듣고, 남자의 마지막 말의 의도로 가장 적절한 것을 고르시오.

① 사과
② 비난
③ 부정
④ 감사
⑤ 인정

6

W Hey, how was your business trip to Europe?

M Oh, it was great. But... _____ _____ _____ in France.

W Oh, I am sorry. So did you go to the police station to report it?

M I did. Luckily, three days later, I _____ _____ _____ _____. But all my money was gone.

W What a pity!

M I know. It was _____ _____ _____.

특정 정보 파악

7 대화를 듣고, 여자가 초대하지 <u>않을</u> 사람을 고르시오.

① Roy
② Jim
③ Paul
④ Daisy
⑤ Samuel

7

W   I wonder *who to invite to my birthday party.
M   In my opinion, Paul and Samuel must come. They are _____ _____ _____.
W   That's right. _____ _____ _____ _____? Daisy?
M   She has to _____ _____ _____ her grandmother.
W   I see. Roy, you're coming, right? _____ _____ _____ _____ your cousin Jim.
M   You got it. He will be happy to hear the news.

*who to [후] [투] → [후루]

할 일 파악

8 대화를 듣고, 남자가 대화 직후에 할 일로 가장 적절한 것을 고르시오.

① 길 건너기
② 버스에서 내리기
③ 자동차 운전하기
④ 경찰에 신고하기
⑤ 친구에게 전화하기

8

M   Excuse me. Does this go to K Mall?
W   No. I think you're _____ _____ _____ _____.
M   Oh, no! What should I do now?
W   You should _____ _____ _____ _____ _____ _____ and cross the street.
M   And then?
W   Get on the bus with the same number going in _____ _____ _____.
M   Thank you.

언급 유무 파악

9 대화를 듣고, 여자가 학교 축제에 관해 언급하지 <u>않은</u> 것을 고르시오.

① 백일장   ② 뮤지컬
③ 무료 음식   ④ 댄스 공연
⑤ 노래 콘테스트

> ♥ **must have p.p.**
> : '~했음에 틀림없다', '반드시 ~했을 것 이다'라는 의미로 현재를 기준으로 과거 의 상태나 행동이 거의 확실함을 나타낼 때 쓰는 표현이다.

9

M   Lisa, _____ _____ _____ _____ told me that your school festival was great.
W   Yes, it was! There were a lot of activities _____ _____ musicals and dance performances. We got a free lunch, too.
M   Sounds great. Were there _____ _____ _____?
W   Yes, there was a singing contest. _____ _____ _____ that my friends were so talented at singing.
M   The festival ♥ must have been exciting.
W   Yeah. You can say that again.

화제 · 주제 파악

10 다음을 듣고, 남자가 하는 말의 내용으로 가장 적절한 것을 고르시오.

① 시장이 열리는 원리
② 자선 행사의 주의 사항
③ 불우 어린이 돕기 행사
④ 재활용을 하는 이유
⑤ 에너지를 보존하는 방법

10

M We are planning to _____ _____ in our community who don't have enough food to eat and _____ _____ _____. That's why our school is having a flea market. Please drop off any items which you don't use anymore at the gym. Other students will be able to buy them. _____ _____ _____ to buy what students give to us. All the money we get from you _____ _____ _____ on children in need.

내용 불일치 파악

11 다음을 듣고, 건강 상담 웹사이트에 대한 내용과 일치하지 <u>않는</u> 것을 고르시오.

① 상담 비용은 무료이다.
② 온라인에 접속해야 한다.
③ 유명한 의사들과 상담이 가능하다.
④ 웹주소는 www.anyhealth.com이다.
⑤ 검색창에 병원 위치를 입력할 수 있다.

11 🇬🇧

W Are you wondering _____ _____ _____ healthy or not? Go online, and you can talk with the most famous doctors in the world. You can meet our doctors online _____ _____ _____. Write down your worries and questions in the search window. The service is free thanks to _____ _____ _____. Just turn on your computer and _____ _____ on our website. The address of our website is www.anyhealth.com.

목적 파악

12 대화를 듣고, 여자가 전화를 건 목적으로 가장 적절한 것을 고르시오.

① 사고 소식을 알리기 위해서
② 메시지를 받고 싶지 않아서
③ 인원 점검을 확인하기 위해서
④ 가족의 행사를 공지하기 위해서
⑤ 안전사고에 대해 경고하기 위해서

12 🇬🇧

M Hello. Dr. Liam's office.

W Hello. _____ _____ _____ _____ April, please?

M She's not in now. Who's calling, please?

W This is her mother, Maggie Evans. Excuse me, but I'm calling because April _____ _____ _____ _____.

M Oh, Mrs. Evans. May I _____ _____ _____?

W Yes, please. Tell her that her grandmother had an accident in the morning.

M I'm sorry to hear that. I'll give her the message when she gets back.

숫자 정보 파악

13 대화를 듣고, 두 사람이 만날 시각을 고르시오.

① 9시
② 9시 30분
③ 10시
④ 10시 13분
⑤ 10시 30분

13

W Do you want to _____ _____ with me this Saturday?

M Sounds great. Where do you want to go?

W I heard Tyson's Center is a nice place to buy clothes and shoes.

M _____ _____ _____ there before, but okay. What time shall we meet?

W How about at nine thirty? The shopping mall opens at ten.

M That's _____ _____ _____ _____. Can we meet thirty minutes after the mall opens?

W Okay. See you then.

관계 추론

14 대화를 듣고, 두 사람의 관계로 가장 적절한 것을 고르시오.

① 상점 주인 — 직원
② 은행 직원 — 고객
③ 우체국 직원 — 고객
④ 비행기 승무원 — 승객
⑤ 관제탑 직원 — 기술자

♥ **depend on ~**
: '~에 의존하다', '~에 달려 있다'라는 의미로 on 뒤에 오는 명사의 중요성을 강조할 때 쓰는 표현이다.

14

M Hello. I'd like to _____ _____ _____ to Korea.

W How would you like to *send it?

M _____ _____ _____ _____. How long will it take to get there by airplane?

W Two days.

M Then airmail, please. How much is it?

W It ♥ depends on the weight of the parcel. _____ _____ _____ _____ _____, please.

M Sure.

*send it [센드] [잇] → [센딧]

부탁한 일 파악

15 대화를 듣고, 남자가 여자에게 부탁한 일로 가장 적절한 것을 고르시오.

① 숙제를 대신 해주기
② 도서관 자리 맡기
③ 책을 반납하기
④ 도서관에서 책 대출하기
⑤ 식사에 친구를 초대하기

15

M Sarah, would you do me a favor?

W Sure. What's up?

M I need to borrow a book at the library to do my homework. But _____ _____ _____ _____ _____.

W What is that?

M I _____ _____ _____ five books from the library. It allows each student to borrow no more than _____ _____ _____ _____ _____.

W Oh, do you want me to check out a book for you?

M Yes. That's what I want you to do.

W Okay, I will.

M I'll treat you to lunch tomorrow. Thank you.

이유 추론

16 대화를 듣고, 여자가 꽃을 산 이유로 가장 적절한 것을 고르시오.

① 친구를 문병하기 위해
② 집 거실을 장식하기 위해
③ 아는 사람을 조문하기 위해
④ 부모님의 개업을 축하하기 위해
⑤ 부모님의 결혼기념일을 축하하기 위해

16 🇬🇧

M Hi, Sophia. What are you carrying?

W Hi, Jacob. I _____ _____ _____ for my parents.

M Wow, they're beautiful! Is it your parents' _____ _____?

W No. In fact, they are opening _____ _____ _____ today. I bought the flowers _____ _____ _____ _____ their new business.

M That's great! Where is the shop?

W It's on Fourth Street. Will you go there with me tomorrow?

M I wish I could, but I am going to a concert.

그림 상황 파악

17 다음 그림의 상황에 가장 적절한 대화를 고르시오.

① ② ③ ④ ⑤

♥ **How have you been?**

: 상대방을 오랜만에 만나 안부가 궁금할 경우 쓰이며 '이제까지 어떻게 지냈어?'의 의미이다. 참고로 'How are you?'도 안부를 물을 수 있지만, 현대 영어에서는 보통 인사 표현으로 사용된다.

17

① W _____ _____ is it from here?

M It is a thirty-minute walk.

② W How do you do, Mr. Park?

M Hi. _____ _____ _____ _____ _____, Mrs. Wilson.

③ W ♥How have you been?

M I've been good. _____ _____, _____ _____.

④ W _____ _____ _____ eating here?

M No, *not at all.

⑤ W I have a problem with my throat.

M Are you sick? _____ _____ _____ to a clinic.

*not at all [낫] [엣] [얼] → [나데덜]

언급 유무 파악

18 다음을 듣고, 여자가 Green Papa's에 대해 언급하지 않은 것을 고르시오.

① 음식의 맛
② 친환경 음식
③ 재료의 우수성
④ 재료를 사온 장소
⑤ 유기농 재배의 유무

18

W _____ _____ _____ _____ fast food and snacks? Then come to Green Papa's and enjoy our food. We only use fruits and vegetables grown organically by _____ _____. So we are sure they're fresh and nutritious. In addition, we don't serve any foods like pizza, hamburgers, and doughnuts. _____ _____ _____ to stick to natural foods. So does our food taste good? Yes! Our cooks were trained _____ _____ _____ _____ _____ of people who love green food. Please drop by to check out our food and to see how it tastes.

적절한 응답 찾기

[19-20] 대화를 듣고, 남자의 마지막 말에
이어질 여자의 말로 가장 적절한 것을
고르시오.

19 Woman: _____
　① Thanks for helping me.
　② You had better come here.
　③ I would say you were right.
　④ I was not happy to be here.
　⑤ The next time, I will say it to
　　you.

19

W　Look! There are lots of elephants over there.

M　They are _____ _____ _____ I expected.

W　Yeah. *What a beautiful sight! I like this place.

M　When I asked you to come here, _____ _____
　_____ _____?

W　Well, at the time, I was more interested in other places, like an
　amusement park.

M　Now _____ _____ _____ _____?

W　I would say you were right.

*What a [왓] [어] → [와더]

적절한 응답 찾기

20 Woman: _____
　① You can't miss it.
　② At the end of the hall.
　③ Thanks for advising me.
　④ Professor Lee is not in his office.
　⑤ You can use my phone anytime.

20

M　Excuse me. Can I ask you something?

W　Sure. How can I help you?

M　_____ _____ _____ _____ Professor Lee's
　office. Do you know where it is?

W　_____ _____ _____ Professor Minho Lee?

M　Yes. He's a law professor.

W　His office is _____ _____ _____ _____. You
　can use the elevator or the stairway to get there.

M　Oh, thanks for helping me. Where is the elevator?

W　At the end of the hall.

1 다음을 듣고, 예상되는 런던의 날씨로 가장 적절한 것을 고르시오.

① ② ③

④ ⑤

2 대화를 듣고, 테이블 위의 음식 배치로 가장 적절한 것을 고르시오.

3 대화를 듣고, 여자의 심정으로 가장 적절한 것을 고르시오.
① grateful   ② ashamed
③ sorrowful   ④ exhausted
⑤ frightened

4 대화를 듣고, 여자가 지난 일요일에 한 일로 가장 적절한 것을 고르시오.
① 교회 가기   ② 헌혈하기
③ 낚시하기   ④ 보트 운전하기
⑤ 해물 라면 먹기

5 대화를 듣고, 두 사람이 대화하는 장소로 가장 적절한 곳을 고르시오.
① 공항   ② 은행
③ 기념품 가게   ④ 기차 매표소
⑤ 분실물 센터

6 대화를 듣고, 여자의 마지막 말의 의도로 가장 적절한 것을 고르시오.
① 안심시키기   ② 동의하기   ③ 충고하기
④ 허락하기   ⑤ 감사하기

7 대화를 듣고, 여자가 교실 청소에서 담당한 일을 고르시오.
① 벽에 페인트칠하기   ② 커튼 털어서 달기
③ 바닥 걸레질하기   ④ 유리 창문 닦기
⑤ 칠판 정리하기

8 대화를 듣고, 남자가 대화 직후에 할 일로 가장 적절한 것을 고르시오.
① 식물에 물주기   ② 시든 화분 버리기
③ 화상 연고 바르기   ④ 화분을 실내로 옮기기
⑤ 길가에 떨어진 낙엽 청소하기

9 다음을 듣고, 여자가 학교 영어 신문 기자 모집에 대해 언급하지 않은 것을 고르시오.
① 신청 자격   ② 모집 기한   ③ 신청 방법
④ 하게 될 일 ⑤ 활동 보조금

10 다음을 듣고, 남자가 하는 말의 내용으로 가장 적절한 것을 고르시오.
① 공개 발표를 잘하는 방법
② 올바른 습관을 유지하는 방법
③ 충격적인 경험을 극복하는 방법
④ 친구들과 사이좋게 지내는 방법
⑤ 학교에서 좋은 성적을 받는 방법

11 대화를 듣고, Buy Nothing Day와 일치하지 않는 것을 고르시오.
① 11월 마지막 토요일을 의미한다.
② 소비주의에 대한 저항으로 생겼다.
③ 적게 소비하는 것을 의미한다.
④ 사람들은 신용 카드를 자르기도 한다.
⑤ 1992년 9월, 캐나다에서 설립되었다.

12 대화를 듣고, 두 사람이 미술관을 방문한 목적으로 가장 적절한 것을 고르시오.
① 유화를 좋아해서
② 그림을 구입하려고
③ 일자리를 구하려고
④ 기분 전환을 위해서
⑤ 미술 보고서를 쓰려고

13 대화를 듣고, 여자가 지불해야 할 금액으로 가장 적절한 것을 고르시오.
① $60　　② $80　　③ $100
④ $120　　⑤ $150

14 대화를 듣고, 두 사람의 관계로 가장 적절한 것을 고르시오.
① 작가 — 팬
② 선생님 — 학생
③ 매니저 — 배우
④ 영화감독 — 만화가
⑤ 매표소 직원 — 손님

15 대화를 듣고, 남자가 여자에게 요청한 일로 가장 적절한 것을 고르시오.
① 친구에게 전화하기
② 레몬 스무디 사다 주기
③ 다음에 탈 것 정하기
④ 놀이 기구 대신 줄 서기
⑤ 가게에서 과일 구입하기

16 대화를 듣고, 여자가 멕시코에 가는 이유로 가장 적절한 것을 고르시오.
① 출장을 가야 해서
② 배낭을 구입하려고
③ 비행기 표가 저렴해서
④ 할머니 댁에 방문하려고
⑤ 멕시코 음식을 맛보려고

17 다음 그림의 상황에 가장 적절한 대화를 고르시오.

①　　②　　③　　④　　⑤

18 대화를 듣고, 두 사람이 반려동물을 키울 때 해야 할 일에 관해 언급하지 <u>않은</u> 것을 고르시오.
① 훈련시키기
② 먹이 주기
③ 산책시키기
④ 발 닦아 주기
⑤ 빗질하기

[19~20] 대화를 듣고, 남자의 마지막 말에 이어질 여자의 말로 가장 적절한 것을 고르시오.

19 Woman: _____
① Let's buy a new washing machine.
② There are stains on the bedsheet.
③ Me, too. I hope winter ends soon.
④ That's a great idea. You're a big help.
⑤ I'm glad you're doing my laundry for me.

20 Woman: _____
① We should be quiet in the office.
② Don't worry. Your project is perfect.
③ Stretching can damage your muscles.
④ People need good nutrients to work hard.
⑤ Why not? This exercise is good for your waist.

● 대화를 다시 듣고, 알맞은 것을 고르시오.

1 Will people need umbrellas in Moscow?

☐ Yes   ☐ No

2 The woman is taking a photo of the food.

☐ True   ☐ False

3 Did the woman fail to buy the mug?

☐ Yes   ☐ No

4 What did the man do last Sunday?

☐ went fishing   ☐ donated blood

5 How did the man pay for the train tickets?

☐ by credit card   ☐ with cash

6 The man fell asleep on the bus.

☐ True   ☐ False

7 What did Daniel do?

☐ swept the floor   ☐ mopped the floor

8 The man's plant grows well under the hot sun.

☐ True   ☐ False

9 About what should students write an article?

☐ their future career   ☐ a happy life

10 Proper gestures are useful for public speaking.

☐ True   ☐ False

11 Where was Buy Nothing Day organized?

☐ in Canada   ☐ in Korea

12 What did the woman buy in the gallery?

☐ a brochure   ☐ a work of art

13 Did the woman use the 20% off coupon?

☐ Yes   ☐ No

14 The woman's cartoon will be made into a film.

☐ True   ☐ False

15 How long did the man and the woman wait for their ride?

☐ 30 minutes   ☐ 40 minutes

16 The woman plans to go to Mexico to see her grandma.

☐ True   ☐ False

17 Did the woman turn off her cellphone beforehand?

☐ Yes   ☐ No

18 Did the woman's father allow her to have a dog?

☐ Yes   ☐ No

19 The man helped the woman wash her bedding at his place.

☐ True   ☐ False

20 How long did the man work in the office?

☐ 4 hours   ☐ 6 hours

---

1 다음을 듣고, 예상되는 런던의 날씨로 가장 적절한 것을 고르시오.

① ② ③

④ ⑤

1 🇬🇧

M Now, I will provide you with the weather forecast for some big cities in Europe. In Rome, it's perfect weather _____ _____ _____. You may also need sunglasses. However, Paris and London are _____ _____ _____ _____. In Berlin, rain showers are expected, but it will be sunny in the afternoon. And it will be _____ _____ _____ _____ in Moscow.

---

2 대화를 듣고, 테이블 위의 음식 배치로 가장 적절한 것을 고르시오.

①  ② ③

④ ⑤

💜 **Let's dig in.**

: 음식을 먹기 시작할 때 쓰는 표현으로, '자, 이제 먹자.'라는 뜻이다.

= Let's eat.

= Help yourself.

2

M Whoa, whoa, _____ _____ _____ _____ for a second.

W Why? 💜Let's dig in. I'm hungry.

M Be patient. I'm _____ _____ of the food.

W All right. You've got 10 seconds.

M Can you put the pasta _____ _____ _____?

W Okay. And then?

M Put the _____ _____ on the right side of the pasta.

W I did that. Lastly, I'll put the orange juice to the left of the pasta.

---

3 대화를 듣고, 여자의 심정으로 가장 적절한 것을 고르시오.

① grateful ② ashamed
③ sorrowful ④ exhausted
⑤ frightened

3

W Look at this black mug _____ _____ _____ _____ on it. It's just my type.

M You bought _____ _____ _____ just 4 days ago.

W Who cares? I love this thing. So I'll buy this one.

M Okay. How much is it?

W Let me see. [*Clicking sound*] Argh! They're all _____ _____.

M For sure? Check it again.

W I _____ _____ _____. Look!

M Yeah, right. Say goodbye to the mug.

한 일 파악

4 대화를 듣고, 여자가 지난 일요일에 한 일로 가장 적절한 것을 고르시오.

① 교회 가기　　　② 헌혈하기
③ 낚시하기　　　④ 보트 운전하기
⑤ 해물 라면 먹기

♥ **Good for you.**

: 상대방의 좋은 일에 대해 칭찬하거나 축하할 때 쓰는 표현으로, '잘됐다.'라는 뜻이다.
= Well done.
= You did a good job!

4

M　What did you _____ _____ _____?
W　I went to the Red Cross and _____ _____.
M　Weren't you scared? I'm _____ _____ _____.
W　I'm okay *with them. What did you do?
M　I _____ _____ with my family. I caught lots of fish.
W　♥Good for you.

*with them [위드] [뎀] → [윗뎀]

장소 추론

5 대화를 듣고, 두 사람이 대화하는 장소로 가장 적절한 곳을 고르시오.

① 공항　　　　　② 은행
③ 기념품 가게　　④ 기차 매표소
⑤ 분실물 센터

5　🇬🇧

M　I'd like to buy a one-way ticket to London for the next train.
W　_____ _____ _____ _____ _____
　　_____, by credit card or with cash?
M　Credit card, please.
W　Here is your ticket. The train will _____ _____ platform 7.
M　How long do I have to wait for the train?
W　The train will _____ _____ _____ _____
　　_____.

의도 파악

6 대화를 듣고, 여자의 마지막 말의 의도로 가장 적절한 것을 고르시오.

① 안심시키기　　② 동의하기
③ 충고하기　　　④ 허락하기
⑤ 감사하기

♥ **Pull yourself together.**

: 상대방을 진정시키거나 기운을 북돋아 줄 때 쓰는 표현으로, '진정해.', '마음을 가다듬어 봐.'라는 뜻이다.
= Take it easy.
= Calm down.

6

[*Telephone rings.*]

M　Hello. Mom, I think _____ _____.
W　Calm down. Where are you now?
M　I don't know. I _____ _____ on the bus.
W　Relax, John. Look around and _____ _____ _____
　　_____.
M　It's _____ _____. I'm scared.
W　Stop crying and ♥pull yourself together.

특정 정보 파악

7 대화를 듣고, 여자가 교실 청소에서 담당한 일을 고르시오.

① 벽에 페인트칠하기
② 커튼 털어서 달기
③ 바닥 걸레질하기
④ 유리 창문 닦기
⑤ 칠판 정리하기

7 🇬🇧

M Maria, today is our _____ _____ _____.

W Great! What should I do?

M How about _____ _____ _____?

W Daniel is already doing that. Is there anything else I can do?

M Hmm... Why don't you mop the floor?

W No problem. What will you do?

M I'll _____ _____ _____.

W Okay. Let's _____ _____.

할 일 파악

8 대화를 듣고, 남자가 대화 직후에 할 일로 가장 적절한 것을 고르시오.

① 식물에 물주기
② 시든 화분 버리기
③ 화상 연고 바르기
④ 화분을 실내로 옮기기
⑤ 길가에 떨어진 낙엽 청소하기

♥ What do you mean (by that)?
: 이해가 되지 않아 추가적인 설명이 필요할 때 쓰는 표현으로, '무슨 의미예요?'라는 뜻이다.
= What exactly is it?
= Can you explain it?

8

M I heard you're a plant doctor. Can you help me?

W Sure. _____ _____.

M Look at this plant. Can you see the leaves are dying?

W It looks like the leaves _____ _____.

M ♥What do you mean?

W This plant _____ _____ _____ _____ _____. Too much sunlight is harmful.

M I *got it. I should _____ _____ _____.

*got it [갓] [잇] → [가릿]

언급 유무 파악

9 다음을 듣고, 여자가 학교 영어 신문 기자 모집에 대해 언급하지 **않은** 것을 고르시오.

① 신청 자격   ② 모집 기한
③ 신청 방법   ④ 하게 될 일
⑤ 활동 보조금

9

W Hello, students. We are _____ _____ _____ _____ for the Sowon Middle School English newspaper. You will *write an article about the school. Every student at Sowon Middle School can _____ _____ _____ _____. If you want to join us, please _____ _____ _____ about a happy life and email us by April 7. The email address is englishjournal@school.com.

*write an [라이트] [언] → [라이런]

화제·주제 파악

10 다음을 듣고, 남자가 하는 말의 내용으로 가장 적절한 것을 고르시오.

① 공개 발표를 잘하는 방법
② 올바른 습관을 유지하는 방법
③ 충격적인 경험을 극복하는 방법
④ 친구들과 사이좋게 지내는 방법
⑤ 학교에서 좋은 성적을 받는 방법

10

M Many students are _____ _____ public speaking. But don't worry. Let me give you some real solutions. First of all, you should _____ _____ _____ _____ _____ in advance. Second, don't be afraid of public speaking. Good speaking _____ _____ _____. Lastly, you can say many things with gestures. Use them properly.

내용 불일치 파악

11 대화를 듣고, Buy Nothing Day와 일치하지 <u>않는</u> 것을 고르시오.

① 11월 마지막 토요일을 의미한다.
② 소비주의에 대한 저항으로 생겼다.
③ 적게 소비하는 것을 의미한다.
④ 사람들은 신용 카드를 자르기도 한다.
⑤ 1992년 9월, 캐나다에서 설립되었다.

11

W _____ _____ _____ _____ _____ Buy Nothing Day before?
M Maybe. But I don't know exactly what it is.
W That _____ _____ a protest against consumerism.
M It means spending less, right?
W That's correct. People sometimes _____ _____ their credit cards.
M When and where was it organized?
W It was founded in Canada in September 1992.
M It has a longer history _____ _____ _____.

목적 파악

12 대화를 듣고, 두 사람이 미술관을 방문한 목적으로 가장 적절한 것을 고르시오.

① 유화를 좋아해서
② 그림을 구입하려고
③ 일자리를 구하려고
④ 기분 전환을 위해서
⑤ 미술 보고서를 쓰려고

♥ **Forget it.**
: 강한 부정의 표현으로 '생각도 하지마.', '상상도 하지마.', '(그 생각을) 잊어.'라는 뜻이다.

12

M It was a great exhibition. I love his oil paintings.
W So do I. His paintings are _____ _____ _____ _____ _____.
M Right. If I had lots of money, I would buy one.
W ♥Forget it. They _____ _____ _____ _____. Instead, I'll take this brochure.
M What for?
W We came here _____ _____ _____ _____ and this will be helpful.
M In that case, I should take one, too.

숫자 정보 파악

13 대화를 듣고, 여자가 지불해야 할 금액으로 가장 적절한 것을 고르시오.

① $60
② $80
③ $100
④ $120
⑤ $150

💗 **have an eye for ~**

: 상대방의 안목에 대해 이야기할 때 쓰는 표현으로, '~을 보는 눈이 있다'라는 뜻이다.

= have good taste in ~

13

W　Excuse me. How much is this red dress?

M　It's 50 dollars. You 💗have a good eye for fashion. That is _____ _____ _____ item here.

W　Thanks. Do you have another one with the same design _____ _____ _____ _____?

M　Of course. We have it in orange.

W　I'll _____ _____ _____, too.

M　One red dress and one orange dress, right? That's 100 dollars in total.

W　I have a 20% off coupon. Can I use it?

M　Sorry, but you can't. It was _____ _____ _____.

관계 추론

14 대화를 듣고, 두 사람의 관계로 가장 적절한 것을 고르시오.

① 작가 — 팬
② 선생님 — 학생
③ 매니저 — 배우
④ 영화감독 — 만화가
⑤ 매표소 직원 — 손님

14 🇬🇧

W　Welcome to my office. I'm a _____ _____ _____ _____.

M　I'm honored to meet you.

W　Please have a seat. Let's talk about your work.

M　Sure. Here is the _____ _____ _____.

W　Oh. The illustration _____ _____.

M　I'm glad you like it. I still can't believe that my cartoon will be _____ _____ _____ _____.

W　It will be a great movie. I guarantee you.

요청한 일 파악

15 대화를 듣고, 남자가 여자에게 요청한 일로 가장 적절한 것을 고르시오.

① 친구에게 전화하기
② 레몬 스무디 사다 주기
③ 다음에 탈 것 정하기
④ 놀이 기구 대신 줄 서기
⑤ 가게에서 과일 구입하기

💗 **You're telling me.**

: 상대방의 의견에 동의할 때 쓰는 표현으로, '내 말이 그거야.'라는 뜻이다.

= I (totally) agree with you.

= Same here.

15

W　Wow! There are _____ _____ _____ at the amusement park.

M　💗You're telling me.

W　How long did we wait for the ride?

M　Maybe 40 minutes.

W　_____ _____. I don't want to _____ _____ _____.

M　Well, can you buy me a lemon smoothie? I'll stay in line here.

W　Why not? I'll _____ _____ _____ _____.

이유 추론

16 대화를 듣고, 여자가 멕시코에 가는
이유로 가장 적절한 것을 고르시오.

① 출장을 가야 해서
② 배낭을 구입하려고
③ 비행기 표가 저렴해서
④ 할머니 댁에 방문하려고
⑤ 멕시코 음식을 맛보려고

16

M Zoe, where are you going with that backpack?

W I'm _____ _____ _____.

M Are you going to see your grandma?

W Nope. My grandma _____ _____ Canada now. I'm
going to Mexico _____ _____ _____ _____.

M You poor thing. You work even on the weekend.

W Don't worry *about it. I _____ _____ _____.

*about it [어바웃] [잇] → [어바우릿]

그림 상황 파악

17 다음 그림의 상황에 가장 적절한
대화를 고르시오.

①   ②   ③   ④   ⑤

17

① M _____ _____ _____ _____ that smartphone?

W I bought it at the store downstairs.

② M Do you know the name of the girl with brown hair?

W I think she is a _____ _____ _____.

③ M This movie is boring. Let's get out of here.

W I totally agree with you.

④ M Would you _____ _____ _____ _____?
It's too loud.

W I'm sorry. I thought I had done that.

⑤ M The movie is so exciting. I love it.

W Same here. I especially like _____ _____ _____.

언급 유무 파악

18 대화를 듣고, 두 사람이 반려동물을
키울 때 해야 할 일에 관해 언급하지
않은 것을 고르시오.

① 훈련시키기
② 먹이 주기
③ 산책시키기
④ 발 닦아 주기
⑤ 빗질하기

18

W Dad, can I have a pet? I want a dog.

M A dog? It's so hard to _____ _____ _____ a dog.

W I know. So I looked for a starter guide about getting a dog.

M Sounds interesting. Tell me about it.

W I have to _____ _____ _____ _____
on a leash every day.

M What should you do after taking it for a walk?

W I should _____ _____ _____ and brush
it.

M I think you are ready to have a pet dog.

[19-20] 대화를 듣고, 남자의 마지막 말에 이어질 여자의 말로 가장 적절한 것을 고르시오.

19 Woman: _____
   ① Let's buy a new washing machine.
   ② There are stains on the bedsheet.
   ③ Me, too. I hope winter ends soon.
   ④ That's a great idea. You're a big help.
   ⑤ I'm glad you're doing my laundry for me.

♥ **How about ~?**
: 어떤 것을 제안할 때 쓰는 표현으로, '~는 어때?'라는 뜻이다.
= What about ~?
= Why don't you ~?

20 Woman: _____
   ① We should be quiet in the office.
   ② Don't worry. Your project is perfect.
   ③ Stretching can damage your muscles.
   ④ People need good nutrients to work hard.
   ⑤ Why not? This exercise is good for your waist.

19

M Why do you _____ _____ _____ _____?
W My _____ _____ _____ _____. And I *have to wash my bedding.
M Hmm. Is there anything else you can do?
W Can I do my laundry at your place?
M Sorry. I have plans. ♥How about _____ _____ _____ _____?
W <u>That's a great idea. You're a big help.</u>

*have to [해브] [투] → [햅투]

20

W Collin, _____ _____ _____. You've been working for almost 6 hours.
M I have to finish this project before leaving the office.
W Come on. Let's _____ _____ _____.
M Okay. [*Pause*] Wait! My back hurts.
W It probably hurts because you kept working _____ _____ _____.
M That's possible.
W Look at me and _____ _____ _____ _____.
M In this office? Are you serious?
W <u>Why not? This exercise is good for your waist.</u>

1 다음을 듣고, 내일 광주의 날씨로 가장 적절한 것을 고르시오.

①   ②   ③

④   ⑤

2 대화를 듣고, 남자가 구입할 시계로 가장 적절한 것을 고르시오.

①   ②   ③

④   ⑤

3 대화를 듣고, 여자의 심정으로 가장 적절한 것을 고르시오.
① happy
② jealous
③ nervous
④ frightened
⑤ disappointed

4 대화를 듣고, 여자가 어제 한 일로 가장 적절한 것을 고르시오.
① 동생과 TV 보기
② 동생을 간호하기
③ 엄마와 병원 가기
④ 파티에 가서 즐기기
⑤ 병원에서 자원봉사하기

5 대화를 듣고, 두 사람이 대화하는 장소로 가장 적절한 곳을 고르시오.
① 식당
② 서점
③ 우체국
④ 도서관
⑤ 편의점

6 대화를 듣고, 남자의 마지막 말의 의도로 가장 적절한 것을 고르시오.
① 부탁
② 동의
③ 위로
④ 반대
⑤ 칭찬

7 대화를 듣고, 남자가 들러야 할 장소로 언급하지 않은 것을 고르시오.
① 약국
② 공항
③ 옷가게
④ 문방구
⑤ 버스터미널

8 대화를 듣고, 여자가 대화 직후에 할 일로 가장 적절한 것을 고르시오.
① 자전거 수리하기
② 식료품점에 가기
③ 남자 집에 들르기
④ 유치원에 방문하기
⑤ 친구에게 감사 인사하기

9 다음을 듣고, 남자가 재활용에 대해 언급하지 않은 것을 고르시오.
① 재활용의 중요성
② 쓰레기 수거인의 역할
③ 재활용 물품의 종류
④ 재활용품 배출 요일
⑤ 재활용품 분리배출 방법

10 다음을 듣고, 여자가 하는 말의 내용으로 가장 적절한 것을 고르시오.
① 음식을 소화하는 요령
② 과학 수업의 중요성
③ 유기체의 자연 원리
④ 자연이 인간에게 주는 영향
⑤ 미생물이 인간에 필요한 이유

11 다음을 듣고, 대중 연설 스터디 클럽에 대한 내용으로 일치하지 않는 것을 고르시오.
① 소개자의 이름은 Bob이다.
② 연설을 잘하는 방법을 연구한다.
③ 점심시간에 동아리 방에서 만난다.
④ 수학을 연구하고 함께 문제를 푼다.
⑤ 질문은 이메일을 통해서 할 수 있다.

12 대화를 듣고, 여자가 시청에 가는 목적으로 가장 적절한 것을 고르시오.
① 화장품을 사기 위해서
② 전시회를 홍보하기 위해서
③ 학교의 행사를 알리기 위해서
④ 예술 작품 전시회를 관람하기 위해서
⑤ 미용에 관한 내용을 발표하기 위해서

13 대화를 듣고, 여자가 지불해야 할 금액으로 가장 적절한 것을 고르시오.
① $20　　② $22　　③ $24
④ $25　　⑤ $30

14 대화를 듣고, 두 사람의 관계로 가장 적절한 것을 고르시오.
① 팬 — 영화감독
② 학생 — 관리인
③ 팬 — 영화배우
④ 지휘자 — 음악가
⑤ 극장 직원 — 손님

15 대화를 듣고, 남자가 여자에게 추천한 일로 가장 적절한 것을 고르시오.
① 수업 태도를 바르게 하기
② 학교 시설을 잘 사용하기
③ 국립공원의 수를 조사하기
④ 무료 현장 학습을 신청하기
⑤ 자연 보호에 대한 보고서 쓰기

16 대화를 듣고, 남자가 수학 성적이 좋지 <u>못한</u> 이유로 가장 적절한 것을 고르시오.
① 건강이 좋지 않아서
② 수학에 흥미가 없어서
③ 답안지를 잘못 작성해서
④ 공부를 열심히 하지 않아서
⑤ 전날에 다른 과목을 공부해서

17 다음 그림의 상황에 가장 적절한 대화를 고르시오.

① ② ③ ④ ⑤

18 대화를 듣고, 두 사람에 관해 일치하지 <u>않는</u> 것을 고르시오.
① 남자는 양파를 싫어한다.
② 여자는 남자 옆에 앉아 있다.
③ 남자는 오늘 급식이 마음에 들지 않는다.
④ 여자는 스튜를 만드는 법을 설명한다.
⑤ 여자는 남자가 균형 잡힌 식사를 해야 한다고 생각한다.

[19–20] 대화를 듣고, 여자의 마지막 말에 이어질 남자의 말로 가장 적절한 것을 고르시오.

19 Man: _____
① Those were the days.
② The more, the better.
③ You can say that again.
④ Keep your fingers crossed.
⑤ Keep your chin up. You will be all right.

20 Man: _____
① It's no big deal.
② Long time, no see.
③ Sure. I will help you up.
④ Okay. I will wait for you.
⑤ Wear your safety gear.

Listen and Check

● 대화를 다시 듣고, 알맞은 것을 고르시오.

1 Seoul and Daejeon will get rain on the weekend.
☐ True   ☐ False

2 Does the man want to buy a clock that is dark color?
☐ Yes   ☐ No

3 Did the woman buy skinny jeans?
☐ Yes   ☐ No

4 The woman went to a party last night.
☐ True   ☐ False

5 How much is the late fee per day?
☐ 5 cents   ☐ 10 cents

6 What does the woman want to be?
☐ a lawyer   ☐ a doctor

7 What should the man buy for his mother?
☐ a T-shirt   ☐ medication

8 The man can lend his car to the woman.
☐ True   ☐ False

9 Did the man say he can put recyclable items anywhere outside?
☐ Yes   ☐ No

10 The woman says people can survive without the help of microorganisms.
☐ True   ☐ False

11 Do club members do their activities every Thursday?
☐ Yes   ☐ No

12 The man's parents' wedding anniversary has already passed.
☐ True   ☐ False

13 The woman's child is ten years old now.
☐ True   ☐ False

14 The man wants to be a movie director.
☐ True   ☐ False

15 Is the woman interested in environmental issues?
☐ Yes   ☐ No

16 The man's math score is bad.
☐ True   ☐ False

17 The woman tells the man the answer is number two.
☐ True   ☐ False

18 Why isn't the man eating the school meal?
☐ because he dislikes onions
☐ because he dislikes stew

19 The man's arm is broken.
☐ True   ☐ False

20 The woman doesn't want to take a walk.
☐ True   ☐ False

40

그림 정보 파악

1 다음을 듣고, 내일 광주의 날씨로 가장 적절한 것을 고르시오.

① ② ③

④ ⑤

1

M Hello, everyone. Here is the weather report. In Busan, _____ _____ _____ _____ _____, and we can expect rainy days this weekend. Seoul and Daejeon will also *have a rainy day tomorrow, but they'll _____ _____ _____ on the weekend. In Gwangju, there will be heavy winds tomorrow. But _____ _____ _____ _____ the day after tomorrow.

*have a [해브] [어] → [해뷔]

그림 정보 파악

2 대화를 듣고, 남자가 구입할 시계로 가장 적절한 것을 고르시오.

① ② ③

④ ⑤

2 🇬🇧

W Good morning, sir. What can I do for you?

M I'd like to _____ _____ _____ for my friend for his birthday.

W How about this round one?

M It looks nice.

W And _____ _____ would you like?

M I want to buy one that is a _____ _____.

W Then what about this light blue one? It's _____ _____ _____ _____ here.

M He will *love it. I'll take that one.

*love it [러브] [잇] → [러빗]

심정 추론

3 대화를 듣고, 여자의 심정으로 가장 적절한 것을 고르시오.

① happy
② jealous
③ nervous
④ frightened
⑤ disappointed

3

M How may I help you?

W I'd like to buy some skinny jeans.

M How about _____ _____ _____?

W I like them, but I _____ _____ a blue pair.

M We have brown ones as well. Please _____ _____.

W Thanks. Oh, my. They're _____ _____ _____ _____ to fit into. Do you have a bigger pair?

M Sorry. The brown ones are the last item we have.

W That's too bad. I will drop by another time.

한 일 파악

4 대화를 듣고, 여자가 어제 한 일로 가장 적절한 것을 고르시오.

① 동생과 TV보기
② 동생을 간호하기
③ 엄마와 병원 가기
④ 파티에 가서 즐기기
⑤ 병원에서 자원봉사하기

4

M Hi, Lily. How was the party last night?

W Hey. Actually, I couldn't go to the party.

M Really? You were excited you were going to the party, _____ _____?

W Yes, I was. But my mom got sick, so I had to _____ _____ _____ _____ _____.

M Oh, you're a good girl. Is she okay?

W Yes, she is feeling better now.

M I hope _____ _____ _____ _____.

장소 추론

5 대화를 듣고, 두 사람이 대화하는 장소로 가장 적절한 곳을 고르시오.

① 식당
② 서점
③ 우체국
④ 도서관
⑤ 편의점

5

M Hello. I'd like to _____ _____ _____.

W Okay. Oh, these are overdue.

M Are you serious?

W You were supposed to return them _____ _____ _____.

M How much is the late fee?

W It's 5 cents per day. _____ _____ _____ _____ in overdue fees for each book.

M Okay. Here you are. Can I return books even when the library isn't open?

W Sure. You can use the automatic book return system in this building _____ _____ _____ _____.

의도 파악

6 대화를 듣고, 남자의 마지막 말의 의도로 가장 적절한 것을 고르시오.

① 부탁
② 동의
③ 위로
④ 반대
⑤ 칭찬

6

W What do you want to be in the future?

M Well, I _____ _____ _____ _____ _____.

W Wow, I believe that you can do it.

M Thanks. Then what do you want to be?

W I think that _____ _____ _____ _____ _____. So I'm thinking of becoming a doctor.

M That's a good choice.

특정 정보 파악

7 대화를 듣고, 남자가 들러야 할 장소로 언급하지 <u>않은</u> 것을 고르시오.

① 약국
② 공항
③ 옷가게
④ 문방구
⑤ 버스터미널

7

W Look out, Adam. Be careful!

M Sorry, Susan. I am _____ _____ _____.

W Why are you in such a hurry?

M My mom asked me _____ _____ _____ _____.
So I have to buy it before the drugstore closes.

W Is that all?

M I also need to buy a T-shirt and an eraser. Oh, my! I _____
_____ that I have to *pick up my younger brother at the bus
terminal.

W Oh. You have _____ _____ _____ _____.

*pick up [픽] [업] → [픽껍]

할 일 파악

8 대화를 듣고, 여자가 대화 직후에 할 일로 가장 적절한 것을 고르시오.

① 자전거 수리하기
② 식료품점에 가기
③ 남자 집에 들르기
④ 유치원에 방문하기
⑤ 친구에게 감사 인사하기

♥ **What are friends for?**
: 자신이 도움을 준 친구가 고마움을 표할 때 그에 대한 응답으로 쓸 수 있는 표현으로 '친구 좋다는 게 뭐야?'의 의미이다.

8 🇬🇧

W Hi, Jason. Will you _____ _____ _____ _____?

M What is it?

W I have to move my stuff. Could I _____ _____ _____?

M Sure. But we have to go to my house first. My car is _____
_____ _____.

W Okay. Thank you _____ _____ _____.

M ♥ What are friends for?

언급 유무 파악

9 다음을 듣고, 남자가 재활용에 대해 언급하지 <u>않은</u> 것을 고르시오.

① 재활용의 중요성
② 쓰레기 수거인의 역할
③ 재활용 물품의 종류
④ 재활용품 배출 요일
⑤ 재활용품 분리배출 방법

9

M Hello, everyone. Recently, recycling _____ _____
_____ _____ than ever before for saving the Earth.
It is very important to save the Earth. We can recycle almost
everything, such as cans, bottles, and plastic items. It is
important to put them _____ _____ _____
_____ on a certain day. We should collect those items
*in our houses first and then take them to that place. After that,
garbage collectors will take care of them _____ _____
_____ _____ _____ them.

*in our [인] [아우어] → [이나우어]

화제·주제 파악

10 다음을 듣고, 여자가 하는 말의 내용으로 가장 적절한 것을 고르시오.

① 음식을 소화하는 요령
② 과학 수업의 중요성
③ 유기체의 자연 원리
④ 주위 환경이 인간에게 주는 영향
⑤ 미생물이 인간에게 필요한 이유

10

W Hello, everyone. This is Laura, a science teacher at Moonhwa Middle School. _____ _____ _____ _____ of microorganisms? They *make us healthier. For example, microorganisms work hard _____ _____ _____ to make us breathe, digest food, and produce energy. So don't forget that _____ _____ _____ _____ _____ — _____.

*make us [메이크] [어스] → [메이커스]

내용 불일치 파악

11 다음을 듣고, 대중 연설 스터디 클럽에 대한 내용으로 일치하지 <u>않는</u> 것을 고르시오.

① 소개자의 이름은 Bob이다.
② 연설을 잘하는 방법을 연구한다.
③ 점심시간에 동아리 방에서 만난다.
④ 수학을 연구하고 함께 문제를 푼다.
⑤ 질문은 이메일을 통해서 할 수 있다.

11

M Hi. My name is Bob, and now _____ _____ _____ our public speaking study club to you. It's a club whose members _____ _____ _____ _____ from different people and practice their public speaking skills. If you are interested in learning how to be a good speaker, visit us in room 302. Our regular meetings will be held _____ _____ during lunchtime. Any questions? _____ _____ _____ _____ bobthegreatpublicspeaker@mymail.co.kr.

목적 파악

12 대화를 듣고, 여자가 시청에 가는 목적으로 가장 적절한 것을 고르시오.

① 화장품을 사기 위해서
② 전시회를 홍보하기 위해서
③ 학교의 행사를 알리기 위해서
④ 예술 작품 전시회를 관람하기 위해서
⑤ 미용에 관한 내용을 발표하기 위해서

12 🇬🇧

W Hi, Jack. _____ _____ _____ _____?
M I'm going to the shopping mall to buy a present for my parents. Their wedding anniversary is _____ _____ _____ _____. How about you?
W I'm going to city hall.
M City hall? What are you going there for?
W It is hosting an exhibition _____ _____ _____ some great works of art by famous artists from around the world.
M Great. I hope _____ _____ _____.
W Thanks. See you soon at school.

숫자 정보 파악

13 대화를 듣고, 여자가 지불해야 할 금액으로 가장 적절한 것을 고르시오.

① $20
② $22
③ $24
④ $25
⑤ $30

13

M What can I do for you?

W I'd like _____ _____ for *Beautiful Life*.

M Three adults?

W No. One is for a kid _____ _____.

M Then the adult tickets are eight dollars each, and the kid's ticket _____ _____ _____.

W Great. Here is _____ _____.

M Here is _____ _____. Have a good time.

관계 추론

14 대화를 듣고, 두 사람의 관계로 가장 적절한 것을 고르시오.

① 팬 ― 영화감독
② 학생 ― 관리인
③ 팬 ― 영화배우
④ 지휘자 ― 음악가
⑤ 극장 직원 ― 손님

14

M I can't believe that _____ _____ _____ _____. I love your movies.

W Thank you so much.

M I have watched all of your films. Can I _____ _____ _____?

W Sure. What's your name?

M It's Jason. Thanks. Someday, I want to be _____ _____ _____ _____ _____.

W _____ _____.

M Thank you. I will try my best.

추천한 일 파악

15 대화를 듣고, 남자가 여자에게 추천한 일로 가장 적절한 것을 고르시오.

① 수업 태도를 바르게 하기
② 학교 시설을 잘 사용하기
③ 국립공원의 수를 조사하기
④ 무료 현장 학습을 신청하기
⑤ 자연 보호에 대한 보고서 쓰기

15 🇬🇧

W Good morning, Prof. Jones. How are you?

M I'm good. Thanks.

W I'm a student _____ _____ _____ _____. I liked the story about the environment from your previous lecture.

M Oh, I'm glad to hear you say that.

W I'm very _____ _____ _____ _____, and I want to learn more about them.

M Oh, really? Then how about signing up for a field trip this semester? It is free, and we can look around a national park and feel the importance of nature.

W That sounds great. I will do that _____ _____ _____ _____.

이유 추론

16 대화를 듣고, 남자가 수학 성적이 좋지 못한 이유로 가장 적절한 것을 고르시오.

① 건강이 좋지 않아서
② 수학에 흥미가 없어서
③ 답안지를 잘못 작성해서
④ 공부를 열심히 하지 않아서
⑤ 전날에 다른 과목을 공부해서

16

W Peter, I need to talk to you.

M Mom, you want to _____ _____ _____ _____ on the test, don't you?

W Yes, I do.

M Are you disappointed that the results didn't meet your expectations ?

W That's not it. Why is your math score so bad? I thought _____ _____ _____ _____ _____.

M Actually, I got most of the answers right, but I wrote them in the wrong places on the answer sheet.

W Okay. I will excuse your mistake this time, but _____ _____ _____ on the next examination.

그림 상황 파악

17 다음 그림의 상황에 가장 적절한 대화를 고르시오.

① ② ③ ④ ⑤

17

① W What does _____ _____ _____?

M He is a teacher.

② W _____ _____ _____ _____ the answer here?

M Sure. The answer is number two.

③ W Is it possible to _____ this _____ the frame?

M Absolutely, yes.

④ W Watch out! It is _____ _____ _____!

M Oh, sorry. I will be more careful.

⑤ W Show me your license, please.

M Okay, _____ _____ _____.

내용 불일치 파악

18 대화를 듣고, 두 사람에 관해 일치하지 않는 것을 고르시오.

① 남자는 양파를 싫어한다.
② 여자는 남자 옆에 앉아 있다.
③ 남자는 오늘 급식이 마음에 들지 않는다.
④ 여자는 스튜를 만드는 법을 설명한다.
⑤ 여자는 남자가 균형 잡힌 식사를 해야 한다고 생각한다.

18

W Mike, _____ _____ _____ next to you?

M Sure.

W _____ _____ _____ _____? You don't like today's school meal?

M Actually, I don't like onions. I didn't know that stew has onions in it.

W Come on. I've never heard about stew without onions. I love the smell.

M Everybody _____ _____ _____.

W I agree with you, but you must have a balanced diet.

M I know. My mom _____ _____ _____ to me.

W Okay. Don't eat it if you don't want to.

19

[19~20] 대화를 듣고, 여자의 마지막 말에 이어질 남자의 말로 가장 적절한 것을 고르시오.

19 Man: _____

① Those were the days.

② The more, the better.

③ You can say that again.

④ Keep your fingers crossed.

⑤ Keep your chin up. You will be all right.

19

M   Maggie, have you heard the news about Daniel?

W   What happened to him?

M   He *had a little accident with a motorcycle _____ _____ _____.

W   Oh, my. Is he okay?

M   Fortunately, yes. He just has a few scratches on his arm. _____ _____ _____.

W   He should be very careful on the streets. _____ _____ _____ _____ _____.

M   <u>You can say that again.</u>

*had a [해드] [어] → [해더]

20 Man: _____

① It's no big deal.

② Long time, no see.

③ Sure. I will help you up.

④ Okay. I will wait for you.

⑤ Wear your safety gear.

20 🇬🇧

M   Hi, Emma. How was your day?

W   Excellent. I feel great today because _____ _____ _____ _____ _____.

M   Can we *take a walk in a minute?

W   Sounds good. But _____ _____ _____ _____ _____ before we go out.

M   What's that? Is it urgent?

W   There's a ton of laundry to do, and I have to run the washing machine. _____ _____ _____ in a minute.

M   <u>Okay. I will wait for you.</u>

*take a walk [테이크] [어] [워크] → [테이커웍]

1 다음을 듣고, 목요일의 날씨로 가장 적절한 것을 고르
시오.

①   ②   ③

④   ⑤

2 대화를 듣고, 남자가 선물할 귀걸이로 가장 적절한 것
을 고르시오.

①   ②   ③

④   ⑤

3 대화를 듣고, 여자의 심정으로 가장 적절한 것을 고르
시오.
① scared   ② thrilled   ③ nervous
④ confused   ⑤ depressed

4 대화를 듣고, 남자가 토요일에 한 일로 가장 적절한 것
을 고르시오.
① 오디션 참여하기
② 집에서 휴식하기
③ 결혼식에 참석하기
④ 친구와 생일 파티 하기
⑤ TV 프로그램 시청하기

5 대화를 듣고, 두 사람이 대화하는 장소로 가장 적절한
곳을 고르시오.
① 학교   ② 문구점   ③ 전시회
④ 놀이터   ⑤ 미술 학원

6 대화를 듣고, 여자의 마지막 말의 의도로 가장 적절한
것을 고르시오.
① 동의   ② 축하   ③ 후회
④ 거절   ⑤ 격려

7 대화를 듣고, 여자가 신청하려는 문화 프로그램을 고르
시오.
① 그림 그리기   ② 지우개 만들기
③ 머그컵 만들기   ④ 조각품 만들기
⑤ 도장 만들기

8 대화를 듣고, 여자가 대화 직후에 할 일로 가장 적절한
것을 고르시오.
① 달리기 연습하기   ② 경기에 참여하기
③ 저녁 먹으러 가기   ④ 생일 선물 사러 가기
⑤ 생일 파티 하러 가기

9 대화를 듣고, 두 사람이 집안일 분담에 대해 언급하지
않은 것을 고르시오.
① 설거지   ② 빨래하기
③ 분리수거   ④ 요리하기
⑤ 화장실 청소

10 다음을 듣고, 여자가 하는 말의 내용으로 가장 적절한
것을 고르시오.
① 취업 경쟁의 문제   ② 좋은 직업의 특성
③ 자기 계발의 필요성   ④ 미래의 꿈의 중요성
⑤ 효율적인 시간 관리 방법

11 대화를 듣고, 시장 조사에 대한 내용으로 일치하지 않
는 것을 고르시오.
① 약국 오픈을 위한 조사이다.
② 전화로 설문 조사를 할 계획이다.
③ 외부 지역 위주로 알아보려고 한다.
④ 지역 조사를 끝내고 설문 조사를 한다.
⑤ 조사 대상은 65세 이상의 사람들이다.

12 대화를 듣고, 여자가 수영 강습을 받는 목적으로 가장 적절한 것을 고르시오.
① 살을 빼기 위해서
② 건강을 유지하기 위해서
③ 수영 강사가 되기 위해서
④ 물 공포증을 극복하기 위해서
⑤ 새로운 운동을 해보기 위해서

13 대화를 듣고, 여자가 지불해야 할 금액으로 가장 적절한 것을 고르시오.
① $8　　　② $10　　　③ $12
④ $14　　　⑤ $16

14 대화를 듣고, 두 사람의 관계로 가장 적절한 것을 고르시오.
① 평론가 — 기자
② 감독 — 연기자
③ 편집장 — 작가
④ 연극배우 — 관객
⑤ 라디오 DJ — 청취자

15 대화를 듣고, 남자가 여자에게 요청한 일로 가장 적절한 것을 고르시오.
① 스튜디오 방문하기
② 사진 기술 알려 주기
③ 샘플 사진 찍어 주기
④ 촬영 모델이 되어 주기
⑤ 사진 동아리 가입하기

16 대화를 듣고, 여자가 비행기 표를 취소한 이유로 가장 적절한 것을 고르시오.
① 여행 날짜를 착각해서
② 여행 계획이 변경되어서
③ 개인적인 사정이 생겨서
④ 여행 지역에 문제가 생겨서
⑤ 할인 표를 구입하기 위해서

17 다음 그림의 상황에 가장 적절한 대화를 고르시오.

①　　②　　③　　④　　⑤

18 대화를 듣고, 남자가 비타민 C 섭취에 관해 언급하지 <u>않은</u> 것을 고르시오.
① 비타민 C 섭취 횟수
② 비타민 C 구입 방법
③ 비타민 C 섭취 방법
④ 비타민 C 함유 과일
⑤ 비타민 C 섭취 효능

[19-20] 대화를 듣고, 여자의 마지막 말에 이어질 남자의 말로 가장 적절한 것을 고르시오.

19 Man: _____
① You don't need to get stressed.
② I have the same problem as you.
③ I hope everything gets better soon.
④ I think it's time for you to change your phone.
⑤ You'd better use it one more year.

20 Man: _____
① You are such a great teacher.
② I don't think I can help you with it.
③ Tell me what you really need to do.
④ It takes time to make a good decision.
⑤ I suggest you carry just one big backpack.

Listen and Check

정답 및 해설 *p.025*

● 대화를 다시 듣고, 알맞은 것을 고르시오.

1 The weather report is only for Seoul.
☐ True　　　☐ False

2 Does the man's girlfriend prefer big earrings?
☐ Yes　　　☐ No

3 The woman was late for her job interview.
☐ True　　　☐ False

4 The man and the woman attended the wedding together.
☐ True　　　☐ False

5 Are the man and the woman buying materials for art class?
☐ Yes　　　☐ No

6 The woman gave the stray cat some snacks.
☐ True　　　☐ False

7 Will the man sign up for the stamp class?
☐ Yes　　　☐ No

8 The man and the woman will have dinner together.
☐ True　　　☐ False

9 Which is a part of the woman's housework?
☐ doing the recycling　☐ doing the laundry

10 A good job makes people want to live better.
☐ True　　　☐ False

11 Will the man and the woman call people of all ages?
☐ Yes　　　☐ No

12 What exercise does the man prefer?
☐ swimming
☐ working out at the gym

13 It's the first time for the woman to visit the bakery.
☐ True　　　☐ False

14 The man and the woman are acting partners in the scene.
☐ Yes　　　☐ No

15 What does the woman have an interest in?
☐ modeling　　　☐ taking photos

16 Did the woman know about the promotion?
☐ Yes　　　☐ No

17 The man will order hot chocolate.
☐ True　　　☐ False

18 What is one of the good sides of taking vitamin C?
☐ getting less stressed
☐ getting less tired

19 Did the woman use her cellphone for a long time?
☐ Yes　　　☐ No

20 What is the woman likely to carry around?
☐ a shoulder bag　　　☐ a backpack

그림 정보 파악

1 다음을 듣고, 목요일의 날씨로 가장 적절한 것을 고르시오.

① ② ③

④ ⑤

1

M Hello. This is the weather report for _____ _____ _____ in Seoul. On Monday, the rain will finally stop, and the sun will shine brightly. It will be cloudy and _____ _____ _____ again on Tuesday and Wednesday. The rain will *stop on Thursday, but it _____ _____ _____. On Friday, there will be strong winds, so you _____ _____ _____ when driving. Thank you.

*stop on [스탑] [온] → [스탑뻔]

그림 정보 파악

2 대화를 듣고, 남자가 선물할 귀걸이로 가장 적절한 것을 고르시오.

① ② ③

④ ⑤

2 🇬🇧

W Good afternoon. May I help you?

M I'm looking for some earrings to give to my girlfriend *as a gift.

W I see. Do you have a _____ _____ _____ _____?

M No, but she usually wears small, _____ _____.

W Then what about these small, round ones? They are _____ _____ _____.

M Wow, they _____ _____.

W These are the most popular earrings with women these days.

M I'll take them.

*as a [에즈] [어] → [에저]

심정 추론

3 대화를 듣고, 여자의 심정으로 가장 적절한 것을 고르시오.

① scared ② thrilled
③ nervous ④ confused
⑤ depressed

💗 **What if ~?**
: 어떠한 일이 발생할 것을 가정할 때 사용하는 표현으로, '~면 어쩌지?'라는 뜻이다.

3

W I _____ _____ _____ _____ tomorrow.

M I'm sure you will do well.

W 💗What if I cannot answer a question?

M Don't worry. You can tell the interviewers _____ _____ _____ and feel about it.

W Or _____ _____ I am late for the interview?

M Angela, you worry too much. Everything will be all right.

W Okay. I should _____ _____ _____.

한 일 파악

4 대화를 듣고, 남자가 토요일에 한 일로 가장 적절한 것을 고르시오.

① 오디션 참여하기
② 집에서 휴식하기
③ 결혼식에 참석하기
④ 친구와 생일 파티 하기
⑤ TV 프로그램 시청하기

4

W　Did you watch _____ _____ _____ last Saturday?

M　No, I had to go somewhere.

W　Where did you have to go?

M　I _____ _____ _____ _____.

W　I see. How was it?

M　It was nice. After the wedding, I _____ _____ _____ _____ _____ with some of my other friends.

W　Sounds fun.

장소 추론

5 대화를 듣고, 두 사람이 대화하는 장소로 가장 적절한 곳을 고르시오.

① 학교
② 문구점
③ 전시회
④ 놀이터
⑤ 미술 학원

5

M　What do we need for art class?

W　_____ _____ _____ _____ a canvas. And you?

M　I need _____ pastels _____ a canvas.

W　How about this set with 36 colors? I have the same one.

M　That's cool. Let's _____ _____ _____ now.

W　Here is the size we need to buy.

M　Good. Let's _____ _____ _____.

의도 파악

6 대화를 듣고, 여자의 마지막 말의 의도로 가장 적절한 것을 고르시오.

① 동의　　　② 축하
③ 후회　　　④ 거절
⑤ 격려

♥ **There must be ~.**

: 무언가가 있을 것이라는 강한 추측을 나타낼 때 사용하는 표현으로, '~가 있음에 틀림없다.'라는 뜻이다.

6

W　Look at those cats. They look hungry.

M　I _____ _____ _____ _____ these days.

W　Should I give them _____ _____ _____ _____?

M　No. You can't give animals just any food.

W　Why is that?

M　Some snacks _____ _____ _____ to them.

W　I see. ♥ There must be something we can do.

특성 성보 파악

7 대화를 듣고, 여자가 신청하려는 문화 프로그램을 고르시오.

① 그림 그리기
② 지우개 만들기
③ 머그컵 만들기
④ 조각품 만들기
⑤ 도장 만들기

7

M What activity should I _____ _____ _____ this time?

W How about _____ _____ _____? That was fun.

M I'll think about it. What about you?

W _____ _____ _____ seems interesting. It says you _____ _____ _____ into an eraser and use it like a stamp.

M That's cool.

W I will sign up for it this time.

할 일 파악

8 대화를 듣고, 여자가 대화 직후에 할 일로 가장 적절한 것을 고르시오.

① 달리기 연습하기
② 경기에 참여하기
③ 저녁 먹으러 가기
④ 생일 선물 사러 가기
⑤ 생일 파티 하러 가기

8

M You ran really fast. _____ _____ _____ with practice?

W It's all over now.

M _____ _____ _____ have dinner together?

W Sorry, but I have _____ _____.

M Oh, yes. You said it's your dad's birthday today.

W That's tomorrow, but I *need to _____ _____ _____ for him now.

*need to [니드] [투] → [니투]

언급 유무 파악

9 대화를 듣고, 두 사람이 집안일 분담에 대해 언급하지 않은 것을 고르시오.

① 설거지
② 빨래하기
③ 분리수거
④ 요리하기
⑤ 화장실 청소

9

M What housework do you think you can do?

W I can _____ _____ _____ and do the laundry.

M Then I'll do the recycling and clean the bathroom.

W What about _____ _____ _____?

M Well, let's _____ _____ _____ _____.

W That's a good idea.

화제·주제 파악

10 다음을 듣고, 여자가 하는 말의 내용으로 가장 적절한 것을 고르시오.

① 취업 경쟁의 문제
② 좋은 직업의 특성
③ 자기 계발의 필요성
④ 미래의 꿈의 중요성
⑤ 효율적인 시간 관리 방법

10 🇬🇧

W How do you know if a certain job is good for you? First, a good job never makes you go hungry. It also _____ _____ _____ to live better. It makes you want to _____ _____ and dream about your future life. If you are willing to spend time doing your job better _____ _____ _____, it is a good job for you.

내용 불일치 파악

11 대화를 듣고, 시장 조사에 대한 내용으로 일치하지 <u>않는</u> 것을 고르시오.

① 약국 오픈을 위한 조사이다.
② 전화로 설문 조사를 할 계획이다.
③ 외부 지역 위주로 알아보려고 한다.
④ 지역 조사를 끝내고 설문 조사를 한다.
⑤ 조사 대상은 65세 이상의 사람들이다.

11

M We're going to _____ _____ _____ to open a pharmacy.

W I'll check places with big hospitals in this area.

M When we decide on a place, we need to do a survey.

W I agree with you.

M Remember that our target is _____ _____ _____ _____.

W Okay. How should we _____ _____ _____ _____ people?

M Because they are elderly, it would be _____ _____ _____ _____.

W I got it.

목적 파악

12 대화를 듣고, 여자가 수영 강습을 받는 목적으로 가장 적절한 것을 고르시오.

① 살을 빼기 위해서
② 건강을 유지하기 위해서
③ 수영 강사가 되기 위해서
④ 물 공포증을 극복하기 위해서
⑤ 새로운 운동을 해보기 위해서

💬 **I agree that + S + V**

: 동의를 나타낼 때 사용하는 표현으로, '~가 …하는 것을 동의하다'라는 뜻이다.

12

M Miranda, I *heard you started to _____ _____ _____.

W Yes, I did.

M Is there a reason why you picked swimming?

W I tried many *kinds of exercise, but I think I'm _____ _____ _____ _____ _____.

M I understand. I like to _____ _____ _____ _____ _____.

W Okay. I'm doing this to keep myself healthy now.

M 💬 I agree that health is really important.

*heard you [헐드] [유] → [헐쥬]
*kinds of [카인즈] [어브] → [카인저브]

숫자 정보 파악

13 대화를 듣고, 여자가 지불해야 할 금액으로 가장 적절한 것을 고르시오.

① $8
② $10
③ $12
④ $14
⑤ $16

13

M　Hi. How can I help you?

W　How much is one macaroon?

M　It's _____ _____ _____ _____ and five dollars for a set of three macaroons.

W　Then please give me three sets and one additional macaroon.

M　This is _____ _____ _____ to our bakery, right?

W　That's right.

M　We're offering a one-dollar discount for _____ _____ _____ _____. So the total is sixteen dollars.

W　Wow, really? Thank you so much.

관계 추론

14 대화를 듣고, 두 사람의 관계로 가장 적절한 것을 고르시오.

① 평론가 — 기자
② 감독 — 연기자
③ 편집장 — 작가
④ 연극배우 — 관객
⑤ 라디오 DJ — 청취자

14

W　This scene feels so hard.

M　You should _____ _____ _____. You should pretend like you don't feel sad.

W　How can I make the audience notice my hidden feelings?

M　_____ _____ _____ _____ _____.

W　Should I _____ _____ _____ and walk very slowly?

M　That sounds nice.

W　Okay. I'll try _____ _____ _____.

요청한 일 파악

15 대화를 듣고, 남자가 여자에게 요청한 일로 가장 적절한 것을 고르시오.

① 스튜디오 방문하기
② 사진 기술 알려 주기
③ 샘플 사진 찍어 주기
④ 촬영 모델이 되어 주기
⑤ 사진 동아리 가입하기

15　🇬🇧

M　Lily, you are interested in photography, _____ _____?

W　Yes, I am. Why do you ask?

M　Our studio is planning to _____ _____ _____ _____, and we _____ _____ _____.

W　Are you asking me to be a model?

M　Will you? I can *teach you many photography skills.

W　Okay. I _____ _____ _____.

M　You will meet a hair designer and a makeup artist that day.

W　I'm so excited.

*teach you [티치] [유] → [티츄]

이유 추론

16 대화를 듣고, 여자가 비행기 표를 취소한 이유로 가장 적절한 것을 고르시오.

① 여행 날짜를 착각해서
② 여행 계획이 변경되어서
③ 개인적인 사정이 생겨서
④ 여행 지역에 문제가 생겨서
⑤ 할인 표를 구입하기 위해서

16

W Do you have plans for this summer vacation?

M Yes. I'm going to Hong Kong.

W I also bought _____ _____ _____ to Hong Kong.

M Now there is _____ _____ _____ online.

W Really? What *is it?

M If you reserve a ticket, you can _____ _____ _____ _____.

W Oh, no! I should cancel mine and _____ _____ _____.

*is it [이즈] [잇] → [이짓]

그림 상황 파악

17 다음 그림의 상황에 가장 적절한 대화를 고르시오.

① ② ③ ④ ⑤

17

① **M** _____ _____ _____ _____?
  W It's okay.

② **M** What do you want to drink?
  W I want _____ _____ _____.

③ **M** Which do you prefer, candy or chocolate?
  W I like _____ _____.

④ **M** What happened to your leg?
  W I _____ _____ _____ at school.

⑤ **M** Are you hungry now?
  W Yes, _____ _____.

언급 유무 파악

18 대화를 듣고, 남자가 비타민 C 섭취에 관해 언급하지 않은 것을 고르시오.

① 비타민 C 섭취 횟수
② 비타민 C 구입 방법
③ 비타민 C 섭취 방법
④ 비타민 C 함유 과일
⑤ 비타민 C 섭취 효능

♥ **Absolutely.**
: 원래 의미는 '절대적으로.', '매우.'인데, 문장의 앞에 쓰여서 강한 긍정이나 확신을 나타낼 때 쓰인다.

18

W What is good about vitamin C?

M It _____ _____ _____ _____and keeps me from getting too tired.

W Do you have to *take it every day?

M _____ _____. If you're not comfortable with _____ _____, you can eat fruit.

W Oh, I love fruit. Which ones contain a lot of vitamin C?

M Oranges, strawberries, and kiwis have a lot of it.

W Maybe I _____ _____ _____.

M ♥ Absolutely.

*take it [테이크] [잇] → [테이킷]

적절한 응답 찾기

[19~20] 대화를 듣고, 여자의 마지막 말에 이어질 남자의 말로 가장 적절한 것을 고르시오.

19 Man: _____
① You don't need to get stressed.
② I have the same problem as you.
③ I hope everything gets better soon.
④ I think it's time for you to change your phone.
⑤ You'd better use it one more year.

적절한 응답 찾기

20 Man: _____
① You are such a great teacher.
② I don't think I can help you with it.
③ Tell me what you really need to do.
④ It takes time to make a good decision.
⑤ I suggest you carry just one big backpack.

♥ **I can't help it.**
: 다른 선택 사항이 없다고 얘기할 때 사용하는 표현으로, '어쩔 수 없다.'라는 뜻이다.
= It can't be helped.

19

W _____ _____ _____ _____ faster and faster.

M How long _____ _____ _____ your cellphone?

W I've *had it for more than three years.

M Wow. You've had it for a very long time.

W Should I _____ _____ _____ *with a new one?

M I think it's time for you to change your phone.

*had it [해드] [잇] → [해딧]
*with a [위드] [어] → [위더]

20 🇬🇧

W I have so many things _____ _____ _____ .

M What are all these for?

W They are for my classes.

M Do you _____ _____ _____ _____ every day?

W Yes, I do. My hands _____ _____ _____ .

M I can tell that. Your bag _____ _____ _____ .

W It is. But ♥ I can't help it.

M I suggest you carry just one big backpack.

1 다음을 듣고, 내일의 날씨로 가장 적절한 것을 고르시오.

① ② ③

④ ⑤

2 대화를 듣고, 남자가 구입할 넥타이로 가장 적절한 것을 고르시오.

① ② ③

④ ⑤

3 대화를 듣고, 여자의 심정으로 가장 적절한 것을 고르시오.

① proud ② bored ③ relieved
④ nervous ⑤ satisfied

4 대화를 듣고, 여자가 주말에 한 일로 가장 적절한 것을 고르시오.
① 공원 산책하기
② 최신 영화 보기
③ 가족과 여행하기
④ 천문대 방문하기
⑤ 가족과 오페라 보기

5 대화를 듣고, 두 사람이 대화하는 장소로 가장 적절한 곳을 고르시오.
① 병원 ② 꽃가게 ③ 경찰서
④ 기차역 ⑤ 열대 우림

6 대화를 듣고, 여자의 마지막 말의 의도로 가장 적절한 것을 고르시오.
① 사과 ② 감사 ③ 분노
④ 만족 ⑤ 격려

7 대화를 듣고, 여자가 사용하지 않을 재료를 고르시오.
① 치즈 ② 버섯 ③ 우유
④ 양념 ⑤ 옥수수

8 대화를 듣고, 남자가 대화 직후에 할 일로 가장 적절한 것을 고르시오.
① 산책하기 ② 자전거 타기
③ 편의점 가기 ④ 식료품 사러 가기
⑤ 요가 수업 등록하기

9 대화를 듣고, 여자가 병원에서 지켜야 할 사항으로 언급하지 않은 것을 고르시오.
① 조용히 활동하기
② 가족 이야기 삼가기
③ 예의 바르게 행동하기
④ 위생 상태를 청결히 하기
⑤ 의료 장비 주의해서 다루기

10 다음을 듣고, 남자가 하는 말의 내용으로 가장 적절한 것을 고르시오.
① 수업 규칙 ② 환경 보호
③ 여가 활동 ④ 수업 과정
⑤ 성적 향상 비결

11 다음을 듣고, 캠핑에 대한 내용과 일치하지 않는 것을 고르시오.
① 이틀간의 캠핑이다.
② 내일 아침 9시에 운동장에서 만난다.
③ 여분의 따뜻한 옷을 가져와야 한다.
④ 야영 시 그룹에서 이탈하지 않는다.
⑤ 무리에서 이탈 시 휴대폰으로 도움을 청한다.

12 대화를 듣고, 여자가 전화를 건 목적으로 가장 적절한 것을 고르시오.
① 일기 예보를 알리기 위해서
② 안부 인사를 전하기 위해서
③ 분실물을 찾아 주기 위해서
④ 버스 정류장의 위치를 몰라서
⑤ 우산을 가져다 달라고 하기 위해서

13 대화를 듣고, 두 사람이 만날 시각을 고르시오.
① 12시 30분 ② 1시
③ 1시 13분 ④ 1시 30분
⑤ 1시 40분

14 대화를 듣고, 두 사람의 관계로 가장 적절한 것을 고르시오.
① 경찰관 ― 시민
② 은행 직원 ― 고객
③ 학교 직원 ― 학부모
④ 기술자 ― 가게 주인
⑤ 편의점 직원 ― 손님

15 대화를 듣고, 여자가 남자에게 부탁한 일로 가장 적절한 것을 고르시오.
① 부모님 태워 드리기
② 업무 시간 분담하기
③ 세탁소에 옷 맡기기
④ 오늘 할 일 기억하기
⑤ 중요한 사람과 통화하기

16 대화를 듣고, 여자가 남자의 제안을 <u>거절한</u> 이유로 가장 적절한 것을 고르시오.
① 몸이 좋지 않아서
② 숙제의 양이 적어서
③ 공평하지 않기 때문에
④ 마감 기한이 이미 지나서
⑤ 부모님이 아프기 때문에

17 다음 그림의 상황에 가장 적절한 대화를 고르시오.

① ② ③ ④ ⑤

18 다음을 듣고, 여자가 오늘 한 일에 대해 언급하지 <u>않은</u> 것을 고르시오.
① 딸 놀이 공원 데려다주기
② 친구들과 점심 먹기
③ 병원에서 아버지 보기
④ 세탁소에서 물건 찾아오기
⑤ 저녁 준비하기

[19-20] 대화를 듣고, 남자의 마지막 말에 이어질 여자의 말로 가장 적절한 것을 고르시오.

19 Woman: _____
① You can say that again.
② I want to have a boyfriend.
③ Oh, my. What should I do now?
④ How good! Actually, I was very worried.
⑤ Time flies, so everything will be fine later.

20 Woman: _____
① Could you say that again?
② I am happy to see you again.
③ I can't wait. Where is the book?
④ You can make a card at the front desk.
⑤ That's great. I would like to make one then.

Listen and Check

● 대화를 다시 듣고, 알맞은 것을 고르시오.

1 It will rain on the weekend.

☐ True   ☐ False

2 Does the woman want to buy a tie for her dad?

☐ Yes   ☐ No

3 What did man and the woman find?

☐ the road   ☐ the light

4 The man went to the opera with the woman.

☐ True   ☐ False

5 The woman sends some flowers to her aunt.

☐ True   ☐ False

6 Does the woman have a singing contest today?

☐ Yes   ☐ No

7 What does the woman make?

☐ mushroom soup   ☐ corn soup

8 Has the woman done yoga before?

☐ Yes   ☐ No

9 The man can talk about his family with old people in the hospital.

☐ True   ☐ False

10 There are no rules for the man's class.

☐ Yes   ☐ No

11 Campers should bring warm clothes because it can be cold at night.

☐ True   ☐ False

12 Where should the man go to give the umbrella to the woman?

☐ school   ☐ the bus station

13 Are the man and the woman going to meet on Saturday?

☐ Yes   ☐ No

14 What did the man show the woman?

☐ a credit card   ☐ an ID card

15 The woman didn't know the man was busy.

☐ True   ☐ False

16 Did the woman give the man more time?

☐ Yes   ☐ No

17 The man brought his wallet.

☐ True   ☐ False

18 Why did the woman go to the amusement park again?

☐ to pick up her daughter

☐ to meet her friends

19 The boy with the man's girlfriend was her younger brother.

☐ True   ☐ False

20 If the woman makes a membership card, can she get a new book for free?

☐ Yes   ☐ No

그림 정보 파악

1 다음을 듣고, 내일의 날씨로 가장 적절한 것을 고르시오.

① ② ③

④ ⑤

1

W Good morning. This is the weekly weather report. We had _____ _____ _____. But *if you are planning to do outdoor activities tomorrow, you're very lucky. It's going to be sunny and mild! Bright sunshine will be all yours tomorrow. However, it's going to rain _____ _____ _____ _____ the day after tomorrow. It'll clear up on the weekend. I hope you have _____ _____ _____ and see you next time.

*if you [이프] [유] → [이퓨]

그림 정보 파악

2 대화를 듣고, 남자가 구입할 넥타이로 가장 적절한 것을 고르시오.

① ② ③

④ ⑤

2

M Sandra, _____ _____ _____ a tie for Dad. How about this one?

W Striped patterns are a bit boring. Get him a tie with _____ _____. How about this one?

M I don't think he'd like animals.

W Then what about these ones with wave patterns?

M Oh, I like them. But _____ _____ _____ a tie with a flower pattern?

W Maybe not. Well, I believe a wave pattern is better. _____ _____ _____ get that one with *waves on it?

M Okay. I hope he likes it.

*waves on it [웨이브스] [언] [잇] → [웨이브써닛]

심정 추론

3 대화를 듣고, 여자의 심정으로 가장 적절한 것을 고르시오.

① proud   ② bored
③ relieved   ④ nervous
⑤ satisfied

💙 **I have no idea.**

: 상대방이 의견을 요청하거나 질문을 할 때 '나는 전혀 모른다.'는 의미로 사용된다.

3

W Mark, where are we going? I think _____ _____ _____.

M I don't know. I can't find the road.

W And it's getting darker.

M I am sure we are taking _____ _____ _____. What should we do?

W 💙 I have no idea. I feel cold and hungry.

M Look! I can _____ _____ _____ over there.

W Oh. We are saved. _____ _____ _____ to the light.

M Yes. We could ask that person how to get home.

한 일 파악

4 대화를 듣고, 여자가 주말에 한 일로 가장 적절한 것을 고르시오.

① 공원 산책하기
② 최신 영화 보기
③ 가족과 여행하기
④ 천문대 방문하기
⑤ 가족과 오페라 보기

4

M   How was your weekend?

W   I spent the entire time with my family.

M   _____ _____ _____ _____ with your family?

W   My parents and I _____ _____ _____ dinner. And then we went to an opera.

M   An opera! It _____ _____ _____ fantastic.

W   Yes. We enjoyed it very much. How was your weekend?

M   I walked my dog in the park. It was _____ _____ _____ _____.

W   You're right. I was happy to see the clear blue sky.

장소 추론

5 대화를 듣고, 두 사람이 대화하는 장소로 가장 적절한 곳을 고르시오.

① 병원
② 꽃가게
③ 경찰서
④ 기차역
⑤ 열대 우림

5

W   Can I help you?

M   I'd like to send a plant to my aunt. She is _____ _____ _____ _____.

W   I see. How about this plant? It is very popular for store openings.

M   It's wonderful. I'll buy it.

W   Good. _____ _____ _____ _____ _____?

M   To Brown Bakery. It's ten blocks away from here. Here is the address.

W   Okay. It _____ _____ _____ *within an hour.

M   Thanks a lot.

*within an hour [위드인] [언] [아우어] → [위던아워]

의도 파악

6 대화를 듣고, 여자의 마지막 말의 의도로 가장 적절한 것을 고르시오.

① 사과   ② 감사
③ 분노   ④ 만족
⑤ 격려

♥ **Come on.**
: 상대방을 격려하거나 어떤 행동을 재촉하거나 상대방을 가볍게 질책할 때 사용되는 표현이다.

6 🇬🇧

W   You have a long face. Is there something wrong?

M   You know, I have a _____ _____ _____. I'm nervous.

W   ♥Come on. You practiced a lot. I'm sure you will do well.

M   But I get the lyrics wrong again and again. I am afraid I _____ _____ _____.

W   I think you'd better try to be _____ _____ the contest.

M   Okay. I'll try.

W   Do not worry too much. I believe you will be _____ _____ _____ _____ _____ _____.

특정 정보 파악

7 대화를 듣고, 여자가 사용하지 <u>않을</u> 재료를 고르시오.

① 치즈　　② 버섯
③ 우유　　④ 양념
⑤ 옥수수

7

M　What are you doing? Cooking?

W　Hi, Dad. I am making some soup for Mom. You know ＿＿＿＿＿ ＿＿＿＿＿ ＿＿＿＿＿ ＿＿＿＿＿ and hasn't eaten anything today.

M　Oh, that's my lovely daughter. What did you put in the soup?

W　I put butter, milk, and some seasonings in it. ＿＿＿＿＿ ＿＿＿＿＿ ＿＿＿＿＿.

M　Perfect. ＿＿＿＿＿ ＿＿＿＿＿ ＿＿＿＿＿ ＿＿＿＿＿ some corn. Your mom likes to *eat it.

W　Oh, I almost forgot. Thanks for the advice.

*eat it [잇] [잇] → [이릿]

할 일 파악

8 대화를 듣고, 남자가 대화 직후에 할 일로 가장 적절한 것을 고르시오.

① 산책하기
② 자전거 타기
③ 편의점 가기
④ 식료품 사러 가기
⑤ 요가 수업 등록하기

8 🇬🇧

W　I'm ＿＿＿＿＿ ＿＿＿＿＿ ＿＿＿＿＿ these days.

M　So am I. Because of that, I'm taking a yoga class to relax.

W　Really? I ＿＿＿＿＿ ＿＿＿＿＿ ＿＿＿＿＿ ＿＿＿＿＿. Does it help?

M　Yes, it does. By the way, how about going for a walk? I think it will be ＿＿＿＿＿ ＿＿＿＿＿ ＿＿＿＿＿ to relax.

W　I agree. There is a park near my house. I should go to the park with you this evening.

M　Okay. Let's go. But before that, we have to drop by the store to ＿＿＿＿＿ ＿＿＿＿＿ ＿＿＿＿＿.

W　I see.

언급 유무 파악

9 대화를 듣고, 여자가 병원에서 지켜야 할 사항으로 언급하지 <u>않은</u> 것을 고르시오.

① 조용히 활동하기
② 가족 이야기 삼가기
③ 예의 바르게 행동하기
④ 위생 상태를 청결히 하기
⑤ 의료 장비 주의해서 다루기

9

W　Welcome, volunteers. I'm Sally O'Brien, the chief nurse.

M　Hello. ＿＿＿＿＿ ＿＿＿＿＿ ＿＿＿＿＿ ＿＿＿＿＿ to follow in this hospital?

W　Thanks for asking that. First, you should be quiet. And you know, you should be ＿＿＿＿＿ ＿＿＿＿＿ ＿＿＿＿＿ ＿＿＿＿＿.

M　I see. Is there anything else?

W　You should handle the medical devices carefully, and you had better not talk about your families. ＿＿＿＿＿ ＿＿＿＿＿ ＿＿＿＿＿ ＿＿＿＿＿ the old people here have no families.

M　Okay. We fully understand.

화제·주제 파악

10 다음을 듣고, 남자가 하는 말의 내용으로 가장 적절한 것을 고르시오.

① 수업 규칙   ② 환경 보호
③ 여가 활동   ④ 수업 과정
⑤ 성적 향상 비결

10

M Hi, everyone. I'm your new English teacher, Mr. Collins. Before we start studying, I want to let you know _____ _____ _____ for my class. Please be on time for class and be seated before class begins. You have to _____ _____ _____ _____ _____ and notebooks on your desk. Raise your hand when you have a question. I welcome any questions about the class. That's all I _____ _____ _____ _____. Thank you.

내용 불일치 파악

11 다음을 듣고, 캠핑에 대한 내용과 일치하지 <u>않는</u> 것을 고르시오.

① 이틀간의 캠핑이다.
② 내일 아침 9시에 운동장에서 만난다.
③ 여분의 따뜻한 옷을 가져와야 한다.
④ 야영 시 그룹에서 이탈하지 않는다.
⑤ 무리에서 이탈 시 휴대폰으로 도움을 청한다.

11

W Hello, campers! Are you excited about our two-day camping trip? I'd like to *give you _____ _____ _____. First, we'll meet here at the playground at nine o'clock tomorrow morning. Please don't be late as our buses are going to leave on time. Second, _____ _____ _____ _____ extra warm clothes. It'll be quite cold in the mountains at night. Lastly, never leave your group _____ _____ _____ _____ _____. If you get separated from the others, immediately shout for help. That's all.

*give you [기브] [유] → [기뷰]

목적 파악

12 대화를 듣고, 여자가 전화를 건 목적으로 가장 적절한 것을 고르시오.

① 일기 예보를 알리기 위해서
② 안부 인사를 전하기 위해서
③ 분실물을 찾아 주기 위해서
④ 버스 정류장의 위치를 몰라서
⑤ 우산을 가져다 달라고 하기 위해서

12

[Telephone rings.]

M Hello.

W Hi, Uncle Sam! This is Jane!

M Hi, Jane. Is there a problem?

W It's pouring now, but I don't have an umbrella. I called Mom and Dad, but _____ _____ _____.

M Do you _____ _____ _____ _____ _____ an umbrella?

W Yes, please. I'm at the bus stop _____ _____.

M Okay. I'll be there soon.

숫자 정보 파악

13 대화를 듣고, 두 사람이 만날 시각을 고르시오.

① 12시 30분 ② 1시
③ 1시 13분 ④ 1시 30분
⑤ 1시 40분

♥ **No problem.**

: 상대방의 부탁이나 제안에 긍정적으로 응답할 때 쓰는 표현으로 '문제없어.', '괜찮아.'라는 의미이다. 상대방이 고마움 또는 미안함을 표현했을 때에도 흔히 쓰인다.

13

W Jack, I'm going to an art gallery to see a Van Gogh exhibition on Saturday. _____ _____ _____ _____ _____ with me?

M A Van Gogh exhibition? He is one of my favorite artists. _____ _____ _____ _____ _____ ?

W Let's meet *in front of the subway station at one thirty.

M Can we meet a bit earlier? My taekwondo lesson finishes around twelve thirty, and it takes only ten minutes to get there.

W Then how about at one? I need to be at home by twelve thirty _____ _____ _____ _____ .

M ♥No problem. I'll see you on Saturday.

*in front of [인] [프런트] [어브] → [인프런텁]

관계 추론

14 대화를 듣고, 두 사람의 관계로 가장 적절한 것을 고르시오.

① 경찰관 ─ 시민
② 은행 직원 ─ 고객
③ 학교 직원 ─ 학부모
④ 기술자 ─ 가게 주인
⑤ 편의점 직원 ─ 손님

♥ **Here you go.**

: 상대방에게 무엇을 전달할 때 쓰는 표현으로 '자, 여기 있어.' 정도의 의미이다.

14

W Number 27, please. Hi! What can I do for you?

M I am here _____ _____ _____ _____ .

W How much would you like to *take out?

M I need to withdraw $500.

W Oh, I see. _____ _____ _____ your ID, please?

M Sure. ♥Here you go.

W Thanks. _____ _____ _____ your PIN here?

M Absolutely.

*take out [테이크] [아웃] → [테카웃]

부탁한 일 파악

15 대화를 듣고, 여자가 남자에게 부탁한 일로 가장 적절한 것을 고르시오.

① 부모님 태워 드리기
② 업무 시간 분담하기
③ 세탁소에 옷 맡기기
④ 오늘 할 일 기억하기
⑤ 중요한 사람과 통화하기

♥ **Never mind.**

: '신경 쓰지 마.'라는 의미이며, 상대방을 위로하거나 격려, 상대방이 미안해할 때 사용하는 표현이다.

---

15 🇬🇧

W Honey, do you remember I asked you to _____ _____ _____ _____ this morning?

M No. What was it?

W I asked you to take my clothes _____ _____ _____ .

M I'm sorry, but I _____ _____ _____ to do it. I had to go to work, meet important people, and pick up our kids today.

W I know _____ _____ .

M Yeah, sorry. But it's true that I have a lot of things to do.

W I understand. ♥Never mind.

이유 추론

16 대화를 듣고, 여자가 남자의 제안을 거절한 이유로 가장 적절한 것을 고르시오.

① 몸이 좋지 않아서
② 숙제의 양이 적어서
③ 공평하지 않기 때문에
④ 마감 기한이 이미 지나서
⑤ 부모님이 아프기 때문에

16 🇬🇧

M Hello, Ms. Parker. Do you have a minute to talk with me?

W Sure. What is it?

M I _____ _____ my homework yet. I need more time.

W Can I ask why?

M Well, my mom got so sick last weekend that I _____ _____ _____ _____ _____ her. That's why.

W I'm sorry to hear that. But I can't give you more time because it is _____ _____ to the other students.

M But...

W Plus, you still have five days to _____ _____ _____. So try your best.

그림 상황 파악

17 다음 그림의 상황에 가장 적절한 대화를 고르시오.

① ② ③ ④ ⑤

17

① W Your wallet is nice. Where did you buy it?
  M Thanks. I bought it at a _____ _____.

② W Are you new here?
  M Yes, I am. _____ _____ _____ _____?

③ W Here it is, sir.
  M Oops. I _____ _____ _____ behind at my house.

④ W How much is it?
  M It's fifty dollars. That's a _____ _____.

⑤ W Next, please.
  M Yes. I'd like to _____ _____ _____ on these pants.

언급 유무 파악

18 다음을 듣고, 여자가 오늘 한 일에 대해 언급하지 <u>않은</u> 것을 고르시오.

① 딸 놀이 공원 데려다주기
② 친구들과 점심 먹기
③ 병원에서 아버지 보기
④ 세탁소에서 물건 찾아오기
⑤ 저녁 준비하기

18

W Today was a busy day for me. I drove my daughter _____ _____ _____ early in the morning. On my way back home, I went to the hospital to see my dad. He is staying in the general hospital in our town. I had a lunch meeting with my friends. I went to the amusement park again _____ _____ _____ _____ at two p.m. After I came back home, I prepared for dinner and _____ _____ _____.

[19-20] 대화를 듣고, 남자의 마지막 말에
이어질 여자의 말로 가장 적절한 것을
고르시오.

19 Woman: _____
① You can say that again.
② I want to have a boyfriend.
③ Oh, my. What should I do
   now?
④ How good! Actually, I was
   very worried.
⑤ Time flies, so everything will
   be fine later.

19

W Do you know what? I _____ _____ _____ Sujin on
  the street.
M Did you? How was she?
W She looked all right. But...
M You are _____ _____ _____. What happened?
W She was _____ _____ _____ _____. They
  seemed very close. Is your relationship okay?
M Ha-ha. Don't worry. Maybe he is her older brother Taeho,
  _____ _____ _____ _____.
W How good! Actually, I was very worried.

---

20 Woman: _____
① Could you say that again?
② I am happy to see you again.
③ I can't wait. Where is the
   book?
④ You can make a card at the
   front desk.
⑤ That's great. I would like to
   make one then.

20

M Hello. May I help you?
W Yes. I _____ _____ _____ the bestselling books
  these days.
M Go straight about twenty meters. You can _____ _____
  _____ _____.
W Oh, thank you. This bookstore is very big.
M Right. _____ _____ _____ _____. Do you have
  a bookstore membership card? If you *have one, you can buy
  books _____ _____ _____.
W That's great. I would like to make one then.

*have one [해브] [원] → [해뷘]

1 다음을 듣고, 방콕의 날씨로 가장 적절한 것을 고르시오.

① ② ③ ④ ⑤

2 대화를 듣고, 테이블 위의 물건 배치로 가장 적절한 것을 고르시오.

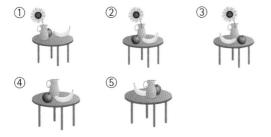

① ② ③ ④ ⑤

3 대화를 듣고, 여자의 심정으로 가장 적절한 것을 고르시오.
① excited　　　② irritated
③ confused　　④ sorrowful
⑤ indifferent

4 대화를 듣고, 여자가 지난 토요일에 한 일로 가장 적절한 것을 고르시오.
① 스테이크 먹기　　② 바다에서 수영하기
③ 스노클링 하기　　④ 오페라 관람하기
⑤ 집에서 푹 자기

5 대화를 듣고, 두 사람이 대화하는 장소로 가장 적절한 곳을 고르시오.
① 공항　　　　　② 사진관
③ 여행사　　　　④ 카메라 상점
⑤ 여권 발급 기관

6 대화를 듣고, 여자의 마지막 말의 의도로 가장 적절한 것을 고르시오.
① 분노　　　② 조언　　　③ 격려
④ 동의　　　⑤ 거절

7 대화를 듣고, 여자가 오케스트라에서 연주할 악기를 고르시오.
① 호른　　　② 첼로　　　③ 피아노
④ 플루트　　⑤ 바이올린

8 대화를 듣고, 남자가 대화 직후에 할 일로 가장 적절한 것을 고르시오.
① 종이꽃 접기　　　② 방 청소하기
③ 풍선에 바람 넣기　④ 공항에 마중 가기
⑤ 케이크 사러 가기

9 다음을 듣고, 여자가 에펠 탑에 대해 언급하지 않은 것을 고르시오.
① 파리에서 볼 수 있다.
② 관광객들에게 유명하다.
③ 철로 만들어진 건축물이다.
④ 불빛 때문에 밤에 예쁘다.
⑤ 사랑의 상징이라고 알려졌다.

10 다음을 듣고, 남자가 하는 말의 내용으로 가장 적절한 것을 고르시오.
① 인터뷰를 잘하는 방법　② 편식을 고치는 방법
③ 질문의 중요성　　　　④ 외부 강사 초청 강의 안내
⑤ 직업을 찾을 때 고려해야 할 것

11 대화를 듣고, 여자가 언급한 내용과 일치하지 않는 것을 고르시오.
① 여자는 15분 전에 개를 잃어버렸다.
② 개는 하얀 털을 가지고 있다.
③ 개는 노란색 옷을 입고 있다.
④ 개는 자신의 이름을 부르면 온다.
⑤ 개를 찾으면 전화해 달라고 했다.

12 대화를 듣고, 여자가 명동을 방문한 목적으로 가장 적절한 것을 고르시오.

① 친구를 만나려고
② 가방을 교환하려고
③ 물감을 구입하려고
④ 머리를 손질하려고
⑤ 원피스를 구입하려고

13 대화를 듣고, 여자가 지불해야 할 금액으로 가장 적절한 것을 고르시오.

① $250   ② $270   ③ $300
④ $330   ⑤ $350

14 대화를 듣고, 두 사람의 관계로 가장 적절한 것을 고르시오.

① 소방관 — 행인
② 공무원 — 시민
③ 운전기사 — 승객
④ 가게 점원 — 손님
⑤ 매표소 직원 — 소비자

15 대화를 듣고, 남자가 여자에게 요청한 일로 가장 적절한 것을 고르시오.

① 서둘러 집에 오기
② 아기 달래주기
③ 병원 예약하기
④ 저녁 준비하기
⑤ 식료품 사오기

16 대화를 듣고, 여자가 보고서를 제출하지 <u>못한</u> 이유로 가장 적절한 것을 고르시오.

① 집에 두고 와서
② 병원에 입원해서
③ 친구에게 빌려줘서
④ 할머니가 돌아가셔서
⑤ 동생 돌보느라 바빠서

17 다음 그림의 상황에 가장 적절한 대화를 고르시오.

①   ②   ③   ④   ⑤

18 대화를 듣고, 두 사람이 사업가 Mr. Harris에 관해 언급하지 <u>않은</u> 것을 고르시오.

① 부유하고 성공한 사업가이다.
② 현재의 나이는 30대이다.
③ 가난한 집에서 태어났다.
④ 2개 국어를 말할 수 있다.
⑤ 기사에 소개되었다.

[19~20] 대화를 듣고, 남자의 마지막 말에 이어질 여자의 말로 가장 적절한 것을 고르시오.

19 Woman: _____

① Okay. Let's go now. I'm starving.
② Sorry, but I don't need any plastic bags.
③ That is an interesting way to recycle waste.
④ Be my guest. You're going to be a big help.
⑤ Don't throw that cigarette butt on the ground.

20 Woman: _____

① No more. Keep your word.
② Son, let me fix your computer.
③ Playing computer games is my hobby.
④ Too much coffee may disturb your sleep.
⑤ Don't worry. I'll lend you some more game CDs.

Listen and Check

● 대화를 다시 듣고, 알맞은 것을 고르시오.

1 The man is reporting the world weather forecast.

☐ True　　　☐ False

2 What did the man prepare a banana for?

☐ eating　　　☐ drawing

3 Who won the final baseball game?

☐ the Boston Red Sox

☐ the New York Yankees

4 What did the man do last Sunday?

☐ ate steak　　　☐ swam

5 Why did the woman take a picture?

☐ for fun　　　☐ for a passport

6 Who has an English test tomorrow?

☐ the man　　　☐ the woman

7 Has the man taken lessons for the violin before?

☐ Yes　　　☐ No

8 The man forgot to bring the cake.

☐ True　　　☐ False

9 The Eiffel Tower is covered with lots of lights.

☐ True　　　☐ False

10 Why did Ms. Sewell visit the school?

☐ to give a lecture　　　☐ to ask questions

11 Where did the woman lose her dog?

☐ at the park　　　☐ in the parking lot

12 Does Hazel live in Myeongdong?

☐ Yes　　　☐ No

13 Did the woman buy a bicycle helmet, too?

☐ Yes　　　☐ No

14 The bus driver didn't take money from passengers.

☐ True　　　☐ False

15 Anna and her baby had to stay home.

☐ True　　　☐ False

16 Until when should the woman hand in her report?

☐ Wednesday　　　☐ Friday

17 The sign says "Disabled Parking Only."

☐ True　　　☐ False

18 Mr. Harris can speak German.

☐ True　　　☐ False

19 Does the woman hate seeing litter on the ground?

☐ Yes　　　☐ No

20 What time is it now?

☐ 9:00 p.m.　　　☐ 12:00 a.m.

그림 정보 파악

1 다음을 듣고, 방콕의 날씨로 가장 적절한 것을 고르시오.

① ② ③

④ ⑤

♥ **It's time for ~.**

: 어떤 일을 해야 한다고 알려줄 때 쓰는 표현으로, '~할 시간이야.'라는 뜻이다.

1

M ♥ It's time for the world weather report. Let's look at the _____ _____ in Asia. Seoul will have _____ _____ _____ _____ today. Both Hanoi and Manila will be warm and sunny though. Bangkok is _____ _____ _____. In Taipei, the skies will be cloudy. That's it for the weather report.

그림 정보 파악

2 대화를 듣고, 테이블 위의 물건 배치로 가장 적절한 것을 고르시오.

① ② ③

④ ⑤

2

M Today, we will draw still objects. Look at the table.

W Sir, I'm afraid that I can't see _____ _____ _____.

M Really? Let me _____ _____ _____ in front of the vase.

W Can you move the banana next to the apple?

M To the right or the left?

W The right side, sir. And can you _____ _____ _____ _____ _____ _____?

M No problem. [*Pause*] Now it's done.

W Thank you so much.

심정 추론

3 대화를 듣고, 여자의 심정으로 가장 적절한 것을 고르시오.

① excited ② irritated
③ confused ④ sorrowful
⑤ indifferent

♥ **What a shame.**

: 어떤 일에 대한 유감이나 아쉬움을 나타낼 때 쓰는 표현으로, '안됐다.', '아쉽다.'라는 뜻이다.

= That's too bad.

3

M Is there _____ _____ on TV?

W I'm watching the final baseball game between the Boston Red Sox and the New York Yankees.

M Oh. _____ _____ _____ about the game. I'm a huge fan of the New York Yankees.

W ♥ What a shame. You are my enemy.

M Wait! Oh, no. The batter for the Red Sox _____ _____ _____ _____.

W Yes! Finally, the Red Sox have defeated the Yankees.

M I can't *believe it.

*believe it [빌리브] [잇] → [빌리빗]

한 일 파악

4 대화를 듣고, 여자가 지난 토요일에 한 일로 가장 적절한 것을 고르시오.

① 스테이크 먹기
② 바다에서 수영하기
③ 스노클링 하기
④ 오페라 관람하기
⑤ 집에서 푹 자기

4 🇬🇧

W How was your last Saturday?

M It was fun. I _____ _____ and snorkeling in the sea.

W I love _____ _____ _____ _____ _____, too.

M Go with me the next time. What did you do last Saturday?

W I went to _____ _____ _____. It was fantastic.

M I didn't know you are into opera.

장소 추론

5 대화를 듣고, 두 사람이 대화하는 장소로 가장 적절한 곳을 고르시오.

① 공항
② 사진관
③ 여행사
④ 카메라 상점
⑤ 여권 발급기관

5

W Hello. I want to _____ _____ _____ _____.

M Okay. Come inside when you are ready.

W All right. Should I sit here?

M Good. Look at the camera. Smile. [*Shutter sounds*] You're all done.

W Thank you. When can I _____ _____ _____?

M It will *take a day to print the photos.

W Okay. _____ _____ _____ tomorrow afternoon.

*take a [테이크] [어] → [테커]

의도 파악

6 대화를 듣고, 여자의 마지막 말의 의도로 가장 적절한 것을 고르시오.

① 분노　　　② 조언
③ 격려　　　④ 동의
⑤ 거절

♥ **Sorry to bother you.**
: 누군가를 방해해서 미안하다고 말할 때 쓰는 표현으로, '성가시게 해서 미안해.'라는 뜻이다.

6

M Mirae, can you _____ _____ _____?

W ♥Sorry to bother you.

M I'm a little nervous because I _____ _____ _____ _____ tomorrow.

W Do you want something to eat?

M No, thanks. I need to _____ _____ _____.

W Cheer up! I'm sure you will do well.

7 대화를 듣고, 여자가 오케스트라에서 연주할 악기를 고르시오.

① 호른
② 첼로
③ 피아노
④ 플루트
⑤ 바이올린

7

M   The school orchestra is _____ _____ _____ _____ this Saturday.

W   I know. Actually, I am a member of the orchestra.

M   Really? What do you play?

W   I _____ _____ _____. Well, I heard your hobby is playing the violin, right?

M   That's true. I took lessons for the violin and the flute.

W   You must be _____ _____ _____ _____.

8 대화를 듣고, 남자가 대화 직후에 할 일로 가장 적절한 것을 고르시오.

① 종이꽃 접기
② 방 청소하기
③ 풍선에 바람 넣기
④ 공항에 마중 가기
⑤ 케이크 사러 가기

8 🇬🇧

M   Colorful balloons and paper flowers _____ _____.

W   Nice, huh? I have decorated it for 2 hours.

M   _____ _____ Jina will like it.

W   Jack, where's the cake? You promised to bring it today.

M   I totally forgot about it. I'll run to the bakery.

W   Hurry. Jina arrived at the airport _____ _____ _____ _____.

M   No problem. I won't _____ _____ _____ _____.

9 다음을 듣고, 여자가 에펠 탑에 대해 언급하지 <u>않은</u> 것을 고르시오.

① 파리에서 볼 수 있다.
② 관광객들에게 유명하다.
③ 철로 만들어진 건축물이다.
④ 불빛 때문에 밤에 예쁘다.
⑤ 사랑의 상징이라고 알려졌다.

9

W   I want to tell you about the Eiffel Tower. You can see it in Paris, France. It is so famous that tourists _____ _____ _____ _____ _____ visit Paris. Because the Eiffel Tower _____ _____ _____ lots of lights, it *looks so romantic and pretty at night. So it has become a _____ _____ _____.

*looks so [룩스] [쏘우] → [룩쏘]

10

화제·주제 파악

10 다음을 듣고, 남자가 하는 말의 내용으로 가장 적절한 것을 고르시오.

① 인터뷰를 잘하는 방법
② 편식을 고치는 방법
③ 질문의 중요성
④ 외부 강사 초청 강의 안내
⑤ 직업을 찾을 때 고려해야 할 것

M   Good morning, students. Attention, please. After lunch, we're going to have a _____ _____ in the auditorium. Ms. Sewell from a law firm will visit our school to give a lecture. She is a lawyer, so she will _____ _____ _____ _____.
After listening to her lecture, you can *ask her whatever you want. It will be a good opportunity _____ _____ _____ _____ _____ _____.

*ask her [애스크] [헐] → [애스컬]

11

내용 불일치 파악

11 대화를 듣고, 여자가 언급한 내용과 일치하지 <u>않는</u> 것을 고르시오.

① 여자는 15분 전에 개를 잃어버렸다.
② 개는 하얀 털을 가지고 있다.
③ 개는 노란색 옷을 입고 있다.
④ 개는 자신의 이름을 부르면 온다.
⑤ 개를 찾으면 전화해 달라고 했다.

♥ **I got it.**
: 상대방의 말이 무슨 의미인지 이해했다고 말하고 싶을 때 쓰는 표현으로, '이해했어.'라는 뜻이다.
= I understand.

W   Can you help me? I lost my dog at the park about 50 minutes ago.
M   That's terrible. I'll _____ _____ _____ _____ your dog.
W   She has white fur and is wearing yellow clothes.
M   Okay. What's her name?
W   Bubble. _____ _____ _____ _____, she will come to you.
M   She is so clever! Don't worry. _____ _____ _____ _____.
W   Thank you. If you find her, call me, please.
M   ♥ I got it.

12

목적 파악

12 대화를 듣고, 여자가 명동을 방문한 목적으로 가장 적절한 것을 고르시오.

① 친구를 만나려고
② 가발을 교환하려고
③ 물감을 구입하려고
④ 머리를 손질하려고
⑤ 원피스를 구입하려고

M   Hazel, _____ _____ _____ _____ here for?
W   I came to Myeongdong to do my hair.
M   But you don't live here. Isn't it far from your place?
W   Right. But I _____ _____ _____. This hairdresser is really good.
M   How would like your hair done?
W   Hmm... I'm thinking of _____ _____ _____ _____ _____ and changing my hair color.
M   That will look nice.

13

숫자 정보 파악

13 대화를 듣고, 여자가 지불해야 할 금액으로 가장 적절한 것을 고르시오.

① $250
② $270
③ $300
④ $330
⑤ $350

W Good evening. Can you _____ _____ _____ for me?

M Sure. Well, how do you like this one?

W It looks nice. How much is it?

M The original price is 300 dollars, but we can _____ _____ _____ _____ _____ .

W That's a great deal. I'm definitely going to get that.

M How about a helmet? _____ _____ _____ _____ is important.

W I agree. How much is it in total?

M All together, it's 350 dollars.

14

관계 추론

14 대화를 듣고, 두 사람의 관계로 가장 적절한 것을 고르시오.

① 소방관 — 행인
② 공무원 — 시민
③ 운전기사 — 승객
④ 가게 점원 — 손님
⑤ 매표소 직원 — 소비자

🌱 **That's a relief.**

: 안도나 안심을 나타낼 때 쓰는 표현으로, '다행이다.'라는 뜻이다.
= It's a good thing.
= What a relief!

W Excuse me. Does this bus go to Gangneung?

M Yes. _____ _____ _____ _____ . We are leaving soon.

W That's great. How much is it?

M We don't _____ _____ _____ _____ . You have to buy a bus ticket at the office.

W Oh, dear. Can you wait for me just for a second?

M Okay. The ticket office is _____ _____ _____ _____ . It's close.

W ♥That's a relief. Thanks.

15 🇬🇧

요청한 일 파악

15 대화를 듣고, 남자가 여자에게 요청한 일로 가장 적절한 것을 고르시오.

① 서둘러 집에 오기
② 아기 달래주기
③ 병원 예약하기
④ 저녁 준비하기
⑤ 식료품 사오기

[*Cellphone rings.*]

W Hi, honey. What's up?

M Anna, are you _____ _____ _____ _____ now?

W I've _____ _____ . Did something bad happen?

M Daisy kept crying, so I had to _____ _____ with her. I didn't buy any groceries.

W Okay. Do you want me to buy some groceries?

M That's correct. _____ _____ _____ buying some onions, carrots, and eggs?

W Not at all. See you soon.

이유 추론

16 대화를 듣고, 여자가 보고서를 제출하지 <u>못한</u> 이유로 가장 적절한 것을 고르시오.

① 집에 두고 와서
② 병원에 입원해서
③ 친구에게 빌려줘서
④ 할머니가 돌아가셔서
⑤ 동생 돌보느라 바빠서

🤍 **Take your time.**
: 당황해서 서두르고 있는 상대방에게 시간을 가지고 차분히 하라고 말할 때 쓰는 표현으로, '천천히 해.'라는 뜻이다.

16

M Hayeon, all the students turned in their reports except you.

W Sorry, sir. But I _____ _____ _____.

M You are not going to tell me that you were sick, are you?

W No. In fact, my grandmother _____ _____ last week.

M Oh, I'm sorry to hear that. 🤍Take your time and _____ _____ _____ _____ by Friday.

W Thank you for understanding.

그림 상황 파악

17 다음 그림의 상황에 가장 적절한 대화를 고르시오.

① ② ③ ④ ⑤

🤍 **I didn't mean it.**
: 의도하지 않았던 일이 생겼을 때 쓰는 표현으로, '그럴 생각은 아니었어.'라는 뜻이다.

17

① M Come closer. There is _____ _____ behind your car.

  W Are you sure? Okay.

② M Hey, you can't park your car here. This is for the disabled.

  W Sorry. I _____ _____ _____ _____.

③ M _____ _____ *with your car?

  W The car won't start.

④ M Look at you. Somebody bought _____ _____ _____.

  W Get in the car. Let's go for a drive.

⑤ M Excuse me, but you are _____ _____ my foot.

  W Sorry. 🤍I didn't mean it.

*with your [위드] [유얼] → [위듀얼]

언급 유무 파악

18 대화를 듣고, 두 사람이 사업가 Mr. Harris에 관해 언급하지 <u>않은</u> 것을 고르시오.

① 부유하고 성공한 사업가이다.
② 현재의 나이는 30대이다.
③ 가난한 집에서 태어났다.
④ 4개 국어를 말할 수 있다.
⑤ 기사에 소개되었다.

18 🇬🇧

M What are you reading?

W It's about Mr. Harris, a _____ _____ _____ _____.

M Why is he in the article? Did he do something special?

W He was _____ _____ _____ _____ _____, but he runs 3 hotels in his early 30s.

M Hmm... That's impressive.

W He can speak 3 languages: English, German, and Spanish.

M I guess he studied hard at school.

W That's _____ _____ _____.

적절한 응답 찾기

[19-20] 대화를 듣고, 남자의 마지막 말에 이어질 여자의 말로 가장 적절한 것을 고르시오.

19 Woman: _____
   ① Okay. Let's go now. I'm starving.
   ② Sorry, but I don't need any plastic bags.
   ③ That is an interesting way to recycle waste.
   ④ Be my guest. You're going to be a big help.
   ⑤ Don't throw that cigarette butt on the ground.

19

M What are you _____ _____ _____ _____ _____?

W Garbage. I just _____ _____ _____ on the ground.

M Do you think you can clean very much?

W I don't think so. But at least I can make the street look better.

M You are so kind. _____ _____ _____ _____?

W <u>Be my guest. You're going to be a big help.</u>

적절한 응답 찾기

20 Woman: _____
   ① No more. Keep your word.
   ② Son, let me fix your computer.
   ③ Playing computer games is my hobby.
   ④ Too much coffee may disturb your sleep.
   ⑤ Don't worry. I'll lend you some more game CDs.

♥ **That's another story.**
   : 말하는 내용이 현재 대화 중인 내용과 다른 별개의 이야기라고 말할 때 쓰는 표현으로, '그건 별개의 이야기야.'라는 뜻이다.
   = That's a different story.

20

W Matthew, are you still _____ _____ _____ _____ _____?

M Sorry, Mom. Just 5 more minutes.

W You promised me that you would finish playing the computer game at 9:00 p.m.

M I know. But I _____ _____ _____ _____ in math this semester.

W So what? ♥ That's another story.

M And this game CD is not mine. I have to return it tomorrow.

W It's midnight. It's _____ _____ _____ _____.

M Please, just 5 more minutes.

W <u>No more. Keep your word.</u>

1 다음을 듣고, 내일의 날씨로 가장 적절한 것을 고르시오.

①   ②   ③

④   ⑤

2 대화를 듣고, 여자가 살 장난감으로 가장 적절한 것을 고르시오.

①   ②   ③

④   ⑤

3 대화를 듣고, 남자의 심정으로 가장 적절한 것을 고르시오.
① envious   ② nervous
③ pleased   ④ satisfied
⑤ disappointed

4 다음을 듣고, 여자가 주말에 한 일로 가장 적절한 것을 고르시오.
① 집에서 독서하기
② 조부모님 방문하기
③ 친척 집을 방문하기
④ 주말 농장 견학 가기
⑤ 친구와 도서관 가기

5 대화를 듣고, 두 사람이 대화하는 장소로 가장 적절한 것을 고르시오.
① 병원   ② 카페   ③ 상점
④ 편의점   ⑤ 양호실

6 대화를 듣고, 여자의 마지막 말의 의도로 가장 적절한 것을 고르시오.
① 거절   ② 사과   ③ 감사
④ 승낙   ⑤ 요청

7 대화를 듣고, 두 사람이 생강에 대해 언급하지 않은 것을 고르시오.
① 맛   ② 향   ③ 효능
④ 관련 음식   ⑤ 원산지

8 대화를 듣고, 여자가 대화 직후에 할 일로 가장 적절한 것을 고르시오.
① 밥 짓기   ② 달걀 사기
③ 점심 먹기   ④ 축구 하기
⑤ 친구들에게 전화하기

9 다음을 듣고, 남자가 언어 과정에 대해 언급하지 않은 것을 고르시오.
① 개설된 과정의 종류   ② 수강 신청 방법
③ 강사들의 출신지   ④ 영문법 과정 수강료
⑤ 새 언어 과정이 시작된 요일

10 다음을 듣고, 여자가 하는 말의 내용으로 가장 적절한 것을 고르시오.
① 제품 서비스의 개선 촉구
② 구매와 감정 사이의 관계
③ 제품 구매 이후의 수리 방법
④ 광고의 긍정적 역할과 주의할 점
⑤ 대중 매체 이용을 제한하는 방법

11 다음을 듣고, 학교 축제에 대한 내용으로 일치하지 않는 것을 고르시오.
① 도시락으로 식사가 제공된다.
② 내일 학교 체육관에서 열린다.
③ 축제는 오후 3시에 끝날 것이다.
④ 축제 동안에 점심을 먹을 것이다.
⑤ 축제 마지막에 특별 경품이 제공될 것이다.

정답 및 해설 *p.035*

12 대화를 듣고, 여자가 전화를 건 목적으로 가장 적절한 것을 고르시오.
① 엄마를 급히 찾으려고
② 병이 났음을 알리려고
③ 자전거의 수리를 맡기려고
④ 잃어버린 전화기를 찾으려고
⑤ 병원에 데려다줄 것을 요청하려고

13 대화를 듣고, 남자가 지불할 금액을 고르시오.
① 6달러 　　　　② 6달러 50센트
③ 7달러 　　　　④ 7달러 50센트
⑤ 8달러

14 대화를 듣고 두 사람의 관계로 가장 적절한 것을 고르시오.
① 아빠 — 딸
② 경찰 — 시민
③ 축구 선수 — 관객
④ 택시 운전사 — 승객
⑤ 직장 상사 — 부하 직원

15 대화를 듣고, 남자가 여자에게 부탁한 일로 가장 적절한 것을 고르시오.
① 여행지 물어보기
② 아침에 깨워 주기
③ 알람 시계 구매하기
④ 비행시간 확인하기
⑤ 아침 식사 준비하기

16 대화를 듣고, 남자가 스쿨버스를 타지 않은 이유로 가장 적절한 것을 고르시오.
① 아침에 늦어서
② 자전거를 타려고
③ 친구 집에 들르려고
④ 학교가 가까워 걷기 위해
⑤ 운동을 위해 다른 곳에 들러서

17 다음 그림 상황에 가장 적절한 대화를 고르시오.

① 　　② 　　③ 　　④ 　　⑤

18 다음을 듣고, 실험실에서 지켜야 할 내용으로 언급하지 않은 것을 고르시오.
① 음식을 가져오지 않는다.
② 허락 없이 들어오지 않는다.
③ 선반의 물건들을 만지지 않는다.
④ 병 속의 내용물을 맛보지 않는다.
⑤ 선반의 물건들을 촬영하지 않는다.

[19-20] 대화를 듣고, 여자의 마지막 말에 이어질 남자의 말로 가장 적절한 것을 고르시오.

19 Man: _____
① Let me think about it.
② I am sorry for being late.
③ I disagree with your proposal.
④ I am looking forward to it as well.
⑤ I can help you anytime you want.

20 Man: _____
① Maybe you are right.
② When is the project due?
③ How about talking with her?
④ What is your phone number?
⑤ I was surprised to hear from you.

Listen and Check

● 대화를 다시 듣고, 알맞은 것을 고르시오.

1 It will snow next Sunday.

☐ True ☐ False

2 Why didn't the woman want to buy the kids' car at first?

☐ because she didn't have enough money

☐ because her son is too young

3 The man is worried that he can't give good answers to the interviewers.

☐ Yes ☐ No

4 What did the man do last weekend?

☐ visited his parents' farm

☐ had dinner with his family

5 Is the man's temperature fine?

☐ Yes ☐ No

6 Will the man send an invitation by mobile phone?

☐ Yes ☐ No

7 Korean traditional foods contain plenty of ginger.

☐ True ☐ False

8 What will the woman do first at the class party?

☐ make egg fried rice ☐ play soccer

9 A Spanish beginner course started this Monday.

☐ True ☐ False

10 Does the woman say people must not buy any products after watching advertisements?

☐ Yes ☐ No

11 The students can get special gifts at the end of the event.

☐ True ☐ False

12 The woman already called his mom.

☐ Yes ☐ No

13 What did the man order?

☐ a roast beef sandwich and mango juice

☐ a roast beef sandwich and French fries

14 How long did it take the woman to get a cab?

☐ around 20 minutes ☐ around 30 minutes

15 The man and the woman will leave at five thirty.

☐ True ☐ False

16 Does the man get tired easily in class because he goes to school by bike?

☐ Yes ☐ No

17 The woman already has new shoes.

☐ True ☐ False

18 People cannot eat or drink in the lab.

☐ True ☐ False

19 Does the man know the exact way to go to the museum?

☐ Yes ☐ No

20 The man has not been able to contact Cathy since last week.

☐ True ☐ False

그림 정보 파악

1 다음을 듣고, 내일의 날씨로 가장 적절한 것을 고르시오.

① ② ③

④ ⑤

1

M   Hello. This is the weather forecast center. The rain _____ _____ _____ _____ will continue until tonight and will stop then. Cloudy weather is expected throughout tomorrow. The temperature is expected to be three degrees Celsius, and there will be _____ _____ overnight. The temperature will gradually drop next week and get colder. _____ _____ _____ _____ a snow day next weekend.

그림 정보 파악

2 대화를 듣고, 여자가 살 장난감으로 가장 적절한 것을 고르시오.

① ② ③

④ ⑤

2

W   I'm looking for a Children's Day present for my five-year-old son.

M   How about a toy robot, a dinosaur action toy figure, or a kids' puzzle?

W   I bought _____ _____ _____ for him last year.

M   How about a kids' car then?

W   I think he is _____ _____ _____ _____ _____ _____.

M   No. A five-year-old boy can play with it safely. It's really fun and very _____ _____ _____.

W   Okay. My son will *love it.

*love it [러브] [잇]→ [러빗]

심정 추론

3 대화를 듣고, 남자의 심정으로 가장 적절한 것을 고르시오.

① envious
② nervous
③ pleased
④ satisfied
⑤ disappointed

3 🇬🇧

W   Hi, Steve. How are the preparations for your interview going?

M   Actually, they're not going well.

W   _____ _____ _____?

M   I am afraid I will make a mistake in front of the interviewers.

W   Hey, it's all in the preparation. I know _____ _____ _____ _____ a lot.

M   But I might not be able to answer when I'm asked an unexpected question.

W   Don't worry too much. Just take a deep breath _____ _____ _____. You can do it.

M   Okay. Thanks for the advice.

한 일 파악

4 다음을 듣고, 여자가 주말에 한 일로
가장 적절한 것을 고르시오.

① 집에서 독서하기
② 조부모님 방문하기
③ 친척 집을 방문하기
④ 주말 농장 견학 가기
⑤ 친구와 도서관

4

W What did you do last weekend?

M I _____ _____ _____ _____ and had dinner
with my family.

W What a lovely weekend you had!

M How about you?

W My appointment _____ _____. So I stayed at home and
read some books.

M Oh, did you? But it wasn't that bad _____ _____
_____ _____ _____, right?

W Yeah. I *enjoyed it.

*enjoyed it [인조이드] [잇] → [인조이딧]

장소 추론

5 대화를 듣고, 두 사람이 대화하는
장소로 가장 적절한 곳을 고르시오.

① 병원
② 카페
③ 상점
④ 편의점
⑤ 양호실

5

W How may I help you?

M _____ _____ _____ _____ _____.

W Since when?

M I got caught outside in a cold shower yesterday. I have had a
runny nose _____ _____ _____.

W Let me take your temperature first.

M Thank you.

W [*Pause*] I think your temperature is fine. Take these prescription
pills and _____ _____ _____.

M Okay, I will.

의도 파악

6 다음을 듣고, 여자의 마지막 말의
의도로 가장 적절한 것을 고르시오.

① 거절
② 사과
③ 감사
④ 승낙
⑤ 요청

♥ **Why not?**
: '왜 안되니?'라는 의미를 가지고 있으
며, 상황에 따라 '당연히 되지.'라는 의미
의 긍정을 나타내는 표현으로 사용된다.

6

[*Telephone rings.*]

W Hello.

M Hi. This is Jack. Are you busy this Saturday?

W No. _____ _____ _____ _____?

M I'd like to invite you to my birthday party. Can you come?

W Wow! I'd love to. _____ _____ _____?

M At a seafood buffet. I'm going to send you an invitation card.
There are details about the party *on it.

W Okay.

M _____ _____ _____ _____ by mobile phone?

W ♥Why not?

*on it [언] [잇] → [어닛]

언급 유무 파악

7 대화를 듣고, 두 사람이 생강에 대해
언급하지 <u>않은</u> 것을 고르시오.

① 맛
② 향
③ 효능
④ 관련 음식
⑤ 원산지

7 🇬🇧

W   Do you like ginger?

M   No, I do not. In fact, it smells bad _____ _____
_____.

W   But it is very good for your health.

M   I know. Ginger also helps food taste better. _____
_____ _____ _____ _____ _____?

W   It helps lower blood sugar levels, and it is also good for
digestion.

M   I heard Korean traditional foods contain plenty of ginger.

W   That's right. For example, people around the world know kimchi
_____ _____ _____ _____. So it is a healthy
food.

할 일 파악

8 대화를 듣고, 여자가 대화 직후에 할
일로 가장 적절한 것을 고르시오.

① 밥 짓기
② 달걀 사기
③ 점심 먹기
④ 축구 하기
⑤ 친구들에게 전화하기

8

W   Dad, we are having a class party tomorrow.

M   _____ _____ _____. What are you going to do?

W   We are planning to play soccer first and then _____
_____ _____.

M   Really? Do you need _____ _____ _____?

W   I need to bring some rice and eggs. We're making egg fried rice.

M   We have rice, but there are no eggs at home. You _____
_____ _____ _____.

W   Okay, I will. I can't wait for tomorrow.

언급 유무 파악

9 다음을 듣고, 남자가 언어 과정에 대해
언급하지 <u>않은</u> 것을 고르시오.

① 개설된 과정의 종류
② 수강 신청 방법
③ 강사들의 출신지
④ 영문법 과정 수강료
⑤ 새 언어 과정이 시작된 요일

9

M   Hello, everyone! I am happy _____ _____ _____
_____ that some new language courses started last
Monday. We now have a Spanish beginner course. We are
also providing our students with a free basic English grammar
course. The teachers _____ _____ _____
_____ teaching, and they _____ _____ _____
_____ your language skills. If you are interested in them,
please visit the student council.

화제·주제 파악

10 다음을 듣고, 여자가 하는 말의 내용으로 가장 적절한 것을 고르시오.

① 제품 서비스의 개선 촉구
② 구매와 감정 사이의 관계
③ 제품 구매 이후의 수리 방법
④ 광고의 긍정적 역할과 주의할 점
⑤ 대중 매체 이용을 제한하는 방법

10 🇬🇧

W We are exposed to a lot of advertisements on TV, in the newspaper, and on the radio. People can _____ _____ _____ _____ and services from advertisements. _____ _____, advertisements tell us that we'll feel much better if we use certain products. They can *make us buy them. That means we are living in a very convenient world. Advertisements can make people buy things they don't even need. But we should be careful _____ _____ _____ _____ _____.

*make us [메이크] [어스] → [메커스]

내용 불일치 파악

11 다음을 듣고, 학교 축제에 대한 내용으로 일치하지 <u>않는</u> 것을 고르시오.

① 도시락으로 식사가 제공된다.
② 내일 학교 체육관에서 열린다.
③ 축제는 오후 3시에 끝날 것이다.
④ 축제 동안에 점심을 먹을 것이다.
⑤ 축제 마지막에 특별 경품이 제공될 것이다.

11

M Hello, Hopkins Middle School students. I have an announcement _____ _____ _____ _____. As you know, the festival will be held in the gym tomorrow. There will be performances such as dancing, singing, and a magic show. _____ _____ _____ _____ 10:00 a.m. and ends at 3:00 p.m. During the festival, we will eat lunch provided by the school cafeteria cooks. _____ _____ the special door prizes and gift bags. They will be given to students at the *end of the event.

*end of [엔드] [어브] → [엔더브]

목적 파악

12 대화를 듣고, 여자가 전화를 건 목적으로 가장 적절한 것을 고르시오.

① 엄마를 급히 찾으려고
② 병이 났음을 알리려고
③ 자전거의 수리를 맡기려고
④ 잃어버린 전화기를 찾으려고
⑤ 병원에 데려다줄 것을 요청하려고

12

W Hello, Mike. This is Claire.
M Hi, Claire. What happened? Your voice sounds strange.
W _____ _____ _____ _____ _____.
M What? Are you hurt a lot?
W Yes. I hurt my leg, so I am having trouble walking. So _____ _____ _____ _____ to the hospital?
M Oh, heavens! Why don't you call your mom?
W I did, but she didn't answer the phone.
M Wait! I'll go there and take you _____ _____ _____.

숫자 정보 파악

13 대화를 듣고, 남자가 지불할 금액을
고르시오.

① 6달러
② 6달러 50센트
③ 7달러
④ 7달러 50센트
⑤ 8달러

13

W   _____ _____ _____ to order?

M   Yes. I'd like a roast beef sandwich and French fries, please.

W   The roast beef sandwich is five dollars, and the French fries are
one dollar fifty cents. _____ _____ _____?

M   Let me think... Mango juice, please.

W   Mango juice is one dollar. So the total is seven dollars and fifty.

M   Oh, sorry. I only have seven dollars. Please _____ _____
_____ _____.

W   Sure.

관계 추론

14 대화를 듣고 두 사람의 관계로 가장
적절한 것을 고르시오.

① 아빠 – 딸
② 경찰 – 시민
③ 축구 선수 – 관객
④ 택시 운전사 – 승객
⑤ 직장 상사 – 부하 직원

14

M   Where would you like to go?

W   The World Cup stadium, please. It's hard to get a cab around
here. _____ _____ _____ _____ _____
_____ for me to catch a cab.

M   This is a busy time of day. Fasten your seatbelt. _____
_____ _____!

W   Do you think we can get there in twenty minutes? I have an
appointment at 6:00.

M   Well, I'm afraid not. There's a lot of traffic. But _____
_____ _____ _____.

W   Okay. Thanks.

부탁한 일 파악

15 대화를 듣고, 남자가 여자에게 부탁한
일로 가장 적절한 것을 고르시오.

① 여행지 물어보기
② 아침에 깨워 주기
③ 알람 시계 구매하기
④ 비행시간 확인하기
⑤ 아침 식사 준비하기

♥ **Sleep tight.**

: 과거 침대가 튼튼하지 못해 침대에서
자는 사람을 묶어야 안전하게 잘 수 있다
는 것에서 유래하여 지금은 '잘 자.'의 의
미로 사용된다.

15 🇬🇧

M   Mom, what time are we leaving tomorrow?

W   Our flight departs at ten in the morning, so we should start early.
Maybe _____ _____ _____ at six.

M   Wow, that's too early. Then I should go to bed now.

W   Yes, that's a good idea.

M   Can you _____ _____ _____ tomorrow morning?
I'm not sure I will be able to _____ _____ _____.

W   Okay. I will wake you up at five.

M   It takes only thirty minutes for me to get ready. _____
_____ _____ if you woke me up at five thirty.

W   Okay. ♥ Sleep tight.

이유 추론

16 대화를 듣고, 남자가 스쿨버스를 타지 <u>않은</u> 이유로 가장 적절한 것을 고르시오.

① 아침에 늦어서
② 자전거를 타려고
③ 친구 집에 들르려고
④ 학교가 가까워 걷기 위해
⑤ 운동을 위해 다른 곳에 들러서

16

W Harry, why didn't you take the school bus this morning?

M I decided to _____ _____ _____ to school.

W What? Did you *get up late and miss the bus?

M No, it's not that. I've decided to exercise twice a week.

W Wow. _____ _____ _____ _____ _____ to get to school by bike? Isn't cycling there too hard?

M I guess it takes about thirty minutes. After the ride, I _____ _____ and can focus on class better. _____ _____ _____ join me?

W I'd love to!

*get up [겟] [업] → [게럽]

그림 상황 파악

17 다음 그림의 상황에 가장 적절한 대화를 고르시오.

① ② ③ ④ ⑤

17

① W Dad, I really want to buy that pair of shoes!

  M You _____ _____ _____ at the house!

② W I think I lost my phone. I can't find it in my bag.

  M Do you want me to _____ _____ _____?

③ W I bought this pair of shoes. _____ _____ _____ _____?

  M They're really cool. Where did you buy them?

④ W Can you show me around the mall?

  M I am afraid I _____ _____ _____ to do that.

⑤ W Dad, look at the beautiful store.

  M Yeah. There are various items _____ _____ _____.

언급 유무 파악

18 다음을 듣고, 실험실에서 지켜야 할 내용으로 언급하지 <u>않은</u> 것을 고르시오.

① 음식을 가져오지 않는다.
② 허락 없이 들어오지 않는다.
③ 선반의 물건들을 만지지 않는다.
④ 병 속의 내용물을 맛보지 않는다.
⑤ 선반의 물건들을 촬영하지 않는다.

18

W It's time to _____ _____ _____ _____ in the science club. Now I'd like to talk about the lab rules with you. First, you can't bring _____ _____ _____ _____ _____ into the lab. Second, don't enter the lab without asking a teacher for permission. Third, please don't touch anything on the shelves. Fourth, _____ _____ _____ _____ in the bottles. Lastly, while doing an experiment, listen to your teacher carefully. If you follow these rules, we will be able to do interesting experiments safely.

[19~20] 대화를 듣고, 여자의 마지막 말에 이어질 남자의 말로 가장 적절한 것을 고르시오.

19 Man: _____
　　① Let me think about it.
　　② I am sorry for being late.
　　③ I disagree with your proposal.
　　④ I am looking forward to it as well.
　　⑤ I can help you anytime you want.

19

M　Jason said you are looking for me. What's up?
W　Do you _____ _____ _____ _____?
M　Maybe. Why?
W　I have to go to the national museum in Seoul. I _____ _____ _____ _____ _____.
M　That's awesome. I am planning to go there, too.
W　Really? What a coincidence! Do you know how to get there?
M　I'm not sure. I'll _____ _____ _____ _____ on the museum's homepage before Thursday.
W　Thanks. We will have a great time there.
M　I am looking forward to it as well.

20 Man: _____
　　① Maybe you are right.
　　② When is the project due?
　　③ How about talking with her?
　　④ What is your phone number?
　　⑤ I was surprised to hear from you.

20

W　Hi, Chris. You have a long face. Is there something wrong?
M　I never thought it would be hard for me _____ _____ _____ _____ _____ with Cathy.
W　Cathy? What's wrong with her?
M　She's been out of contact since yesterday. We were scheduled to work together yesterday. But she never showed up.
W　You _____ _____ _____ _____.
M　She never answers my phone calls, my messages, and my e-mails.
W　I know how you feel. But it's important for you to persuade her to do it _____ _____ _____ _____ before the deadline.
M　Maybe you are right.

1 다음을 듣고, 싱가포르의 내일 날씨로 가장 적절한 것을 고르시오.

①   ②   ③

④ ⑤

2 대화를 듣고, 남자가 구입할 코트로 가장 적절한 것을 고르시오.

① ② ③

④ ⑤

3 대화를 듣고, 여자의 심정으로 가장 적절한 것을 고르시오.
① shy ② sad ③ bored
④ anxious ⑤ satisfied

4 대화를 듣고, 남자가 오늘 한 일로 가장 적절한 것을 고르시오.
① 친구 만나기
② 동물원 가기
③ 농장 체험 하기
④ 농장 일 돕기
⑤ 집 청소하기

5 대화를 듣고, 두 사람이 대화하는 장소로 가장 적절한 곳을 고르시오.
① 학교 ② 놀이터 ③ 버스 안
④ 버스 정류장 ⑤ 택시 정류장

6 대화를 듣고, 남자의 마지막 말의 의도로 가장 적절한 것을 고르시오.
① 동의 ② 축하 ③ 격려
④ 조언 ⑤ 사과

7 대화를 듣고, 여자가 이번 년도에 도전할 활동을 고르시오.
① 열기구 타기 ② 외국어 배우기
③ 번지 점프 하기 ④ 배낭여행 떠나기
⑤ 패러글라이딩 타기

8 대화를 듣고, 여자가 대화 직후에 할 일로 가장 적절한 것을 고르시오.
① 우체국 방문하기 ② 우편 번호 검색하기
③ 직원에게 질문하기 ④ 적절한 상자 고르기
⑤ 수령인 주소 기입하기

9 대화를 듣고, 남자가 전자 기기에 대해 언급하지 <u>않은</u> 것을 고르시오.
① 기기의 무게 ② 기기의 용도
③ 기기 가격 ④ 기기 출시 연도
⑤ 구매 가능 장소

10 다음을 듣고, 여자가 하는 말의 내용으로 가장 적절한 것을 고르시오.
① 건강의 비결 ② 정보 습득 방법
③ 독서의 중요성 ④ 지혜로운 사람
⑤ 좋은 책의 기준

11 대화를 듣고, 패키지여행에 대한 내용으로 일치하지 <u>않는</u> 것을 고르시오.
① 총 여행 기간은 일주일이다.
② 다른 기간보다 저렴한 여행 상품이다.
③ 패키지여행을 가는 총 인원은 20명이다.
④ 이번 달에 New York으로 가는 여행이나.
⑤ 자유 여행을 할 수 있는 하루가 주어진다.

12 대화를 듣고, 여자가 백화점을 가는 목적으로 가장 적절한 것을 고르시오.
① 반품하기 위해서
② 운동을 하기 위해서
③ 스트레스를 풀기 위해서
④ 새로운 옷을 보기 위해서
⑤ 필요한 물건을 사기 위해서

13 대화를 듣고, 여자가 지불해야 할 금액으로 가장 적절한 것을 고르시오.
① $8   ② $11   ③ $13
④ $15   ⑤ $17

14 대화를 듣고, 두 사람의 관계로 가장 적절한 것을 고르시오.
① 부모 — 자식
② 의사 — 환자
③ 약사 — 고객
④ 편의점 — 고객
⑤ 선생님 — 학생

15 대화를 듣고, 남자가 여자에게 요청한 일로 가장 적절한 것을 고르시오.
① 모금하기
② 아이 보살피기
③ 봉사 활동 가기
④ 바자회 도와주기
⑤ 전시회 방문하기

16 대화를 듣고, 여자가 원피스 구입을 망설이는 이유로 가장 적절한 것을 고르시오.
① 너무 화려해서
② 가격이 비싸서
③ 실용적이지 않아서
④ 사이즈가 맞지 않아서
⑤ 가격 비교를 하고 싶어서

17 다음 그림의 상황에 가장 적절한 대화를 고르시오.

①   ②   ③   ④   ⑤

18 대화를 듣고, 남자가 응용 프로그램 개발 대회에 관해 언급하지 <u>않은</u> 것을 고르시오.
① 대회까지 남은 기간
② 대회 우승 상금
③ 참여 팀들의 개발 항목
④ 대회에 참여하는 팀의 수
⑤ 남자가 속한 팀의 멤버 수

[19~20] 대화를 듣고, 여자의 마지막 말에 이어질 남자의 말로 가장 적절한 것을 고르시오.

19 Man: _____
① I can't agree more.
② Don't be so selfish.
③ I hope things get better.
④ Why didn't you tell me?
⑤ You know you don't need it.

20 Man: _____
① That's not a big deal.
② You don't have to do that.
③ You'd better talk to a doctor.
④ Laughter is the best medicine.
⑤ I can no longer think about it.

Listen and Check

● 대화를 다시 듣고, 알맞은 것을 고르시오.

1 The weather in Hong Kong is windy.
☐ True ☐ False

2 Does the man prefer the coat with patterns?
☐ Yes ☐ No

3 The woman feels excited about transferring to another school.
☐ True ☐ False

4 What did the man help with on his grandfather's farm?
☐ feeding animals ☐ watering plants

5 How will they go to school today?
☐ bus ☐ taxi

6 They will prepare for a presentation together.
☐ True ☐ False

7 Did the man go backpacking in Europe?
☐ Yes ☐ No

8 The woman knows the recipient's zip code.
☐ True ☐ False

9 What can the man do with the device?
☐ watch movies ☐ draw pictures

10 Books can comfort readers.
☐ True ☐ False

11 How many days are given for free traveling?
☐ one day ☐ two days

12 What does the man suggest the woman do?
☐ go shopping ☐ exercise

13 The woman paid for things without any coupons.
☐ True ☐ False

14 What problem does the man have?
☐ taking pills ☐ falling asleep

15 Did they plan the bazaar together from the beginning?
☐ Yes ☐ No

16 What does the man think about the dress?
☐ It is attractive. ☐ It is unpractical.

17 The man wants to buy a plain helmet.
☐ True ☐ False

18 They have one month left until the competition.
☐ True ☐ False

19 Where will the woman use the coffee machine?
☐ in her workroom ☐ at her home

20 What is the woman afraid of doing?
☐ seeing a doctor ☐ losing weight

그림 정보 파악

1 다음을 듣고, 싱가포르의 내일 날씨로 가장 적절한 것을 고르시오.

①  ② ③

④ ⑤

1

M Good evening. I'm Carl Park from the weather center. This is the forecast for _____ _____ _____ _____ tomorrow. In Bangkok, it will be warm and sunny. In Hong Kong, it will be a little _____ _____ _____. There will be _____ _____ _____ in the afternoon in Singapore. In Manila, the weather will be cloudy. Thank you.

그림 정보 파악

2 대화를 듣고, 남자가 구입할 코트로 가장 적절한 것을 고르시오.

① ② ③

④ ⑤

2 🇬🇧

W Good afternoon. What are you looking for?
M I'm _____ _____ a coat for myself.
W How about the length of the coat?
M I'd like to _____ _____ _____ _____.
W How about this? It has a classic checkered pattern.
M I like the _____ _____ _____ _____. Do you have that style *with a bigger collar?
W Yes, we do. It's _____ _____ _____ this month.
M I love the design. I'll take it.

*with a [위드] [어] → [위더]

심정 추론

3 대화를 듣고, 여자의 심정으로 가장 적절한 것을 고르시오.

① shy ② sad
③ bored ④ anxious
⑤ satisfied

3

W What are you writing?
M I'm _____ _____ _____ _____ to you.
W You are _____ _____ _____.
M Don't be. We can still see each other.
W I know. But I'm going to _____ _____ _____ and school so much.
M You will _____ _____ _____ there, too.
W I'm not sure.

한 일 파악

4 대화를 듣고, 남자가 오늘 한 일로 가장 적절한 것을 고르시오.

① 친구 만나기
② 동물원 가기
③ 농장 체험 하기
④ 농장 일 돕기
⑤ 집 청소하기

4 🇬🇧

W Why _____ _____ _____ _____ this morning?

M I had to go to my grandfather's farm.

W Why did you go there?

M He _____ _____ _____ _____ him with some work.

W What did you do there?

M I _____ _____ _____ _____ _____. I fed them and cleaned their cages. It was really hard.

W You had a long day.

장소 추론

5 대화를 듣고, 두 사람이 대화하는 장소로 가장 적절한 곳을 고르시오.

① 학교
② 놀이터
③ 버스 안
④ 버스 정류장
⑤ 택시 정류장

5

W _____ _____ _____ are here.

M Hmm... I _____ _____ _____ _____ for school today.

W Why's that?

M I need to talk to Mrs. Kim before my first class.

W Because this *bus is already full, we should wait for _____ _____ _____.

M Why don't we _____ _____ _____ today?

W Okay. There is one over there.

*bus is [버쓰] [이즈] → [버씨즈]

의도 파악

6 대화를 듣고, 남자의 마지막 말의 의도로 가장 적절한 것을 고르시오.

① 동의   ② 축하
③ 격려   ④ 조언
⑤ 사과

💙 **Two heads are better than one.**
: '백지장도 맞들면 낫다.'라는 뜻으로 두 사람의 지혜가 한 사람의 지혜보다 낫다는 의미이다.

6

W I have so many things to finish by tomorrow.

M What do you have to do?

W I need to _____ _____ _____ _____ and prepare for a presentation.

M It sounds like you have lots of work to do. Are you doing everything _____ _____ _____?

W Yes, I am.

M You'd _____ _____ _____ _____. 💙Two heads are better than one.

특정 정보 파악

7 대화를 듣고, 여자가 이번 년도에 도전할 활동을 고르시오.

① 열기구 타기
② 외국어 배우기
③ 번지 점프 하기
④ 배낭여행 떠나기
⑤ 패러글라이딩 타기

♥ **Give it a try.**
: 상대방에게 무언가를 도전해볼 것을 격려할 때 사용하는 표현으로, '시도해 봐.', '한번 해봐.'라는 뜻이다.

7 🇬🇧

W What should I do this year?

M You _____ _____ _____ _____ for two months last year, right?

W Right. That was such an _____ _____ in my life.

M What is it that you're the most *afraid of but long for?

W It's taking _____ _____ _____ _____.

M ♥Give it a try!

W Hmm... I'll _____ _____ _____ to do it.

*afraid of [어프레이드] [오브] → [어프레이더브]

할 일 파악

8 대화를 듣고, 여자가 대화 직후에 할 일로 가장 적절한 것을 고르시오.

① 우체국 방문하기
② 우편 번호 검색하기
③ 직원에게 질문하기
④ 적절한 상자 고르기
⑤ 수령인 주소 기입하기

8

M Hello. Are you going to _____ _____ _____?

W Yes, I am.

M Please choose a box that is _____ _____ _____ for the things you are sending.

W Okay. And what if I don't know the _____ _____ _____?

M I'll help you with that when you _____ _____ _____ _____ with his address on it.

W Thank you.

언급 유무 파악

9 대화를 듣고, 남자가 전자 기기에 대해 언급하지 <u>않은</u> 것을 고르시오.

① 기기의 무게
② 기기의 용도
③ 기기 가격
④ 기기 출시 연도
⑤ 구매 가능 장소

9

M I want to buy _____ _____ _____.

W What do you do with it?

M I can _____ _____ _____ on it anywhere I go.

W That's cool.

M It's _____ _____ _____ only 120 dollars *because it _____ _____ two years ago.

W What a good price! I want to buy one, too.

*because it [비커즈] [잇] → [비커짓]

화제·주제 파악

10 다음을 듣고, 여자가 하는 말의 내용으로 가장 적절한 것을 고르시오.

① 건강의 비결
② 정보 습득 방법
③ 독서의 중요성
④ 지혜로운 사람
⑤ 좋은 책의 기준

10

W How often do you read books? What kinds of books do you usually read? Books _____ _____ _____ in life. They *give you knowledge and new information and sometimes _____ _____ _____ messages. You should keep them nearby so that you can read anytime you want. Books will _____ _____ healthier, wiser, and _____ _____.

*give you [기브] [유] → [기뷰]

내용 불일치 파악

11 대화를 듣고, 패키지여행에 대한 내용으로 일치하지 <u>않는</u> 것을 고르시오.

① 총 여행 기간은 일주일이다.
② 다른 기간보다 저렴한 여행 상품이다.
③ 패키지여행을 가는 총 인원은 20명이다.
④ 이번 달에 New York으로 가는 여행이다.
⑤ 자유 여행을 할 수 있는 하루가 주어진다.

11

M We're _____ _____ _____ _____ _____ to New York this month, right?
W Yes. We depart on the tenth and come back on the seventeenth.
M _____ _____ _____ are there on the tour?
W There are twenty.
M Are we allowed to visit places we want to by ourselves?
W We are _____ _____ _____ _____ to do whatever we want and to go wherever we want.
M I'm _____ _____!

목적 파악

12 대화를 듣고, 여자가 백화점을 가는 목적으로 가장 적절한 것을 고르시오.

① 반품하기 위해서
② 운동을 하기 위해서
③ 스트레스를 풀기 위해서
④ 새로운 옷을 보기 위해서
⑤ 필요한 물건을 사기 위해서

♥ **I recommend that + S + V**
: 제안을 나타낼 때 사용하는 표현으로, '~가 …할 것을 제안하다'라는 뜻이다.

12

W I'm going to the department store _____ _____.
M You just went there yesterday.
W I'm just _____ _____ _____ my stress.
M You're _____ _____ _____ _____.
W But I don't know any other way to do it.
M ♥I recommend that you exercise. Regular exercise _____ _____ _____.

13 대화를 듣고, 여자가 지불해야 할 금액으로 가장 적절한 것을 고르시오.

① $8   ② $11
③ $13   ④ $15
⑤ $17

13

M　Hello. _____ _____ _____ _____ _____?

W　How much is this headband?

M　It's _____ _____.

W　What about _____ _____?

M　They are seven dollars per set.

W　I'll buy _____ _____ and _____ _____ _____ earrings. Here's a two-dollar discount coupon.

M　Thank you. Here are your things.

---

14 대화를 듣고, 두 사람의 관계로 가장 적절한 것을 고르시오.

① 부모 — 자식
② 의사 — 환자
③ 약사 — 고객
④ 편의점 — 고객
⑤ 선생님 — 학생

14

M　I _____ _____ _____ _____ falling asleep.

W　Hmm... Take this small pill an hour before you go to bed.

M　I will.

W　And take one thirty minutes _____ _____ _____.

M　What will happen if I take one after skipping a meal?

W　You can _____ _____ _____ *if you take it on an empty stomach.

M　Okay. I will eat whatever I can before I *take a pill.

W　_____ _____ _____ if you don't get better after a few days.

*if you [이프] [유] → [이퓨]
*take a [테이크] [어] → [테이커]

---

15 대화를 듣고, 남자가 여자에게 요청한 일로 가장 적절한 것을 고르시오.

① 모금하기
② 아이 보살피기
③ 봉사 활동 가기
④ 바자회 도와주기
⑤ 전시회 방문하기

♥ **Could you give me a hand?**
: 상대방에게 도움을 신청할 때 사용하는 표현으로, '도와줄 수 있니?'라는 뜻이다. 여기서 'give me a hand'는 손을 내민다는 것으로 도움을 준다는 의미이다.

15

M　Do you have any plans for this Saturday?

W　No, I've got _____ _____ _____ _____.

M　♥Could you give me a hand with the preparations for my bazaar?

W　What is the bazaar for?

M　This is for _____ _____ _____ _____ _____ in need of treatment.

W　Then I will gladly join you.

M　Thanks. You can help me _____ _____ _____ _____.

16 대화를 듣고, 여자가 원피스 구입을
망설이는 이유로 가장 적절한 것을
고르시오.

① 너무 화려해서
② 가격이 비싸서
③ 실용적이지 않아서
④ 사이즈가 맞지 않아서
⑤ 가격 비교를 하고 싶어서

16 🇬🇧

W   This dress looks beautiful. I'd like to _____ _____
_____ .

M   All right. I want to see you in the dress.

W   [*Pause*] What do you think?

M   You _____ _____ .

W   Isn't the flower pattern _____ _____ ?

M   I think you can wear it on _____ _____ _____
_____ you want to change your mood.

W   I love it, but it doesn't seem that practical.

---

17 다음 그림의 상황에 가장 적절한
대화를 고르시오.

①   ②   ③   ④   ⑤

17

① W   How was my performance?
   M   It was _____ .
② W   This is _____ _____ _____ now.
   M   I love it.
③ W   What about this helmet?
   M   I'd like to have one with a _____ _____ _____ .
④ W   It _____ _____ when I had an accident.
   M   Don't worry. I can fix it.
⑤ W   Are you _____ _____ _____ ?
   M   Yes, please.

---

18 대화를 듣고, 남자가 응용 프로그램
개발 대회에 관해 언급하지 <u>않은</u> 것을
고르시오.

① 대회까지 남은 기간
② 대회 우승 상금
③ 참여 팀들의 개발 항목
④ 대회에 참여하는 팀의 수
⑤ 남자가 속한 팀의 멤버 수

♥ **Exactly.**
 : 상대방의 하는 말에 맞장구를 치며 강
한 공감을 나타낼 때 사용하는 표현으로,
'맞아.', '바로 그거야.'라는 뜻이다.

18

W   We need to talk about the application development competition.

M   ♥Exactly.

W   _____ _____ _____ are competing?

M   Four, including us.

W   What are _____ _____ _____ ?

M   They are games, online learning, and video editing.

W   We three should _____ _____ _____ a really
creative idea.

M   We still have two months till the contest. We can _____
_____ _____ .

[19-20] 대화를 듣고, 여자의 마지막 말에 이어질 남자의 말로 가장 적절한 것을 고르시오.

19 Man: _____
① I can't agree more.
② Don't be so selfish.
③ I hope things get better.
④ Why didn't you tell me?
⑤ You know you don't need it.

19

W   I'm going to buy a coffee machine.
M   Where will you *use it?
W   Just _____ _____ _____.
M   So you *need it for yourself.
W   Well, if visitors come, then I might _____ _____ _____ _____ for three or four people.
M   A _____ _____ _____ _____.
W   That big one looks cool _____.
M   You know you don't need it.

*use it [유즈] [잇] → [유짓]
*need it [니드] [잇] → [니딧]

20 Man: _____
① That's not a big deal.
② You don't have to do that.
③ You'd better talk to a doctor.
④ Laughter is the best medicine.
⑤ I can no longer think about it.

20

W   Jake, I _____ _____ _____ these days.
M   What happened?
W   _____ _____. I just don't want to do anything and can't stop crying.
M   Oh, no.
W   I don't want to eat either. I already _____ _____ _____ this week.
M   Have you *seen a doctor?
W   I'm _____ _____ _____ _____.
M   You'd better talk to a doctor.

*seen a [신] [어] → [시너]

1 다음을 듣고, 일요일의 날씨로 가장 적절한 것을 고르시오.

①   ②   ③

④   ⑤

2 대화를 듣고, 남자가 구입할 케이크로 가장 적절한 것을 고르시오.

①   ②   ③

④   ⑤

3 대화를 듣고, 여자의 심정으로 가장 적절한 것을 고르시오.
① tired   ② bored   ③ curious
④ serious   ⑤ disappointed

4 대화를 듣고, 여자가 어제 한 일로 가장 적절한 것을 고르시오.
① 캠핑 장비 구매하기
② 가족과 이야기하기
③ 캠핑 장비 점검하기
④ 우체국에서 물건 찾기
⑤ 친구의 소원 들어주기

5 대화를 듣고, 두 사람이 대화하는 장소로 가장 적절한 곳을 고르시오.
① 기차역   ② 시장   ③ 상점
④ 학교   ⑤ 공항

6 대화를 듣고, 남자의 마지막 말의 의도로 가장 적절한 것을 고르시오.
① 승낙   ② 요청   ③ 감사
④ 거절   ⑤ 조언

7 대화를 듣고, 여자가 먹지 않는 음식을 고르시오.
① 야채   ② 새우   ③ 초밥
④ 조개   ⑤ 생선

8 대화를 듣고, 남자가 수면을 취하기 위해 할 일로 가장 적절한 것을 고르시오.
① 샤워를 하기   ② 명상을 하기
③ 운동을 하기   ④ 독서를 하기
⑤ 우유를 마시기

9 다음을 듣고, 여자가 좋은 성적을 위한 조언으로 언급하지 않은 것을 고르시오.
① 수업 듣기   ② 다양한 학습 방법 찾기
③ 식사 거르지 않기   ④ 친구와 함께 공부하기
⑤ 선생님에게 도움 요청하기

10 다음을 듣고, 남자가 하는 말의 내용으로 가장 적절한 것을 고르시오.
① 첨단 기계의 유용성
② 뇌가 기억을 하는 원리
③ 집중을 위한 바른 자세
④ 많은 정보를 분석하는 방법
⑤ 스마트폰 사용의 단점

11 다음을 듣고, 안내 방송에 대한 내용과 일치하지 않는 것을 고르시오.
① 내일 야구 결승전이 열린다.
② 먹을 음식을 가져와도 된다.
③ 내일의 오후 수업은 취소된다.
④ 결승전은 1시 30분에 시작된다.
⑤ 학교 야구팀이 준결승에서 승리했다.

12 대화를 듣고, 여자가 전화를 건 목적으로 가장 적절한 것을 고르시오.
① 식당 예약을 확인하기 위해서
② 모임 일정을 변경하기 위해서
③ 식당의 위치를 물어보기 위해서
④ 식당까지의 교통편을 알기 위해서
⑤ 백화점이 언제 개장하는지 알기 위해서

13 대화를 듣고, 남자가 학교를 출발할 시각을 고르시오.
① 2시 50분 ② 3시
③ 3시 10분 ④ 3시 50분
⑤ 4시

14 대화를 듣고, 두 사람의 관계로 가장 적절한 것을 고르시오.
① 상담사 — 의뢰인
② 선생님 — 학부모
③ 은행 직원 — 고객
④ 문구점 주인 — 학생
⑤ 보석 가게 직원 — 손님

15 대화를 듣고, 남자가 여자에게 부탁한 일로 가장 적절한 것을 고르시오.
① 발표에 참여하기
② 프로그램 가르쳐 주기
③ 발표 주제의 자료 찾기
④ 컴퓨터의 문제 발견하기
⑤ 담당 선생님께 연락하기

16 대화를 듣고, 여자가 당황한 이유로 가장 적절한 것을 고르시오.
① 택시비가 비싸서
② 다른 택시를 타서
③ 엄마가 집에 안 계셔서
④ 지갑을 도서관에 놓고 와서
⑤ 돈을 빌려달라고 부탁받아서

17 다음 그림의 상황에 가장 적절한 대화를 고르시오.

① ② ③ ④ ⑤

18 다음을 듣고, 여자가 새로운 학교에 대해 언급하지 않은 것을 고르시오.
① 학년 당 적은 학급 수
② 많은 스포츠 클럽
③ 선생님들의 친절함
④ 가입하고 싶은 클럽
⑤ 학교와 집 사이의 거리

[19-20] 대화를 듣고, 남자의 마지막 말에 이어질 여자의 말로 가장 적절한 것을 고르시오.

19 Woman: _____
① What brings you here?
② I have never been to Japan.
③ I can give you a call soon.
④ I hope you have a nice trip to Japan.
⑤ I am visiting my uncle who lives in Japan.

20 Woman: _____
① You can count on me.
② Let me tell you how to do it.
③ We should always recycle old items.
④ Upcycling is what I have heard about.
⑤ I am interested in hearing more about that.

Listen and Check

● 대화를 다시 듣고, 알맞은 것을 고르시오.

1 It will be cloudy and rainy on Friday.

☐ True ☐ False

2 Does the man's sister like dolls but not fruit?

☐ Yes ☐ No

3 The woman couldn't get a ticket.

☐ True ☐ False

4 Does the woman's family go camping every month?

☐ Yes ☐ No

5 When can the man and the woman visit the duty-free shop?

☐ when they leave
☐ when they come back

6 Aiden can't check Victoria's homework today because he is too busy.

☐ True ☐ False

7 Can the woman eat seafood other than shrimp?

☐ Yes ☐ No

8 What did the man already do to sleep well?

☐ do exercise ☐ take a shower

9 Is using flashcards the best way to memorize because all students use them?

☐ Yes ☐ No

10 Why should we try to reduce the amount of time we use their smartphones?

☐ because they can get a lot of information
☐ because their brains can get duller

11 Does the school prepare some food for students?

☐ Yes ☐ No

12 The restaurant is on Third Avenue.

☐ True ☐ False

13 The man has a fever and a headache.

☐ True ☐ False

14 Is the man more interested in gold than silver?

☐ Yes ☐ No

15 Does the man know how to use the presentation program?

☐ Yes ☐ No

16 What did the woman ask her mother to do?

☐ to wait in front of her house
☐ to find her purse in the house

17 The woman thinks the music that the man is listening to is noisy.

☐ True ☐ False

18 The woman's new school only has three grades.

☐ True ☐ False

19 Do the man and the woman know each other?

☐ Yes ☐ No

20 The woman knows a lot about upcycling.

☐ True ☐ False

그림 정보 파악

1 다음을 듣고, 일요일의 날씨로 가장 적절한 것을 고르시오.

①   ②   ③

④   ⑤

1

W Now, it's time for the weather report. Yesterday, the clouds _____ _____, and we'll have sunny skies from now until Thursday. But on Friday, it will be _____ _____ _____ _____. And there is a good *chance of rain on Saturday. _____ _____ _____ _____ before Sunday, and we will have a fine, clear day on Sunday.

*chance of [챈스] [어브] → [챈써브]

그림 정보 파악

2 대화를 듣고, 남자가 구입할 케이크로 가장 적절한 것을 고르시오.

①   ②   ③

④   ⑤

2

M I need to buy a cake for my sister's birthday party. _____ _____ _____ I get?

W She likes fruit, so I think this one is the best.

M Hmm. Actually, I want _____ _____ _____.

W How about this one _____ _____ _____ in the middle? It looks like a big castle.

M But she _____ _____ _____. I think I'll get this one.

W A doll? It's very cute. She will like it!

M Yes. I hope it is a special cake for her.

심정 추론

3 대화를 듣고, 여자의 심정으로 가장 적절한 것을 고르시오.

① tired
② bored
③ curious
④ serious
⑤ disappointed

3 🇬🇧

M What are you doing here? I thought you went to see the movie *Avengers*.

W I _____ _____, _____ the tickets were all sold out. I am sad.

M Oh, that's too bad. You really wanted to see it.

W Yes, I did. I didn't think there would be _____ _____ _____ _____ _____ that movie.

M You should buy tickets in advance.

W You are right. I will do that _____ _____ _____.

한 일 파악

4 대화를 듣고, 여자가 어제 한 일로 가장
적절한 것을 고르시오.

① 캠핑 장비 구매하기
② 가족과 이야기하기
③ 캠핑 장비 점검하기
④ 우체국에서 물건 찾기
⑤ 친구의 소원 들어주기

4 🇬🇧

M Hi, Grace. What did you do yesterday?

W I _____ _____ _____ my mom.

M Great. What did you buy?

W I bought a new tent and chairs _____ _____ _____

_____.

M Are you going camping soon?

W Yes. My family _____ _____ _____ _____.

M Sounds great. _____ _____ my family went camping
like your family.

장소 추론

5 대화를 듣고, 두 사람이 대화하는
장소로 가장 적절한 곳을 고르시오.

① 기차역
② 시장
③ 상점
④ 학교
⑤ 공항

5

W We've checked in and are all _____ _____ _____.

M Before that, I want to look around the duty-free shops. Can I?

W _____ _____ _____. I am not sure that we have
much time to spend at the shops. Our departure time _____

_____ _____.

M Let me check the boarding time again. You're right. We are
running *out of time.

W Yes. We can drop by the duty-free shops _____ _____

_____ _____.

M Okay. I can't wait to get on the airplane.

*out of [아웃] [어브] → [아우러브]

의도 파악

6 대화를 듣고, 남자의 마지막 말의
의도로 가장 적절한 것을 고르시오.

① 승낙
② 요청
③ 감사
④ 거절
⑤ 조언

6

W Hi, Aiden. You've come at just the right time!

M _____ _____ _____ _____, Victoria?

W I need your help. I just finished my history assignment. Can you
*check it _____ _____ _____ _____?

M When _____ _____ _____ _____ hand it in?

W By tomorrow.

M I am very busy right now. But I can do it tonight.

*check it [체크] [잇] → [체킷]

특정 정보 파악

7 대화를 듣고, 여자가 먹지 <u>않는</u> 음식을 고르시오.

① 야채　　　② 새우
③ 초밥　　　④ 조개
⑤ 생선

♥ **What a day!**

: 하루를 모두 지내고 그 날을 돌이켜보며 기쁨과 어려움을 나타낼 때 쓴다. 문맥에 따라서 기쁨을 나타내는지 어려움을 나타내는지 파악하는 것이 중요하다.

7

M　♥What a day! Why don't we eat out today?

W　That's good. _____ _____ _____ _____ for dinner?

M　I heard a seafood restaurant opened down on the corner. I think we can eat sushi, vegetables, and seafood there.

W　_____ _____ _____ that I am allergic to shrimp?

M　Oh, sorry. But you can eat any seafood _____ _____ shrimp, can't you?

W　Right. Let's eat there.

M　Okay.

할 일 파악

8 대화를 듣고, 남자가 수면을 취하기 위해 할 일로 가장 적절한 것을 고르시오.

① 샤워를 하기
② 명상을 하기
③ 운동을 하기
④ 독서를 하기
⑤ 우유를 마시기

8

W　Mark, you look tired. Did you _____ _____ _____ last night?

M　No, I didn't. I have a sleeping problem these days. So I always _____ _____.

W　Why don't you _____ _____ _____ before going to bed?

M　I tried, but _____ _____ _____ for me.

W　Then how about _____?

M　Good idea! I will *run on a treadmill after dinner starting tomorrow.

*run on [런] [언] → [러넌]

언급 유무 파악

9 다음을 듣고, 여자가 좋은 성적을 위한 조언으로 언급하지 <u>않은</u> 것을 고르시오.

① 수업 듣기
② 다양한 학습 방법 찾기
③ 식사 거르지 않기
④ 친구와 함께 공부하기
⑤ 선생님에게 도움 요청하기

9

W　Do you really want to get good grades and have the willpower _____ _____ _____? Here are some tips. First, don't skip meals. Second, there are _____ _____ _____ _____, so you need to find your own learning style. For example, some students do better at memorizing by using charts and flashcards. But _____ _____. Lastly, you can study well by listening to lectures. You need to ask your parents or a teacher to _____ _____ _____ your style.

10 다음을 듣고, 남자가 하는 말의 내용으로 가장 적절한 것을 고르시오.

① 첨단 기계의 유용성
② 뇌가 기억을 하는 원리
③ 집중을 위한 바른 자세
④ 많은 정보를 분석하는 방법
⑤ 스마트폰 사용의 단점

10

M These days, most teenagers use smartphones. We can get _____ _____ _____ _____ easily by using them. But they have some bad points, too. First, we spend too much time _____ _____ _____. So we often feel less focused on our studies and jobs. Second, our brains get duller because we don't use them to memorize numbers anymore. Therefore, _____ _____ _____ _____ _____ our smartphones less.

11 다음을 듣고, 안내 방송에 대한 내용과 일치하지 <u>않는</u> 것을 고르시오.

① 내일 야구 결승전이 열린다.
② 먹을 음식을 가져와도 된다.
③ 내일의 오후 수업은 취소된다.
④ 결승전은 1시 30분에 시작된다.
⑤ 학교 야구팀이 준결승에서 승리했다.

11 🇬🇧

W This is a school announcement. Good news, everyone! Our school baseball team _____ _____ _____ _____. So in order to cheer for our school team in the final round, we are going to _____ _____ _____ _____ tomorrow and go to the Daejeon ballpark. We'll leave our school for the stadium at around one thirty. The final game begins at two. _____ _____ _____ _____ _____ to eat. Let's root *for our baseball team!

*for our [풔얼] [아우어] → [풔라우어]

12 대화를 듣고, 여자가 전화를 건 목적으로 가장 적절한 것을 고르시오.

① 식당 예약을 확인하기 위해서
② 모임 일정을 변경하기 위해서
③ 식당의 위치를 물어보기 위해서
④ 식당까지의 교통편을 알기 위해서
⑤ 백화점이 언제 개장하는지 알기 위해서

12

M Sky Restaurant. How can I help you?

W Hello. I have a reservation for 6:00 p.m. The name is Paula.

M Paula at 6:00 p.m. Yes, I can see _____ _____ _____. Do you want to change it?

W No. I've never been to your restaurant before. Is it on Third Street?

M No. It's _____ _____ _____ of Fifth Avenue and Apple Street.

W Oh, I see. Is it near the department store?

M Yes. It's just _____ _____ _____ from it.

W Thank you. See you soon.

숫자 정보 파악

13 대화를 듣고, 남자가 학교를 출발할
시각을 고르시오.

① 2시 50분
② 3시
③ 3시 10분
④ 3시 50분
⑤ 4시

13

M Hello, Ms. Brown. May I go home early?

W Sit down here. Are you feeling bad?

M Yes, a little. _____ _____ _____ _____ and a
headache. I think I've got the flu.

W School *ends at 4:00 p.m. When do you want to go home?

M It is three now. I want to _____ _____ _____
_____.

W Okay. Then I'll call your mother and tell her you are going
home early today. You should _____ _____ _____
_____. All right?

M Thank you.

*ends at [앤즈] [앳] → [앤잿]

관계 추론

14 대화를 듣고, 두 사람의 관계로 가장
적절한 것을 고르시오.

① 상담사 – 의뢰인
② 선생님 – 학부모
③ 은행 직원 – 고객
④ 문구점 주인 – 학생
⑤ 보석 가게 직원 – 손님

14

M Excuse me. Can you show me _____ _____?

W Sure. Which are you interested in, gold or silver?

M _____ _____ _____ _____.

W Then I'd like to recommend this one. _____ _____
_____, and it's only $75.

M Oh, it's beautiful. It's exactly what I want. I'll take it.

W Okay. Do you _____ _____ _____?

M No, I don't. Thank you.

부탁한 일 파악

15 대화를 듣고, 남자가 여자에게 부탁한
일로 가장 적절한 것을 고르시오.

① 발표에 참여하기
② 프로그램 가르쳐 주기
③ 발표 주제의 자료 찾기
④ 컴퓨터의 문제 발견하기
⑤ 담당 선생님께 연락하기

15 🇬🇧

M Kelly, could you _____ _____ _____ _____?

W Sure. What is it?

M I have a presentation about World War II tomorrow.

W You've done a lot of presentations before.

M _____ _____ _____ _____ I have to use the
PowerPoint program. I don't know how to use it.

W Then maybe it's time for you _____ _____ _____.

M That's right. Do you have time to teach me?

W Of course. What are friends for?

이유 추론

16 대화를 듣고, 여자가 당황한 이유로
가장 적절한 것을 고르시오.

① 택시비가 비싸서
② 다른 택시를 타서
③ 엄마가 집에 안 계셔서
④ 지갑을 도서관에 놓고 와서
⑤ 돈을 빌려달라고 부탁받아서

16

W   George, I was very embarrassed yesterday.

M   _____ _____?

W   I was going home by taxi when I suddenly realized I had
_____ _____ _____ in the library.

M   So what did you do?

W   I called my mom and _____ _____ _____
_____ _____ _____ in front of the house with some
money.

M   Was she at home?

W   Luckily, yes.

M   That's good!

그림 상황 파악

17 다음 그림의 상황에 가장 적절한
대화를 고르시오.

① ② ③ ④ ⑤

♥ **I couldn't agree more.**

: '더 이상 동의할 수 없어.'라는 의미로 상
대방의 말에 전적으로 찬성할 때 사용하
는 표현이다.

17

① W   Do you know _____ _____ _____ _____?

M   I have no idea.

② W   Excuse me. Could you turn down the volume?

M   Oh, sorry. _____ _____ _____ _____.

③ W   I think we should _____ _____ _____ in the library.

M   ♥ I couldn't agree more.

④ W   Do you have some time?

M   Actually, I am _____ _____ _____ _____.

⑤ W   _____ _____ _____ your headset for a moment?

M   Sure. Here *it is.

*it is [잇] [이즈] → [이리즈]

언급 유무 파악

18 다음을 듣고, 여자가 새로운 학교에
대해 언급하지 않은 것을 고르시오.

① 학년 당 적은 학급 수
② 많은 스포츠 클럽
③ 선생님들의 친절함
④ 가입하고 싶은 클럽
⑤ 학교와 집 사이의 거리

18

W   Dear Ethan. One month has passed _____ _____
_____ _____. How are my old friends? Tell them I
miss them. I like my new school. My new school is a little
different. First, each grade has only three classes. So I know
almost everyone's name now. And the teachers are _____
_____ _____ _____. They are trying to teach me
what I don't know. Lastly, there are many sports clubs. I want to
join the badminton club. _____ _____ _____ your
news soon. Bye.

적절한 응답 찾기

[19-20] 대화를 듣고, 남자의 마지막 말에 이어질 여자의 말로 가장 적절한 것을 고르시오.

19 Woman: _____

① What brings you here?

② I have never been to Japan.

③ I can give you a call soon.

④ I hope you have a nice trip to Japan.

⑤ I am visiting my uncle who lives in Japan.

19 🇬🇧

W   Excuse me. _____ _____ _____ _____?

M   Well, you are... Are you May? Clover Elementary School?

W   That's right, Steve. _____ _____, _____ _____.

M   How *have you been?

W   I have been good. I can't believe we are meeting here in Japan.

M   _____ _____. I have been traveling for 5 days. _____ _____ _____?

W   I am visiting my uncle who lives in Japan.

*have you [해브] [유] → [해뷰]

적절한 응답 찾기

20 Woman: _____

① You can count on me.

② Let me tell you how to do it.

③ We should always recycle old items.

④ Upcycling is what I have heard about.

⑤ I am interested in hearing more about that.

♥ Shall I ~ ?

: '내가 ~할까?'라는 의미로 'Will I ~?' 보다 상대방에게 겸손하게 요청이나 허락을 구하는 표현으로 사용된다.

20

M   Have you ever heard about upcycling?

W   What? Upcycling? Not recycling?

M   It's upcycling. ♥Shall I tell you what it is?

W   Please. What is it?

M   Upcycling is _____ _____ recycling as both are about reusing items.

W   What is the difference then?

M   We can do upcycling _____ _____ _____ make used items better ones.

W   For example?

M   Do you have old jeans? We can _____ _____ _____ _____ _____ _____ _____.

W   I am interested in hearing more about that.

1 다음을 듣고, 서울의 내일 날씨로 가장 적절한 것을 고르시오.

①   ②   ③

④   ⑤

2 대화를 듣고, 테이블에 놓인 귀금속의 배치로 가장 적절한 것을 고르시오.

①   ②   ③

④   ⑤

3 대화를 듣고, 여자의 심정으로 가장 적절한 것을 고르시오.
① relaxed   ② touched
③ ashamed   ④ comfortable
⑤ disappointed

4 대화를 듣고, 여자가 일요일에 한 일로 가장 적절한 것을 고르시오.
① 용돈 저축하기   ② 박물관에 가기
③ 기차 여행하기   ④ 아르바이트하기
⑤ 역사 보고서 쓰기

5 대화를 듣고, 두 사람이 대화하는 장소로 가장 적절한 곳을 고르시오.
① 동물원   ② 백화점
③ 동물병원   ④ 경찰서
⑤ 미용실

6 대화를 듣고, 여자의 마지막 말의 의도로 가장 적절한 것을 고르시오.
① 동의   ② 거절   ③ 실망
④ 축하   ⑤ 격려

7 대화를 듣고, 여자가 거리 축제에서 참여하게 될 활동을 고르시오.
① 행사 진행자   ② 페이스 페인팅
③ 쿠키 만들기   ④ 마카롱 판매
⑤ 곤충 종류 소개

8 대화를 듣고, 남자가 대화 직후에 할 일로 가장 적절한 것을 고르시오.
① 농구하러 가기   ② 아침 먹으러 가기
③ 드라이브하러 가기   ④ 정비소에 차 맡기기
⑤ 운전면허 시험 치르기

9 다음을 듣고, 여자가 학교 운동회에 대해 언급하지 않은 것을 고르시오.
① 내일 학교 운동회가 열린다.
② 오전에 100미터 달리기를 한다.
③ 점심은 학교에서 제공된다.
④ 오후 4시에 축구 경기를 한다.
⑤ 운동회 후에 시상식이 있다.

10 다음을 듣고, 남자가 하는 말의 내용으로 가장 적절한 것을 고르시오.
① 돌잔치   ② 민속촌   ③ 전통 의상
④ 전통 혼례   ⑤ 전통 주택

11 대화를 듣고, 여자가 언급한 내용과 일치하지 않는 것을 고르시오.
① 2월 7일에 출발할 수 있다
② 3일 동안 머무는 여행이다.
③ 항공권이 포함된 여행 상품이다.
④ 호텔에서 아침 식사가 제공된다.
⑤ 개인 경비를 가져와야 한다.

12 대화를 듣고, 여자가 집으로 되돌아온 목적으로 가장 적절한 것을 고르시오.
① 숙제를 두고 나가서
② 장갑을 바꿔 끼려고
③ 목도리를 착용하려고
④ 감기 걸려서 집에서 쉬려고
⑤ 자동차 타고 학교에 가려고

13 대화를 듣고, 여자가 지불해야 할 금액으로 가장 적절한 것을 고르시오.
① $25   ② $45   ③ $50
④ $65   ⑤ $75

14 대화를 듣고, 두 사람의 관계로 가장 적절한 것을 고르시오.
① 은행 직원 ― 손님
② 가게 사장 ― 직원
③ 선생님 ― 학생
④ 경찰관 ― 시민
⑤ 기술자 ― 손님

15 대화를 듣고, 남자가 여자에게 요청한 일로 가장 적절한 것을 고르시오.
① 돈을 투자해 달라고
② 고아원에 방문해 달라고
③ 자원봉사를 허락해 달라고
④ 건강 상태를 확인해 달라고
⑤ 익명으로 기부하게 해달라고

16 대화를 듣고, 여자가 맨발로 걸으려는 이유로 가장 적절한 것을 고르시오.
① 모래를 좋아해서
② 바다로 뛰어들기 위해
③ 몸의 건강을 위해
④ 발을 물에 씻으려고
⑤ 신발이 더러워질까 봐

17 다음 그림의 상황에 가장 적절한 대화를 고르시오.

①   ②   ③   ④   ⑤

18 대화를 듣고, 두 사람이 서울 마라톤에 관해 언급하지 <u>않은</u> 것을 고르시오.
① 참가 비용
② 참여 자격
③ 대회 일정
④ 접수 기간
⑤ 달리는 거리

[19~20] 대화를 듣고, 남자의 마지막 말에 이어질 여자의 말로 가장 적절한 것을 고르시오.

19 Woman: _____
① Okay. I'll give it a try.
② You can be a great writer.
③ I've already turned in my essay.
④ My essay score is lower than yours.
⑤ Don't panic. We've got plenty of time.

20 Woman: _____
① I should get a new cellphone.
② Excuse me, but do I know you?
③ Why not? I'm leaving right now.
④ Don't forget to bring me a present.
⑤ It was fun today. I hope to see you soon.

Listen and Check

● 대화를 다시 듣고, 알맞은 것을 고르시오.

1 Will there be a white Christmas?
☐ Yes ☐ No

2 There are two rings on the table.
☐ True ☐ False

3 Nahyun didn't like the movie *Jessica's Diary*.
☐ True ☐ False

4 What did the man do on Sunday?
☐ went to the museum
☐ did his part-time job

5 Does the woman's cat have a serious disease?
☐ Yes ☐ No

6 What will the man do in front of the audience?
☐ act in a play ☐ play the piano

7 The man will sell cookies and macaroons at the street festival.
☐ True ☐ False

8 Did Youngho pass the driving test?
☐ Yes ☐ No

9 What time are the students going to do tug-of-war?
☐ at 2:00 p.m. ☐ at 4:00 p.m.

10 Babies usually wear *hanbok* at this event.
☐ True ☐ False

11 Is the woman interested in the Taipei package tour?
☐ Yes ☐ No

12 How's the weather outside?
☐ warm ☐ cold

13 What would the woman like to buy?
☐ a phone case ☐ a pencil case

14 The man used the ATMs without any problems.
☐ True ☐ False

15 How much does the man want to donate to the orphanage?
☐ one thousand dollars
☐ ten thousand dollars

16 The woman wanted to walk across the sand beach.
☐ True ☐ False

17 What did the woman drop on the ground?
☐ a muffler ☐ a purse

18 The man is running a full marathon this Sunday.
☐ True ☐ False

19 The man and the woman have to hand in their essays tomorrow.
☐ True ☐ False

20 Did the woman get a text message from Jonathan?
☐ Yes ☐ No

그림 정보 파악

1 다음을 듣고, 서울의 내일 날씨로 가장 적절한 것을 고르시오.

① ② ③

④ ⑤

1

M Merry Christmas, everyone. Today is Christmas Eve. It's afternoon now, and the ＿＿＿＿ ＿＿＿＿ ＿＿＿＿ ＿＿＿＿. It's still sunny, but it will be cloudy this evening. On Christmas Day, as expected, you can ＿＿＿＿ ＿＿＿＿ ＿＿＿＿ to the ground. The day after tomorrow, it will ＿＿＿＿ ＿＿＿＿ and be sunny again.

그림 정보 파악

2 대화를 듣고, 테이블에 놓인 귀금속의 배치로 가장 적절한 것을 고르시오.

① ②  ③

④  ⑤

♥ **Can you please help?**

: 상대방에게 도움을 요청할 때 쓰는 표현으로, '나를 도와주겠니?'라는 뜻이다.

= Will you help me?

= Give me a helping hand.

2 🇬🇧

M To sell jewelry well, we should take nice photos.

W I totally agree with you.

M You are ＿＿＿＿ ＿＿＿＿ ＿＿＿＿ ＿＿＿＿, right? ♥Can you please help?

W All right. Place the flower ring on the table and put the heart-shaped necklace ＿＿＿＿ ＿＿＿＿ ＿＿＿＿ ＿＿＿＿ of the ring.

M Okay. And then?

W Put the star earrings ＿＿＿＿ the ring with the flower design and the heart-shaped necklace.

M Wow, it ＿＿＿＿ ＿＿＿＿ ＿＿＿＿. Nice job!

심정 추론

3 대화를 듣고, 여자의 심정으로 가장 적절한 것을 고르시오.

① relaxed
② touched
③ ashamed
④ comfortable
⑤ disappointed

3

M Nahyun, did you see the movie *Jessica's Diary*?

W Yes, I saw it with my sister last night.

M How was the movie?

W I ＿＿＿＿ ＿＿＿＿ ＿＿＿＿ ＿＿＿＿ the movie.

M *Was it that bad?

W It was the ＿＿＿＿ ＿＿＿＿ ＿＿＿＿ ＿＿＿＿ this year.

M Can you tell me why you didn't like it?

W Above all, the story does not ＿＿＿＿ ＿＿＿＿.

M Oh, I see. I'll ＿＿＿＿ ＿＿＿＿ ＿＿＿＿.

*was it [워즈] [잇] → [워짓]

한 일 파악

4 대화를 듣고, 여자가 일요일에 한 일로 가장 적절한 것을 고르시오.

① 용돈 저축하기
② 박물관에 가기
③ 기차 여행하기
④ 아르바이트하기
⑤ 역사 보고서 쓰기

4

M Pamela, what did you do on the weekend?

W I _____ _____ _____ _____ at a *gas station last Sunday, and I _____ _____ today. And you?

M I _____ _____ _____ _____ for my history report.

W Oh, no! I _____ _____ _____ the report. Is your history report finished?

M Of course. Do you want me to help you to finish your report?

W Please. I'll treat you to a nice dinner later if you do that.

*gas station [개쓰] [스테이션] → [개스테이션]

장소 추론

5 대화를 듣고, 두 사람이 대화하는 장소로 가장 적절한 곳을 고르시오.

① 동물원   ② 백화점
③ 동물병원   ④ 경찰서
⑤ 미용실

♥ **What seems to be the problem?**

: 상대방에게 뭔가 문제가 있거나 상황이 좋지 않아 보일 때 쓰는 표현으로, '무슨 문제가 있나요?', '무엇이 잘못되었나요?' 라는 뜻이다.

= What's the matter?
= Is something wrong (with you)?

5

M Come on in. ♥ What seems to be the problem?

W My cat _____ _____ yesterday. I saw pieces of hair, food, and fluids in her vomit.

M Do you know _____ _____ she vomits?

W Not often. Maybe once a month.

M Then you don't _____ _____ _____ _____ about it. Cats sometimes need to throw up hairballs because they can't digest them.

W I got it. _____ _____ _____.

의도 파악

6 대화를 듣고, 여자의 마지막 말의 의도로 가장 적절한 것을 고르시오.

① 동의   ② 거절
③ 실망   ④ 축하
⑤ 격려

6 🇬🇧

M I've never stood _____ _____ _____ _____ _____ before.

W Relax. You can just play the piano _____ _____.

M _____ _____ I make a mistake in the middle?

W Don't worry. I know you practiced a lot.

M Thank you for _____ _____ _____.

W Show them what you've practiced. I'm sure you will do well.

특정 정보 파악

7 대화를 듣고, 여자가 거리 축제에서
참여하게 될 활동을 고르시오.

① 행사 진행자
② 페이스 페인팅
③ 쿠키 만들기
④ 마카롱 판매
⑤ 곤충 종류 소개

7

W I'm _____ _____ _____ the street festival on
Saturday.

M Same here. Many people will *visit it. I'll sell cookies and
macaroons there.

W Wow! Sounds great.

M What will you do at the street festival?

W I decided to _____ _____ _____.

M It'll be fun. For me, a butterfly, please.

W Sure. I'm going to _____ _____ _____ _____
_____ _____.

*visit it [비짓] [잇] → [비짓]

할 일 파악

8 대화를 듣고, 남자가 대화 직후에 할
일로 가장 적절한 것을 고르시오.

① 농구하러 가기
② 아침 먹으러 가기
③ 드라이브하러 가기
④ 정비소에 차 맡기기
⑤ 운전면허 시험 치르기

8

M Honey, do you know what's wrong with Youngho?

W He _____ _____ _____ _____ today, but he
didn't pass it.

M _____ _____ _____. He was excited that he could
drive my car soon.

W Why don't you take him _____ _____ _____?

M Not today. I took my car to the shop for an inspection.

W Hmm... How about _____ _____ with him?

M That's better. I'll do that.

언급 유무 파악

9 다음을 듣고, 여자가 학교 운동회에
대해 언급하지 않은 것을 고르시오

① 내일 학교 운동회가 열린다.
② 오전에 100미터 달리기를 한다.
③ 점심은 학교에서 제공된다.
④ 오후 4시에 축구 경기를 한다.
⑤ 운동회 후에 시상식이 있다.

9

W Good morning, students. Tomorrow is our _____ _____
_____. I'll let you know the schedule. From 10:00 to 12:00 in
the morning, we'll run some 100-meter races. After that, we will
have lunch. As school lunches will not be provided tomorrow,
you should _____ _____ _____ _____. At
2:00, we are going to do tug-of-war. Lastly, we will play soccer
at 4:00. When the game ends, we'll _____ _____
_____ _____. We'll have fun tomorrow.

화제·주제 파악

10 다음을 듣고, 남자가 하는 말의
내용으로 가장 적절한 것을 고르시오.

① 돌잔치
② 민속촌
③ 전통 의상
④ 전통 혼례
⑤ 전통 주택

10

M This is a Korean tradition for _____ _____ _____ _____
_____ of a baby. The baby wears Korean traditional
clothes, called *hanbok*. In the middle of the party, the baby is
asked to _____ _____ _____ _____ from the
table. People think that the object the baby grabs will tell the
child's future. For example, if the baby picks up money, he will
_____ _____. What is this?

내용 불일치 파악

11 대화를 듣고, 여자가 언급한 내용과
일치하지 <u>않는</u> 것을 고르시오.

① 2월 7일에 출발할 수 있다
② 3일 동안 머무는 여행이다.
③ 항공권이 포함된 여행 상품이다.
④ 호텔에서 아침 식사가 제공된다.
⑤ 개인 경비를 가져와야 한다.

11

W Hello. Joy Travel Agency.

M _____ _____ _____ _____ about the Taipei
package tour.

W When do you want to go?

M On February 7. I want to stay there for 3 days.

W Okay. [*Pause*] _____ _____. How many people?

M 4 adults. Does it include flights, hotels, and meals?

W We will *provide you with the flights and the hotels _____
_____ _____. And you have to cover _____
_____ _____.

M Okay. I see.

*provide you [프로바이드] [유] → [프로바이쥬]

목적 파악

12 대화를 듣고, 여자가 집으로 되돌아온
목적으로 가장 적절한 것을 고르시오.

① 숙제를 두고 나가서
② 장갑을 바꿔 끼려고
③ 목도리를 착용하려고
④ 감기 걸려서 집에서 쉬려고
⑤ 자동차 타고 학교에 가려고

12 🇬🇧

M Janet, why are you home now? I thought you _____
_____ _____.

W I did. But I came back just now, Dad. It's so cold outside.

M Did you come back _____ _____ _____?

W No, I'm wearing gloves now. I _____ _____ _____
my muffler.

M I got it. Here it is. Put on your muffler.

W Thanks, Dad.

M Hurry up. Don't be _____ _____ _____.

숫자 전보 파악

13 대화를 듣고, 여자가 지불해야 할 금액으로 가장 적절한 것을 고르시오.

① $25
② $45
③ $50
④ $65
⑤ $75

13

W   Excuse me, but I'd like to buy a phone case.
M   Okay. _____ _____ _____ cellphone do you have?
W   I have one by the ABC Company.
M   Then _____ _____ _____ from the ones in this section.
W   Let me see. [*Pause*] How much are this one and that one?
M   25 dollars each. If you buy two items, you can _____ _____ _____.
W   That's great. I'll _____ _____ _____.

관계 추론

14 대화를 듣고, 두 사람의 관계로 가장 적절한 것을 고르시오.

① 은행 직원 — 손님
② 가게 사장 — 직원
③ 선생님 — 학생
④ 경찰관 — 시민
⑤ 기술자 — 손님

♥ **It was no use.**
: 어떤 일을 시도해 봤지만 효과가 없을 때 쓰는 표현으로, '소용이 없다.'라는 뜻 이다.
= It was no good.

14

[*Telephone rings.*]
W   This is Hello Bank. How may I help you?
M   I'm calling because I _____ _____ _____ _____ one of your ATMs.
W   _____ _____ is the problem?
M   I put my card into the machine, but the machine _____ _____.
W   _____ _____ _____ _____ the "Cancel" button on the screen?
M   I did. But ♥ it was no use.
W   Okay. I'll send someone there right away.

요청한 일 파악

15 대화를 듣고, 남자가 여자에게 요청한 일로 가장 적절한 것을 고르시오.

① 돈을 투자해 달라고
② 고아원에 방문해 달라고
③ 자원봉사를 허락해 달라고
④ 건강 상태를 확인해 달라고
⑤ 익명으로 기부하게 해달라고

♥ **Would you mind if ~?**
: 상대방의 의견을 구하거나 허락을 요청 할 때 쓰는 표현으로, '~해도 괜찮겠니?' 라는 뜻이다.
= Is it all right if ~?

15

W   How can I help you?
M   Um, I _____ _____ _____ _____ to this orphanage.
W   ♥ Would you mind if I asked you how much?
M   Not really. One thousand dollars, but _____ _____ _____.
W   What is it?
M   All I want is that _____ _____ _____ _____.
W   Okay. I promise you.

16 대화를 듣고, 여자가 맨발로 걸으려는
이유로 가장 적절한 것을 고르시오.

① 모래를 좋아해서

② 바다로 뛰어들기 위해

③ 몸의 건강을 위해

④ 발을 물에 씻으려고

⑤ 신발이 더러워질까 봐

16

M Look at the deep blue sea.

W It's so beautiful. Let's _____ _____ the white sand beach.

M That's a good idea. Why are you _____ _____ your shoes?

W I want to _____ _____ on the sand beach.

M Why? Your feet will get dirty soon.

W Walking barefoot _____ _____ _____ through the body.

M If it's good for my health, then I should _____ _____.

---

17 다음 그림의 상황에 가장 적절한
대화를 고르시오.

① ② ③ ④ ⑤

17

① **M** Your purse is cute. Where did you get it?

  W I bought it when I _____ _____ _____.

② **M** Hey, you just dropped your purse.

  W Thanks for _____ _____ _____.

③ **M** Do not throw trash on the street.

  W Sorry. I _____ do it again.

④ **M** The *ground is _____ _____ shake.

  W I feel it. Is it an earthquake?

⑤ **M** Let's _____ _____ after work.

  W Okay. I need to buy a purse.

*ground is [그라운드] [이즈] → [그라운디즈]

---

18 대화를 듣고, 두 사람이 서울 마라톤에
관해 언급하지 <u>않은</u> 것을 고르시오.

① 참가 비용

② 참여 자격

③ 대회 일정

④ 접수 기간

⑤ 달리는 거리

♥ **Can you tell me more?**

: 상대방의 말에 추가적인 설명을 요청할
때 쓰는 표현으로, '더 말해 줄 수 있니?'
라는 뜻이다.

= Can you explain it more?

18

M I'll take part in the Seoul Marathon _____ _____.

W _____! ♥ Can you tell me more?

M The marathon is open to everyone, and there is _____ _____ _____.

W _____ _____ _____ do participants have to run?

M It's a _____ _____. So maybe 21 kilometers.

W 21 kilometers? Wow! Good luck to you.

적절한 응답 찾기

[19-20] 대화를 듣고, 남자의 마지막 말에 이어질 여자의 말로 가장 적절한 것을 고르시오.

19 Woman: _____

① Okay. I'll give it a try.

② You can be a great writer.

③ I've already turned in my essay.

④ My essay score is lower than yours.

⑤ Don't panic. We've got plenty of time.

19 🇬🇧

M How's your essay going?

W Terrible. I haven't written a single word.

M You should be in a hurry. We have to _____ _____ _____ _____.

W I know. But I don't have any ideas.

M Calm down. You can't _____ _____ _____ _____ at one go.

W You're right. I agree with you.

M Write down _____ _____ _____ _____ on the paper.

W Okay. I'll give it a try.

적절한 응답 찾기

20 Woman: _____

① I should get a new cellphone.

② Excuse me, but do I know you?

③ Why not? I'm leaving right now.

④ Don't forget to bring me a present.

⑤ It was fun today. I hope to see you soon.

💜 **What do you mean by that?**

: 상대방의 말이 이해가 되지 않아 추가적인 설명이 필요할 때 쓰는 표현으로, '무슨 의미니?'라는 뜻이다.

= What exactly is it?

20

[*Cellphone rings.*]

W Hi, Melvin.

M Hazel, what's up? We are waiting for you.

W Waiting for me? 💜What do you mean by that?

M We are _____ _____ _____ _____ for Jonathan's farewell party.

W What? I thought it is going to be next Wednesday.

M No. Jonathan _____ _____ _____. He told me that he sent a text message to you.

W I didn't _____ _____ _____.

M Anyway, can you come here now?

W Why not? I'm leaving right now.

1 다음을 듣고, 예상되는 런던의 날씨로 가장 적절한 것을 고르시오.

2 대화를 듣고, 남자가 만들 쿠션으로 가장 적절한 것을 고르시오.

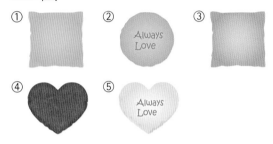

3 대화를 듣고, 남자의 심정으로 가장 적절한 것을 고르시오.
① sorry ② bored ③ proud
④ nervous ⑤ satisfied

4 대화를 듣고, 여자가 축제에서 한 일로 가장 적절한 것을 고르시오.
① 퍼즐 대회 참가
② 수학 시상식 참여
③ 수학의 이론 발표
④ 시 대표로 대회 참여
⑤ 수학에 대한 영화 관람

5 대화를 듣고, 두 사람이 대화하는 장소로 가장 적절한 곳을 고르시오.
① 서점 ② 강당 ③ 도서관
④ 천문대 ⑤ 체육관

6 대화를 듣고, 여자의 마지막 말의 의도로 가장 적절한 것을 고르시오.
① 비난 ② 동의 ③ 사과
④ 충고 ⑤ 감사

7 대화를 듣고, 여자가 중국에 대해 언급하지 않은 것을 고르시오.
① 많은 사람
② 변화 속도
③ 현대식 건물
④ 위험한 교통 상황
⑤ 친절한 사람

8 대화를 듣고, 여자가 대화 직후에 할 일로 가장 적절한 것을 고르시오.
① 다른 상점에 전화하기
② 본사에 사이즈를 문의하기
③ 손님의 영수증을 확인하기
④ 다른 종류의 신발을 가져오기
⑤ 다른 사이즈의 신발을 가져오기

9 다음을 듣고, 남자가 핼러윈에 대해 언급하지 않은 것을 고르시오.
① 기념하는 날짜
② 기념하는 국가
③ 아이들의 활동
④ 즐겨 먹는 음식
⑤ 아시아의 기념 유무

10 다음을 듣고, 여자가 하는 말의 내용으로 가장 적절한 것을 고르시오.
① 안전 교육의 숙지
② 연극을 계획하는 이유
③ 휴대 전화의 기능 설명
④ 연극 관람 시 주의 사항
⑤ 사진 촬영을 할 때 요령

11 다음을 듣고, 수학 여행에 대한 내용으로 일치하지 않는 것을 고르시오.
① 3주 전에 강원도로 갔다.
② 동해안의 일출을 보았다.
③ 호텔 옆에 해변이 있었다.
④ 버스 안에서 음식을 먹었다.
⑤ 저녁을 먹고 공연을 보았다.

12 대화를 듣고, 여자가 전화를 건 목적으로 가장 적절한 것을 고르시오.
① 공연 일정을 변경하려고
② 학교 신문에 광고를 하려고
③ 학교의 방학 날짜를 물어보려고
④ 남자가 어디 있는지를 확인하려고
⑤ 노래 경연 대회에 함께 신청하려고

13 대화를 듣고, 남자가 살 청바지의 가격을 고르시오.
① $25 ② $40 ③ $45
④ $50 ⑤ $90

14 대화를 듣고, 두 사람의 관계로 가장 적절한 것을 고르시오.
① 선생님 — 학부형 ② 경찰관 — 운전자
③ 운전자 — 동승자 ④ 운전 강사 — 학생
⑤ 카레이서 — 정비원

15 대화를 듣고, 남자가 여자에게 부탁한 일로 가장 적절한 것을 고르시오.
① 자리를 맡아주기 ② 소란 피우지 않기
③ 자리를 양보해 주기 ④ 남의 발을 밟지 않기
⑤ 핸드폰을 사용하지 않기

16 대화를 듣고, 콘서트가 취소된 이유로 가장 적절한 것을 고르시오.
① 예약을 하지 못해서 ② 날씨가 좋지 않아서
③ 공연 준비가 부족해서 ④ 극장에 화재가 발생해서
⑤ 공연할 사람이 부상을 당해서

17 다음 그림의 상황에 가장 적절한 대화를 고르시오.

① ② ③ ④ ⑤

18 다음을 듣고, 여자가 오늘 일정에 대해 언급하지 않은 것을 고르시오.
① 지역 식당에서 점심을 먹는다.
② O-World는 입장료가 무료이다.
③ 박물관에서 도시에 대해 배운다.
④ 점심을 먹고, 지역 마을을 잠깐 들른다.
⑤ O-World까지 이동하는데 3시간이 걸린다.

[19~20] 대화를 듣고, 여자의 마지막 말에 이어질 남자의 말로 가장 적절한 것을 고르시오.

19 Man: _____
① I'm thinking about that.
② Please drive me to the hospital.
③ Would you buy me lunch today?
④ Don't worry. It's just a matter of time.
⑤ Can you help me with my homework?

20 Man: _____
① That's fine with me.
② It's very far from here.
③ Tell me what time it is.
④ What makes you think so?
⑤ I am surprised to hear that.

Listen and Check

정답 및 해설 *p.059*

● 대화를 다시 듣고, 알맞은 것을 고르시오.

1 Paris will be cloudy all day long.
☐ True   ☐ False

2 The man and the woman are going to buy a cushion for their mother as a birthday present.
☐ True   ☐ False

3 The man couldn't buy a movie ticket because he didn't have time today.
☐ True   ☐ False

4 Was the woman unable to participate in the puzzle activities?
☐ Yes   ☐ No

5 What did the woman recommend to the man?
☐ the *Harry Potter* series
☐ poetry

6 Could the man hear the music the woman listened to?
☐ Yes   ☐ No

7 How were the buildings in China?
☐ traditional   ☐ modern

8 The man wants to exchange his shoes because they are too big for him.
☐ True   ☐ False

9 Does the man say people in Asia don't celebrate Halloween?
☐ Yes   ☐ No

10 When can a person late for the play enter?
☐ after the curtains go up
☐ during the break time

11 What did the man do at the hotel at night?
☐ watch performances
☐ eat delicious snacks

12 Did the man know there was a singing contest?
☐ Yes   ☐ No

13 Why was the first pair of jeans ninety dollars?
☐ because it was a new product
☐ because it was the regular price

14 The man gave a ticket to the woman because she was driving her car too fast.
☐ True   ☐ False

15 Does the man want to sit next to his wife?
☐ Yes   ☐ No

16 The man knew that the concert was canceled.
☐ True   ☐ False

17 Does the woman know what the man needs?
☐ Yes   ☐ No

18 Where is the first place they will visit?
☐ O-World   ☐ the city museum

19 The man has a stomachache because he ate a lot for lunch.
☐ True   ☐ False

20 The woman's grandfather passed away.
☐ True   ☐ False

그림 정보 파악

1 다음을 듣고, 예상되는 런던의 날씨로 가장 적절한 것을 고르시오.

①   ②   ③

④   ⑤

1

M Good evening! Here is today's world weather report. Today in Seoul, the rain _____ _____ _____ _____ from last night. In New York, there will be showers and thunderstorms _____ _____ _____. The forecast for Paris is mostly cloudy, and the weather will _____ _____ _____.
Snow is expected in London. Thank you for listening and see you next time.

그림 정보 파악

2 대화를 듣고, 남자가 만들 쿠션으로 가장 적절한 것을 고르시오.

①   ②   ③

④   ⑤

🤍 **I'm with you.**

: 상대방에 말에 동의하거나, 상대방의 의견에 따를 경우에 사용된다.
= I couldn't agree more.

2

W Chris, how about making a cushion for Mom _____ _____ _____ _____?

M Sounds great. What *kind of cushion shall we make?

W I'd like to make a square one with a heart in the middle of it.

M Well, how about a heart-shaped one _____ _____ _____ "Always Love" on it?

W Great! That would _____ _____ _____ a square one. 🤍 I'm with you.

M Okay. Let's make it.

*kind of [카인드] [어브] → [카인더브]

심정 추론

3 대화를 듣고, 남자의 심정으로 가장 적절한 것을 고르시오.

① sorry
② bored
③ proud
④ nervous
⑤ satisfied

3

W How can I help you?

M Hello. I'd like _____ _____ _____ _____ _____ *Coco*.

W What time?

M For the seven-thirty show.

W Wait, please... Sorry. _____ _____ _____ _____ for that time. Why don't you book a ticket for tomorrow's showing? There are plenty of seats then.

M But I don't have time for a movie tomorrow. What a pity! Maybe next time.

W I am sorry that _____ _____ _____ _____.

한 일 파악

4 대화를 듣고, 여자가 축제에서 한 일로 가장 적절한 것을 고르시오.

① 퍼즐 대회 참가
② 수학 시상식 참여
③ 수학의 이론 발표
④ 시 대표로 대회 참여
⑤ 수학에 대한 영화 관람

4

M   _____ _____ _____ _____ _____ the city math festival last Saturday.

W   Yes, I did. So many people went to the festival.

M   Were there _____ _____ _____ _____ _____?

W   Yes. There were exciting puzzle games.

M   Oh, I like puzzles. What puzzle did you do?

W   Sadly, I couldn't do any of them. The lines were _____ _____ for me to participate.

M   Then what activity did you do?

W   I watched a movie on math history.

장소 추론

5 대화를 듣고, 두 사람이 대화하는 장소로 가장 적절한 곳을 고르시오.

① 서점
② 강당
③ 도서관
④ 천문대
⑤ 체육관

5

W   Did you find anything good?

M   No, _____ _____ _____.

W   What are you reading these days?

M   Some poetry. The poems I am reading are touching and _____ _____ _____.

W   _____. Did you read the new *Harry Potter* series? I thought the books were really great.

M   Oh, I'll read them the next time. I will pick up *one of _____ _____. Where is the circulation desk?

W   It's _____ _____ _____ _____. Let's go now.

*one of [원] [어브] → [워너브]

의도 파악

6 대화를 듣고, 여자의 마지막 말의 의도로 가장 적절한 것을 고르시오.

① 비난   ② 동의
③ 사과   ④ 충고
⑤ 감사

♥ **Excuse me?**

: 원래는 '실례합니다.'는 의미이지만, 문장의 앞에 쓰여 상대방의 말을 정확하게 듣지 못해 끝을 올려서 말할 경우에 '다시 한번 말씀해 주시겠습니까?'로 사용될 수 있다.

6

M   Heather, why don't you turn down the volume?

W   ♥Excuse me?

M   I said _____ _____ _____ the volume.

W   Why? I'm just listening to music with my earphones.

M   But I can hear your music. It is too loud.

W   Sorry. I didn't know it was bothering you.

M   I think _____ _____ _____ _____ _____ music loudly by using earphones or headphones so that you can protect your ears.

W   I will be more careful _____ _____ _____.

7 대화를 듣고, 여자가 중국에 대해
언급하지 <u>않은</u> 것을 고르시오.

① 많은 사람
② 변화 속도
③ 현대식 건물
④ 위험한 교통 상황
⑤ 친절한 사람

7

M Hi, Esther. How was your field trip to China?

W It was better _____ _____ _____ _____ it to
be. It seems to be changing rapidly. The people were kind, and
the buildings were modern. And...

M And? What were you going to say?

W The people, of course. Wherever I went, there were _____
_____ _____ that I was always careful not to lose sight
of my friends.

M Ha-ha. I understand _____ _____ _____.

8 대화를 듣고, 여자가 대화 직후에 할
일로 가장 적절한 것을 고르시오.

① 다른 상점에 전화하기
② 본사에 사이즈를 문의하기
③ 손님의 영수증을 확인하기
④ 다른 종류의 신발을 가져오기
⑤ 다른 사이즈의 신발을 가져오기

♥ That's very kind of you.
: 상대방의 친절에 대한 감사함을 표현할
때 '당신은 매우 친절하군요.' 정도의 의
미로 쓰인다. 'You are very kind.'도 사
용될 수 있지만, '당신은 (원래) 매우 친절
해요.'처럼 들릴 수 있기 때문에 'That's
very kind of you.'가 상대방의 행위에 대
한 표현으로 더 적절하다.

8

W What can I do for you?

M I'd like to _____ _____ _____.

W What's the problem with them?

M They are size 270, but I think they are too tight for me.

W Then would you like size 275?

M Yes. I'll feel _____ _____ in size 275.

W Wait... Sorry. Because we don't have that size, I have to call
another store _____ _____ _____ _____
_____ _____.

M ♥That's very kind of you. Please do that.

9 다음을 듣고, 남자가 핼러윈에 대해
언급하지 <u>않은</u> 것을 고르시오.

① 기념하는 날짜
② 기념하는 국가
③ 아이들의 활동
④ 즐겨 먹는 음식
⑤ 아시아의 기념 유무

9

M Every year on October thirty-first, people, especially in the
U.S., Canada, and Britain celebrate Halloween. Children
go from house to house and shout, "Trick or treat!" while
wearing costumes _____ _____ _____ _____
_____ ghosts or witches. In the past, people believed
that the souls of dead people wandered around _____
_____ _____. Nowadays, some people in Asia like to
celebrate the day, too. They wear unique costumes _____
_____ _____ with their family members and friends.

화제 · 주제 파악

10 다음을 듣고, 여자가 하는 말의
내용으로 가장 적절한 것을 고르시오.

① 안전 교육의 숙지
② 연극을 계획하는 이유
③ 휴대 전화의 기능 설명
④ 연극 관람 시 주의 사항
⑤ 사진 촬영을 할 때 요령

10

W Welcome to the Grand Theater. The play is about to begin. Please make your way to your seats. The curtains _____ _____ _____ _____ three minutes. Before the play, please turn off your cell phones and remember that _____ _____ _____ _____ in the theater. The play should last for about two hours, and there will be a ten-minute break _____ _____ _____. Anyone who is late for the play will be admitted only during the break time. Please enjoy the play. Thank you.

내용 불일치 파악

11 다음을 듣고, 수학 여행에 대한 내용으로 일치하지 <u>않는</u> 것을 고르시오.

① 3주 전에 강원도로 갔다.
② 동해안의 일출을 보았다.
③ 호텔 옆에 해변이 있었다.
④ 버스 안에서 음식을 먹었다.
⑤ 저녁을 먹고 공연을 보았다.

11

M I went on a school trip to Gangwon-do three weeks ago. My friends and I _____ _____ _____ _____. On the bus, we enjoyed delicious snacks and drinks. When we arrived at the hotel, we cried out of joy _____ _____ _____ _____ _____ right beside it. After we unpacked our stuff, we had dinner. That night, some students and teachers put on terrific performances for us. I was very _____ _____ their singing and dancing were the best.

목적 파악

12 대화를 듣고, 여자가 전화를 건 목적으로 가장 적절한 것을 고르시오.

① 공연 일정을 변경하려고
② 학교 신문에 광고를 하려고
③ 학교의 방학 날짜를 물어보려고
④ 남자가 어디 있는지를 확인하려고
⑤ 노래 경연 대회에 함께 신청하려고

12 🇬🇧

[*Cellphone rings.*]

M Hi, Laura. What's up?

W Hi, Jay. Did you see the notice in the school newspaper?

M _____ _____ _____ _____ _____ _____?

W I mean the one about the singing contest.

M No, _____ _____ _____ _____. When is it?

W November thirtieth. Why don't we enter it together?

M _____ _____ _____.

숫자 정보 파악

13 대화를 듣고, 남자가 살 청바지의 가격을 고르시오.

① $25
② $40
③ $45
④ $50
⑤ $90

13

W May I help you?

M Yes. I like these blue jeans. _____ _____ _____ _____ ?

W They are ninety dollars.

M That's too expensive.

W Right. They are new products. But the pants in that section are _____ _____ _____ _____ .

M That's nice. Oh! These jeans are pretty. But the price tag says they are eighty dollars.

W That is the regular price, but we can give them to you _____ _____ _____ .

M Great. I'll buy them.

관계 추론

14 대화를 듣고, 두 사람의 관계로 가장 적절한 것을 고르시오.

① 선생님 — 학부형
② 경찰관 — 운전자
③ 운전자 — 동승자
④ 운전 강사 — 학생
⑤ 카레이서 — 정비원

14

W What can I do for you?

M Show me your driver's license, please.

W _____ _____ _____ . Was I driving too fast?

M Yes. You were driving ten kilometers per hour over the speed limit. I have to _____ _____ _____ for speeding.

W Oh, I'm sorry. If you *give me a chance this time, I will be more careful the next time.

M I wish I could do that, but I can't. Here's your ticket. Please drive more carefully _____ _____ _____ .

W All right.

*give me [기브] [미] → [김미]

부탁한 일 파악

15 대화를 듣고, 남자가 여자에게 부탁한 일로 가장 적절한 것을 고르시오.

① 자리를 맡아주기
② 소란 피우지 않기
③ 자리를 양보해 주기
④ 남의 발을 밟지 않기
⑤ 핸드폰을 사용하지 않기

15 🇬🇧

M Excuse me. _____ _____ _____ _____ ?

W I beg your pardon?

M Is someone using this seat?

W No. _____ _____ _____ _____ .

M I am very sorry, but would you mind moving over one seat so that my wife and I can sit together?

W No, _____ _____ _____ .

M Thank you very much.

16 대화를 듣고, 콘서트가 취소된 이유로 가장 적절한 것을 고르시오.

① 예약을 하지 못해서
② 날씨가 좋지 않아서
③ 공연 준비가 부족해서
④ 극장에 화재가 발생해서
⑤ 공연할 사람이 부상을 당해서

16

W Paul, did you hear the news?

M No, I didn't. What happened?

W The music concert that we were going to see _____ _____ _____.

M What? Why did that happen?

W There was a fire at the theater last night. The news said _____ _____ _____ _____ by the fire.

M _____ _____ _____? I am so sorry to hear that.

---

17 다음 그림의 상황에 가장 적절한 대화를 고르시오.

① ② ③ ④ ⑤

17

① W What is the weather like outside?

  M _____ _____ _____ there's a lot of rain.

② W Sorry. I *stepped on you.

  M That's okay. _____ _____ _____ _____ _____.

③ W I know what you are _____ _____. Here it is.

  M Oh, it's raining outside. Thank you.

④ W _____ _____ _____ _____ do you like?

  M I love rainy and snowy weather.

⑤ W I'll _____ _____ a uniform for the game.

  M I appreciate it.

*stepped on [스텝트] [언] → [스텝턴]

---

18 다음을 듣고, 여자가 오늘 일정에 대해 언급하지 <u>않은</u> 것을 고르시오.

① 지역 식당에서 점심을 먹는다.
② O-World는 입장료가 무료이다.
③ 박물관에서 도시에 대해 배운다.
④ 점심을 먹고, 지역 마을을 잠깐 들른다.
⑤ O-World까지 이동하는데 3시간이 걸린다.

18

W Hello, everyone. _____ _____ _____ _____ today's schedule. It will take us three hours to get to today's main attraction, O-World. And we'll stop at two places _____ _____ _____. The first is the city museum, where you can learn about our city. We'll have lunch at a famous local restaurant at noon. After lunch, we'll take a short tour of the local village. When we _____ _____ at O-World, it'll be two thirty, and you will be free to _____ _____ the place with your friends.

적절한 응답 찾기

[19~20] 대화를 듣고, 여자의 마지막 말에 이어질 남자의 말로 가장 적절한 것을 고르시오.

19 Man: _____
  ① I'm thinking about that.
  ② Please drive me to the hospital.
  ③ Would you buy me lunch today?
  ④ Don't worry. It's just a matter of time.
  ⑤ Can you help me with my homework?

♥ **might have p.p.**
: 현재를 기준으로 추측하는 동작이나 상태가 이전에 일어났을 경우 사용되며, '~했을지도 모른다', '아마 ~했을 것이다'의 의미로 쓰인다. 여기서 might는 과거 시제가 아니라, 추측의 정도가 조동사 may보다 약해서 쓰였다.
= may have p.p.

19 🇬🇧

W You look a little pale. What's wrong? Are you sick?
M Yeah, I have _____ _____ in my stomach.
W You looked well yesterday. What happened today?
M It started at lunch. The pain is getting worse. I can't _____ _____.
W That's _____ _____. What did you eat for lunch?
M I just had milk and bread. I didn't eat much.
W It's very hot and humid these days. I think that the milk and bread _____ _____ _____ _____ ♥might have been bad. What would you like me to do?
M <u>Please drive me to the hospital.</u>

적절한 응답 찾기

20 Man: _____
  ① That's fine with me.
  ② It's very far from here.
  ③ Tell me what time it is.
  ④ What makes you think so?
  ⑤ I am surprised to hear that.

♥ **May she rest in peace.**
: 어떤 사람(여기서는 여성)이 사망했을 경우 애도를 표현할 때 사용되는 표현이다. '고이 잠드소서.', '고인의 명복을 빕니다.' 정도의 의미로 해석된다.
= Rest in peace.
= R.I.P.

20

W I haven't seen Mike in class for a few days.
M I heard his grandmother _____ _____. So he went to her funeral.
W I am sorry. ♥May she rest in peace.
M Yeah. Why don't we go to the funeral home _____ _____ _____ _____?
W That's a good idea. I am in.
M All right. When is the best time to go to see him?
W I think we can get together _____ _____ _____. How about at three o'clock?
M <u>That's fine with me.</u>

1 다음을 듣고, 일요일 아침 날씨로 가장 적절한 것을 고르시오.

①   ②   ③

④   ⑤

2 대화를 듣고, 남자가 주문하는 음료로 가장 적절한 것을 고르시오.

①   ②   ③

④   ⑤

3 대화를 듣고, 여자의 심정으로 가장 적절한 것을 고르시오.
① upset   ② happy   ③ angry
④ touched   ⑤ disappointed

4 대화를 듣고, 남자가 주말에 한 일로 가장 적절한 것을 고르시오.
① 집에서 휴식하기
② 여행 계획 세우기
③ 리조트 예약하기
④ 홀로 여행 떠나기
⑤ 밀린 과제 끝내기

5 대화를 듣고, 두 사람이 대화하는 장소로 가장 적절한 곳을 고르시오.
① 집   ② 서점   ③ 학교
④ 음식점   ⑤ 빵집

6 대화를 듣고, 남자의 마지막 말의 의도로 가장 적절한 것을 고르시오.
① 격려   ② 후회
③ 축하   ④ 충고
⑤ 제안

7 대화를 듣고, 여자가 가려고 하는 장소를 고르시오.
① 정원   ② 카페
③ 공연장   ④ 영화관
⑤ 호텔

8 대화를 듣고, 여자가 대화 직후에 할 일로 가장 적절한 것을 고르시오.
① 장보기   ② 요리하기
③ 운전하기   ④ 청소하기
⑤ 부모님 뵙기

9 대화를 듣고, 남자가 도서관에 대해 언급하지 않은 것을 고르시오.
① 연체료   ② 폐관 시간
③ 도서관 위치   ④ 책 대여 기간
⑤ 도서관 휴일

10 다음을 듣고, 여자가 하는 말의 내용으로 가장 적절한 것을 고르시오.
① 과거의 실수   ② 기억력 향상법
③ 역사의 중요성   ④ 현대인의 관심사
⑤ 현대 사회의 문제

11 대화를 듣고, 할인 행사에 대한 내용으로 일치하지 않는 것을 고르시오.
① 일주일간 진행된다.
② Rainbow 마트에서 열린다.
③ 장난감이 인기가 많다.
④ 고기와 과일을 할인한다.
⑤ 두 달에 한 번씩 열린다.

12 대화를 듣고, 여자가 프랑스를 가는 목적으로 가장 적절한 것을 고르시오.

① 여행을 가기 위해서
② 친구를 만나기 위해서
③ 쇼핑몰 오픈을 위해서
④ 물건을 사오기 위해서
⑤ 한국 물품을 팔기 위해서

13 대화를 듣고, 여자가 지불해야 할 금액으로 가장 적절한 것을 고르시오.

① $5 　　　　② $7 　　　　③ $10
④ $15 　　　　⑤ $17

14 대화를 듣고, 두 사람의 관계로 가장 적절한 것을 고르시오.

① 아빠 — 아들
② 상사 — 직원
③ 교수 — 대학생
④ 면접관 — 지원자
⑤ 트레이너 — 선수

15 대화를 듣고, 남자가 여자에게 요청한 일로 가장 적절한 것을 고르시오.

① 학교 같이 가기
② 숙제 같이 하기
③ 숙제 대신 제출하기
④ 할아버지 병문안 가기
⑤ 같은 수업에 참여하기

16 대화를 듣고, 여자가 신용 카드를 사용하지 <u>않는</u> 이유로 가장 적절한 것을 고르시오.

① 필요하지 않아서
② 혜택이 많이 없어서
③ 자주 카드를 잃어버려서
④ 과소비를 줄이기 위해서
⑤ 소지하고 있는 카드가 많아서

17 다음 그림의 상황에 가장 적절한 대화를 고르시오.

① 　　② 　　③ 　　④ 　　⑤

18 대화를 듣고, 남자가 체육 대회에 관해 언급하지 <u>않은</u> 것을 고르시오.

① 대회 운동 종목
② 준비된 응원가 수
③ 선생님의 참여 여부
④ 대회가 열리는 요일
⑤ 같은 학년 참여자 수

[19~20] 대화를 듣고, 여자의 마지막 말에 이어질 남자의 말로 가장 적절한 것을 고르시오.

19 Man: _____

① I'm always here for you.
② Wow, you were born to do it.
③ I'll give you what you need.
④ Failure is the mother of success.
⑤ Everyone has their own strengths.

20 Man: _____

① That's too bad.
② I'm relieved to hear that.
③ I'm interested in your job.
④ Please remind me of the date.
⑤ I will respect whatever decision you make.

● 대화를 다시 듣고, 알맞은 것을 고르시오.

1 How is the weather on Saturday morning?

☐ cloudy   ☐ rainy

2 The man likes to have whipped cream on top.

☐ True   ☐ False

3 Did the woman know the man would marry early?

☐ Yes   ☐ No

4 Did the man go to the resort alone?

☐ Yes   ☐ No

5 The woman will buy a croissant and milk.

☐ True   ☐ False

6 Will the man stop doing his homework to watch a movie?

☐ Yes   ☐ No

7 The woman wants to go to a concert hall.

☐ True   ☐ False

8 What will the man do?

☐ clean the house   ☐ go to the market

9 What time is it now?

☐ 8:30 p.m.   ☐ 9:00 p.m.

10 The woman thinks learning history is important.

☐ True   ☐ False

11 Everything in the market is on sale.

☐ True   ☐ False

12 Why is the woman going to France?

☐ to meet friends   ☐ to buy things

13 Has the woman bought things from the store before?

☐ Yes   ☐ No

14 The man is still in college.

☐ True   ☐ False

15 The man's grandfather is very sick.

☐ True   ☐ False

16 Does the man agree with the woman about using a credit card?

☐ Yes   ☐ No

17 The woman's next dental appointment is next Friday.

☐ True   ☐ False

18 What sport do they play on a sports day?

☐ basketball   ☐ volleyball

19 Is the woman happy with her ballet now?

☐ Yes   ☐ No

20 What's the reason the woman wants to change her job?

☐ the low salary   ☐ too much work

그림 정보 파악

1 다음을 듣고, 일요일 아침 날씨로 가장
   적절한 것을 고르시오.

①  ② ③

④ ⑤

1

M Good morning. This is the SBC weather forecast _____
   _____ _____. It will be cloudy in all of Korea. It will rain
   on Saturday morning and _____ _____ on Saturday
   night. But you can _____ _____ _____ again on
   Sunday morning. The weather will get warmer. It will be *perfect
   to _____ _____ _____ _____ in the afternoon.

*perfect to [펄펙트] [투] → [펄펙투]

그림 정보 파악

2 대화를 듣고, 남자가 주문하는 음료로
   가장 적절한 것을 고르시오.

①  ② ③

④ ⑤

2

W Hello. What would you like to order?
M One chocolate frappe, please.
W _____ _____ _____ _____ _____?
M I *want a large.
W _____ _____ _____ _____ have whipped
   cream?
M _____ _____ _____, please.

*want a [원트] [어] → [워너]

심정 추론

3 대화를 듣고, 여자의 심정으로 가장
   적절한 것을 고르시오.

① upset
② happy
③ angry
④ touched
⑤ disappointed

♥ Me neither.
: 상대방의 말에 부정으로 맞장구를 칠
때 사용하는 표현으로, '나도 그렇지 않
아.'라는 뜻이다.

3

W Tomorrow is the big day.
M Yes. I am _____ _____.
W I didn't *expect you _____ _____ _____ _____.
M ♥Me neither.
W Anyway, I'm _____ _____ _____.
M Thanks.
W I hope you _____ _____ _____.

*expect you [익스펙트] [유] → [익스펙츄]

한 일 파악

4 대화를 듣고, 남자가 주말에 한 일로 가장 적절한 것을 고르시오.

① 집에서 휴식하기
② 여행 계획 세우기
③ 리조트 예약하기
④ 홀로 여행 떠나기
⑤ 밀린 과제 끝내기

4

W How was your weekend?

M I went to a resort _____ _____.

W _____ _____?

M I _____ _____ _____ and *focus on myself.

W What did you do there?

M I did everything I wanted to do _____ _____ _____.

W That really sounds peaceful.

*focus on [포커쓰] [온] → [포커쏜]

장소 추론

5 대화를 듣고, 두 사람이 대화하는 장소로 가장 적절한 곳을 고르시오.

① 집
② 서점
③ 학교
④ 음식점
⑤ 빵집

5 🇬🇧

W Wow, they _____ _____.

M What _____ _____ _____?

W I'll get a croissant with strawberry jam inside.

M Is that enough? _____ _____?

W Of course not. I'll also get some butter cookies.

M Okay. Then I'll buy _____ _____ _____ _____.

의도 파악

6 대화를 듣고, 남자의 마지막 말의 의도로 가장 적절한 것을 고르시오.

① 격려　　② 후회
③ 축하　　④ 충고
⑤ 제안

6

W Kevin, why don't we _____ _____ _____ _____?

M Sorry, but I can't. I need to do my science homework.

W You can do it after the movie.

M _____ _____ _____ is the first thing to do.

W You're _____ _____ _____ _____.

M It's better to do important things first.

특정 정보 파악

7 대화를 듣고, 여자가 가려고 하는 장소를 고르시오.

① 정원
② 카페
③ 공연장
④ 영화관
⑤ 호텔

7

W   Guess where I want to go to with you tonight.

M   Okay. You should give me _____ _____ _____.

W   Sure. We can watch a _____ _____ by a jazz band.

M   Hmm, is it _____ _____ _____?

W   No. We _____ _____ _____ cocktails there.

M   It's not a hotel, is it?

W   Yes, it is.

할 일 파악

8 대화를 듣고, 여자가 대화 직후에 할 일로 가장 적절한 것을 고르시오.

① 장보기
② 요리하기
③ 운전하기
④ 청소하기
⑤ 부모님 뵙기

8 🇬🇧

W   Your parents will be here at 6:00 in the evening, right?

M   Yes. _____ _____ _____ _____ for dinner?

W   How about shabu shabu? They both like _____ _____ _____.

M   Sounds great. They will love it.

W   Can you go to the market and _____ _____ _____?
     I will clean the house while you're out.

M   Okay.

언급 유무 파악

9 대화를 듣고, 남자가 도서관에 대해 언급하지 <u>않은</u> 것을 고르시오.

① 연체료
② 폐관 시간
③ 도서관 위치
④ 책 대여 기간
⑤ 도서관 휴일

9

M   Let's hurry. The library closes at 9:00 p.m.

W   Don't worry. We still have _____ _____ _____.

M   If I don't return the books, I have to _____ _____ _____ _____. And it is not open tomorrow because it is closed every Thursday.

W   How much is the late fee?

M   It's _____ _____ _____ _____.

W   For how many days can we borrow a book?

M   We can borrow a book for two weeks.

화제·주제 파악

10 다음을 듣고, 여자가 하는 말의
내용으로 가장 적절한 것을 고르시오.

① 과거의 실수
② 기억력 향상법
③ 역사의 중요성
④ 현대인의 관심사
⑤ 현대 사회의 문제

10

W What do you think about history? Why should we learn history?
_____ _____ _____ is very important. It *tells
us where we come from. It also teaches us how the present
society came to exist. If we want to move forward to _____
_____ _____ _____, we should not forget past
mistakes and problems, so we need to _____ _____
_____ _____ history.

*tells us [텔쓰] [어쓰] → [텔써쓰]

내용 불일치 파악

11 대화를 듣고, 할인 행사에 대한
내용으로 일치하지 않는 것을
고르시오.

① 일주일간 진행된다.
② Rainbow 마트에서 열린다.
③ 장난감이 인기가 많다.
④ 고기와 과일을 할인한다.
⑤ 두 달에 한 번씩 열린다.

11

M Jessie, where are you going?
W I'm going to the Rainbow Mart. It's _____ _____
_____ for one week.
M Is everything on sale?
W No, only meat and fruit _____ _____ _____
_____.
M _____ _____ does the store have this kind of event?
W _____ _____ _____ _____.

목적 파악

12 대화를 듣고, 여자가 프랑스를 가는
목적으로 가장 적절한 것을 고르시오.

① 여행을 가기 위해서
② 친구를 만나기 위해서
③ 쇼핑몰 오픈을 위해서
④ 물건을 사오기 위해서
⑤ 한국 물품을 팔기 위해서

12 🇬🇧

M What are you looking at?
W I'm looking at _____ _____ _____ _____.
M Why are you planning to go there?
W For business. I need to _____ _____ _____ from
Paris to sell.
M Are they for your _____ _____ _____?
W Yes, they are. *Clothes and accessories from Paris are
_____ _____.
M I see.

*clothes and [클로즈] [엔드] → [클로젠]

13 대화를 듣고, 여자가 지불해야 할 금액으로 가장 적절한 것을 고르시오.

① $8   ② $11

③ $12   ④ $15

⑤ $17

13 🇬🇧

M   Hello. What can I do for you?

W   I'm looking for _____ _____ _____.

M   You can see the paper right over there.

W   _____ _____ _____ _____ for A4 and B4-sized paper?

M   It's five dollars for a set of A4-sized paper and seven dollars for a set of B4-sized paper.

W   I'll _____ _____ _____ _____ A4 and one set of B4. I'll _____ _____ _____.

M   Okay. You just used two dollars in points.

---

14 대화를 듣고, 두 사람의 관계로 가장 적절한 것을 고르시오.

① 아빠 — 아들

② 상사 — 직원

③ 교수 — 대학생

④ 면접관 — 지원자

⑤ 트레이너 — 선수

14

W   I see you have a lot of _____ _____ in this field.

M   I started right after I graduated from college.

W   What's your reason for _____ _____ _____ _____ at this company?

M   I love the products your company makes, so I want to work here.

W   Why did you _____ _____ the Design Department?

M   I'm confident I _____ _____ _____ that go well with your company's products.

W   Okay.

---

15 대화를 듣고, 남자가 여자에게 요청한 일로 가장 적절한 것을 고르시오.

① 학교 같이 가기

② 숙제 같이 하기

③ 숙제 대신 제출하기

④ 할아버지 병문안 가기

⑤ 같은 수업에 참여하기

♥ **Don't mention it.**

: 상대방의 감사 인사에 대답할 때 사용하는 표현으로, '천만에.'라는 뜻이다.

= You're welcome.

= Not at all.

15

M   Hannah, I _____ _____ _____ tomorrow.

W   _____ _____?

M   My grandfather's very sick, so I need to go to the hospital.

W   I'm so sorry to hear that. I hope your grandfather gets better soon.

M   Thanks. By the way, can you _____ _____ _____ _____ for me?

W   Of course. I can do that for you.

M   You're _____ _____ _____ _____.

W   ♥ Don't mention it.

이유 추론

16 대화를 듣고, 여자가 신용 카드를 사용하지 <u>않는</u> 이유로 가장 적절한 것을 고르시오.

① 필요하지 않아서
② 혜택이 많이 없어서
③ 자주 카드를 잃어버려서
④ 과소비를 줄이기 위해서
⑤ 소지하고 있는 카드가 많아서

16

M I think I spent too much money this month.

W Are you _____ _____ _____ _____?

M Yes, I am.

W It makes people _____ _____ _____.

M I agree with you.

W That's why I _____ _____ _____ _____. Now I spend far less than before.

M Maybe I should try that, too.

그림 상황 파악

17 다음 그림의 상황에 가장 적절한 대화를 고르시오.

① ② ③ ④ ⑤

17

① W I _____ _____ _____.

　 M Let me see.

② W How about next Friday?

　 M Sorry, but _____ _____ _____.

③ W Hello. How can I *help you?

　 M I'm _____ _____ _____ _____ for my wife.

④ W Do you _____ _____ _____?

　 M No, thank you.

⑤ W How long _____ _____ _____ _____ my turn?

　 M It will be your turn soon.

*help you [헬프] [유] → [헬퓨]

언급 유무 파악

18 대화를 듣고, 남자가 체육 대회에 관해 언급하지 <u>않은</u> 것을 고르시오.

① 대회 운동 종목
② 준비된 응원가 수
③ 선생님의 참여 여부
④ 대회가 열리는 요일
⑤ 같은 학년 참여자 수

18

W Sports day is _____ _____, right?

M Yes, that's right.

W _____ _____ _____ are there in our grade?

M They are about 200.

W *That's a lot. Are our school teachers playing games, too?

M I heard that they will.

W That will be fun. Do you know _____ _____ _____ _____ _____ that day?

M We will have a race and play basketball and soccer.

W We have to _____ _____ _____ _____ for our class.

M Yes, we have to do that.

*that's a [뎃츠] [어] → [뎃처]

[19~20] 대화를 듣고, 여자의 마지막 말에 이어질 남자의 말로 가장 적절한 것을 고르시오.

19 Man: _____
  ① I'm always here for you.
  ② Wow, you were born to do it.
  ③ I'll give you what you need.
  ④ Failure is the mother of
     success.
  ⑤ Everyone has their own
     strengths.

♥ **I wonder if + S + V**
: 무언가에 대한 확신이 들지 않을 때 사용하는 표현으로, '~인지 아닌지 궁금하다'라는 뜻이다. 'if' 대신 'whether'를 쓸 수도 있다.

19

M   How _____ _____ _____?
W   Well, I'm not sure about it.
M   What's wrong?
W   ♥ I wonder if I _____ _____ _____ _____.
M   What makes you think that way?
W   I _____ _____ _____ over and over again.
M   Failure is the mother of success.

20 Man: _____
  ① That's too bad.
  ② I'm relieved to hear that.
  ③ I'm interested in your job.
  ④ Please remind me of the date.
  ⑤ I will respect whatever decision
     you make.

20

W   I'm _____ _____ _____ _____.
M   Why do you want to change jobs?
W   I _____ _____ _____ _____ to do. I no longer
     have free time to do anything I want.
M   But you're _____ _____ _____ _____
     _____.
W   I got lost between happiness and success.
M   I will respect whatever decision you make.

1 다음을 듣고, 금요일의 날씨로 가장 적절한 것을 고르시오.

①   ②   ③

④   ⑤

2 대화를 듣고, 남자가 구입할 케이크로 가장 적절한 것을 고르시오.

①   ②   ③

④   ⑤

3 대화를 듣고, 여자의 심정으로 가장 적절한 것을 고르시오.
① lonely   ② thrilled   ③ grateful
④ nervous   ⑤ satisfied

4 대화를 듣고, 여자가 벽화 그리기 대회에서 한 일로 가장 적절한 것을 고르시오.
① 신문 기사 쓰기   ② 물감 섞기
③ 물 나르기   ④ 고양이 그리기
⑤ 사진 촬영하기

5 대화를 듣고, 두 사람이 대화하는 장소로 가장 적절한 곳을 고르시오.
① 빵집   ② 승강기
③ 도서관   ④ 백화점
⑤ 식료품 가게

6 대화를 듣고, 남자의 마지막 말의 의도로 가장 적절한 것을 고르시오.
① 조언   ② 칭찬   ③ 경고
④ 불평   ⑤ 위로

7 대화를 듣고, 여자가 구입하지 않은 물건을 고르시오.
① 머그컵   ② 오렌지 주스   ③ 탁상시계
④ 액자   ⑤ 담요

8 대화를 듣고, 남자가 대화 직후에 할 일로 가장 적절한 것을 고르시오.
① 저녁 먹기   ② 물 마시기
③ 식물 구입하기   ④ 보고서 끝내기
⑤ 화분에 물 주기

9 대화를 듣고, 여자가 캠핑장에서 지켜야 할 사항으로 언급하지 않은 것을 고르시오.
① 쓰레기 버리지 말 것
② 꽃을 꺾지 말 것
③ 시끄럽게 떠들지 말 것
④ 동생과 싸우지 말 것
⑤ 혼자서 이동하지 말 것

10 다음을 듣고, 남자가 하는 말의 내용으로 가장 적절한 것을 고르시오.
① 손 씻기   ② 태국의 문화
③ 칭찬하는 방법   ④ 몸짓의 다양성
⑤ 발표할 때 주의 사항

11 다음을 듣고, 기숙사의 생활 규칙에 대한 내용과 일치하지 않는 것을 고르시오.
① 학생 카드를 가지고 다녀야 한다.
② 방 열쇠를 잃어버리면 벌금이 있다.
③ 외출 시 문을 잠가야 한다.
④ 반려동물을 키울 수 없다.
⑤ 밤 10시 전에 취침해야 한다.

12 대화를 듣고, 여자가 전화를 건 목적으로 가장 적절한 것을 고르시오.
① 여행을 취소하려고
② 출국 날짜를 늦추려고
③ 여권 번호를 변경하려고
④ 비행시간을 확인하려고
⑤ 여권을 재발급 받으려고

13 대화를 듣고, 두 사람이 만날 시각을 고르시오.
① 2:00 p.m.　　② 2:30 p.m.
③ 3:00 p.m.　　④ 3:30 p.m.
⑤ 4:00 p.m.

14 대화를 듣고, 두 사람의 관계로 가장 적절한 것을 고르시오.
① 운전자 ― 보행자
② 수리 기사 ― 고객
③ 경찰관 ― 시민
④ 판매원 ― 손님
⑤ 선생님 ― 학생

15 대화를 듣고, 남자가 여자에게 부탁한 일로 가장 적절한 것을 고르시오.
① 자신과 결혼하자고
② 결혼반지를 골라달라고
③ 주말에 데이트를 하자고
④ 수학 문제를 풀어 달라고
⑤ 저녁 식사를 만들어 달라고

16 대화를 듣고, 여자가 남자의 제안을 <u>거절한</u> 이유로 가장 적절한 것을 고르시오.
① 집안일이 많아서
② 시간이 맞지 않아서
③ 시계를 수리해야 해서
④ 영화를 좋아하지 않아서
⑤ 중간고사를 준비해야 해서

17 다음 그림의 상황에 가장 적절한 대화를 고르시오.

① ② ③ ④ ⑤

18 다음을 듣고, 여자가 여행에 대해 언급하지 <u>않은</u> 것을 고르시오.
① 날씨
② 음식
③ 박물관
④ 전통 의상
⑤ 여행 간 나라

[19-20] 대화를 듣고, 남자의 마지막 말에 이어질 여자의 말로 가장 적절한 것을 고르시오.

19 Woman: _____
① What about having lunch together?
② Don't worry. I can help you practice.
③ I think you have to prepare some material.
④ Hurry up. We should finish printing it.
⑤ It was nice talking to you. See you later.

20 Woman: _____
① I'll bring some balloons to your party.
② Don't forget to take a pill after dinner.
③ I'm so excited about my birthday party.
④ It's all right. I hope you get better.
⑤ That's okay. We are having Chinese food delivered.

Listen and Check

정답 및 해설 *p.068*

● 대화를 다시 듣고, 알맞은 것을 고르시오.

1 How will the weather be on Thursday?
☐ cloudy   ☐ rainy

2 What kind of cake is sold out?
☐ fruitcakes   ☐ chocolate cakes

3 The woman is looking for her school bag.
☐ True   ☐ False

4 Did the woman's team win second prize in the contest?
☐ Yes   ☐ No

5 Which floor does the woman want to go to?
☐ the sixth floor   ☐ the seventh floor

6 The man went to the sea to watch the sunset.
☐ True   ☐ False

7 What is the color of the mug?
☐ yellow   ☐ black

8 The man didn't water the plant regularly.
☐ True   ☐ False

9 Where is the campsite located?
☐ on a mountain   ☐ by the sea

10 The thumbs-up sign means praise in Thailand.
☐ True   ☐ False

11 What is another use for the student card?
☐ a cash card   ☐ a room key

12 Where did the woman call?
☐ the airline   ☐ the airport

13 When will Taeju go to the dentist?
☐ today   ☐ tomorrow

14 Was the man driving his car?
☐ Yes   ☐ No

15 The woman will help him to buy a ring.
☐ True   ☐ False

16 When will the movie *Sisters* be released?
☐ this Sunday   ☐ this Saturday

17 Where is Charlie running?
☐ in the restaurant   ☐ on the playground

18 What did the woman eat at a restaurant?
☐ *bulgogi*   ☐ *bibimbap*

19 Aiden needs to prepare more material.
☐ True   ☐ False

20 Did Mike attend Mihyun's party?
☐ Yes   ☐ No

그림 정보 파악

1 다음을 듣고, 금요일의 날씨로 가장 적절한 것을 고르시오.

①   ②   ③

④   ⑤

1

W   Good morning. This is the weather forecast for this week. Monday and Tuesday will be rainy. Don't forget to _____ _____ _____. However, it is _____ _____ _____ _____ on Wednesday. On Thursday, it will be _____ _____ _____ _____. This Friday, it will be a bit cold but sunny.

그림 정보 파악

2 대화를 듣고, 남자가 구입할 케이크로 가장 적절한 것을 고르시오.

① ②   ③

④   ⑤

2

M   Excuse me. Is this bakery still open?

W   We will be closing soon. But you've got 30 minutes.

M   That's nice. I need to _____ _____ _____ _____ for my son.

W   Unfortunately, we're _____ _____ of them. How about this fruitcake?

M   My son doesn't like fruit. Anything else?

W   We have a fresh cream cake _____ _____ _____ _____ _____ _____.

M   That's perfect. I'll take it.

심정 추론

3 대화를 듣고, 여자의 심정으로 가장 적절한 것을 고르시오.

① lonely   ② thrilled
③ grateful   ④ nervous
⑤ satisfied

♥ **It must be ~**
: 확신을 나타낼 때 쓰는 표현으로, '~임에 틀림없다'라는 뜻이다.
= I'm sure that S + V

3

W   I can't find my notebook for English class.

M   Did you _____ _____ _____ it to school?

W   I definitely *put it in my bag in the morning.

M   _____ _____. ♥ It must be in your bag then.

W   Nope. [Rustling sounds] See. _____ _____ here.

M   Did you _____ _____ _____ _____ _____ on your desk?

W   Of course, I did.

*put it in [풋] [잇] [인] → [푸리린]

한 일 파악

4 대화를 듣고, 여자가 벽화 그리기 대회에서 한 일로 가장 적절한 것을 고르시오.

① 신문 기사 쓰기
② 물감 섞기
③ 물 나르기
④ 고양이 그리기
⑤ 사진 촬영하기

♥ What for?

: 목적이나 이유를 물어볼 때 쓰는 표현으로, '무엇 때문에?'라는 뜻이다.
= For what reason?
= How come?

4 🇬🇧

M Amazing! You are in the school newspaper.

W My team _____ _____ _____ in the wall painting contest.

M I didn't know _____ _____ _____. Did you draw this cat?

W Actually, I didn't draw any pictures.

M What did you do?

W I helped my team. I _____ _____ _____ _____.

M Water? ♥What for?

W It helps the watercolors get mixed just right.

장소 추론

5 대화를 듣고, 두 사람이 대화하는 장소로 가장 적절한 곳을 고르시오.

① 빵집
② 승강기
③ 도서관
④ 백화점
⑤ 식료품 가게

5

W Thank you for getting the door for me.

M This is what neighbors do. Your hands are full of paper bags.

W Could you please _____ _____ _____ _____ for me?

M No problem. [Pause] Why are you carrying those paper bags?

W I _____ _____ _____ _____ for my twin kids.

M [Ding-dong] Well, _____ _____ _____. Happy birthday to your twins.

W Thank you. Have a great day!

의도 파악

6 대화를 듣고, 남자의 마지막 말의 의도로 가장 적절한 것을 고르시오.

① 조언   ② 칭찬
③ 경고   ④ 불평
⑤ 위로

6

M How have you been doing during summer vacation?

W I went to the East Sea _____ _____ _____ _____.

M Wow! That sounds so great.

W Yeah, it was good _____ _____ _____ _____.

M What happened?

W It was _____ _____ _____, so I could not see anything.

M I'm sorry to hear the sad news.

7 대화를 듣고, 여자가 구입하지 <u>않은</u> 물건을 고르시오.

① 머그컵
② 오렌지 주스
③ 탁상시계
④ 액자
⑤ 담요

---

7 🇬🇧

M Helen, _____ _____ _____ _____?

W I bought some _____ _____ _____ my room.

M Oh. Can I see _____ _____ _____?

W Sure. I bought a black alarm clock, two picture frames, and a blanket.

M They are _____ _____.

W I bought one more thing: a big yellow mug. I'll use it when I drink orange juice.

---

8 대화를 듣고, 남자가 대화 직후에 할 일로 가장 적절한 것을 고르시오.

① 저녁 먹기
② 물 마시기
③ 식물 구입하기
④ 보고서 끝내기
⑤ 화분에 물 주기

♥ **You have a point.**
: 상대방의 의견에 대해 수긍할 때 쓰는 표현으로, '네 말이 맞아.'라는 뜻이다.
= You're right.
= I can't agree with you more.

8

W I think this plant _____ _____ _____ _____.

M Oh, I forgot to *water it.

W You promised me that you'd _____ _____ _____.

M Sorry. But I was _____ _____.

W I understand. But this plant doesn't. It will die without water.

M ♥You have a point. I'll _____ _____ _____.

*water it [워러] [잇] → [워러릿]

---

9 대화를 듣고, 여자가 캠핑장에서 지켜야 할 사항으로 언급하지 <u>않은</u> 것을 고르시오.

① 쓰레기 버리지 말 것
② 꽃을 꺾지 말 것
③ 시끄럽게 떠들지 말 것
④ 혼자서 이동하지 말 것
⑤ 동생과 싸우지 말 것

9

M Mom, I can _____ _____ _____. We are almost there.

W You're right. Do you remember what I told you?

M Of course. Do not _____ _____ _____ _____ _____, and do not pick any flowers.

W And? I told you two more things.

M Let me think. [*Pause*] Do not _____ _____ _____.

W That's important. This campsite is in the middle of the mountains.

M Okay. I'll _____ _____ _____.

W Last one. Don't fight with your brother.

화제·주제 파악

10 다음을 듣고, 남자가 하는 말의 내용으로 가장 적절한 것을 고르시오.

① 손 씻기
② 태국의 문화
③ 칭찬하는 방법
④ 몸짓의 다양성
⑤ 발표할 때 주의 사항

10

M When you talk to someone from another culture, you should remember this. Gestures can _____ _____ _____ in different cultures. For example, the _____ _____ should not be used in Thailand. In Korea, it means _____ _____ _____. However, it's a _____ _____ _____ in Thailand.

내용 불일치 파악

11 다음을 듣고, 기숙사의 생활 규칙에 대한 내용과 일치하지 <u>않는</u> 것을 고르시오.

① 학생 카드를 가지고 다녀야 한다.
② 방 열쇠를 잃어버리면 벌금이 있다.
③ 외출 시 문을 잠가야 한다.
④ 반려동물을 키울 수 없다.
⑤ 밤 10시 전에 취침해야 한다.

♥ **You're not allowed to ~**
: 어떤 행동이나 상황이 허용되지 않을 때 쓰는 표현으로, '~해서는 안 된다.'라는 뜻이다.
= You should not ~.
= You'd better not ~.

11

W Attention, please. Let me tell you the rules for a fun and _____ _____ _____. Always carry your student card. You can use it as your room key. _____ _____ _____ when you go out. ♥ You are not allowed to have any pets. Lastly, you should _____ _____ _____ before 10:00 p.m. Thank you for listening to me.

목적 파악

12 대화를 듣고, 여자가 전화를 건 목적으로 가장 적절한 것을 고르시오.

① 여행을 취소하려고
② 출국 날짜를 늦추려고
③ 여권 번호를 변경하려고
④ 비행시간을 확인하려고
⑤ 여권을 재발급 받으려고

12

[Telephone rings.]

M Good morning. This is Tangerine Airline.

W Hello. _____ _____ if I can change my passport number.

M When is your flight _____ _____ _____?

W A week from now.

M It's possible. _____ _____ _____ _____ _____?

W Because I lost my passport, I _____ _____ _____ _____.

M I see. Please tell me the new number.

W M12345678. Thank you so much.

숫자 정보 파악

13 대화를 듣고, 두 사람이 만날 시각을 고르시오.

① 2:00 p.m.
② 2:30 p.m.
③ 3:00 p.m.
④ 3:30 p.m.
⑤ 4:00 p.m.

♥ **It won't take long.**

: 예상했던 것보다 시간이 길게 소요되지 않을 거라고 말할 때 쓰는 표현으로, '오래 걸리지는 않을 거야.'라는 뜻이다.

= It will be soon.
= It won't be long.

13

W Taeju, what do you do in your free time?

M I usually _____ _____ _____ _____ with my friends.

W It's the same for me. I take badminton lessons.

M Do you? _____ _____ _____ _____ together tomorrow?

W Let's meet at 3:00 p.m.

M I _____ _____ _____ with my dentist at two. But ♥ it won't take long.

W Hmm... How about at 4:00 p.m.?

M That's better. See you then.

관계 추론

14 대화를 듣고, 두 사람의 관계로 가장 적절한 것을 고르시오.

① 운전자 ― 보행자
② 수리 기사 ― 고객
③ 경찰관 ― 시민
④ 판매원 ― 손님
⑤ 선생님 ― 학생

14

[*Screeching brakes*] [*Pause*]

W Watch out! You _____ _____ _____.

M I'm sorry. I *didn't notice your car was coming.

[*Car door opens and closes.*]

W Are you all right?

M I'm okay.

W _____ _____ _____. But it's _____ _____ to use a smartphone while walking on the street.

M I know. I'm sorry.

W When you walk across the road, you should be careful.

M I'll _____ _____ _____ _____.

*didn't notice [디튼트] [노티스] → [디튼노리스]

부탁한 일 파악

15 대화를 듣고, 남자가 여자에게 부탁한 일로 가장 적절한 것을 고르시오.

① 자신과 결혼하자고
② 결혼반지를 골라달라고
③ 주말에 데이트를 하자고
④ 수학 문제를 풀어 달라고
⑤ 저녁 식사를 만들어 달라고

15 🇬🇧

M I want to _____ _____ _____ _____ _____ _____ and make my proposal perfect.

W That's so romantic!

M I know. But I'm so _____ _____ _____. I can't even decide _____ _____ _____ _____.

W That's a big problem. You cannot ask her about that.

M Right. Can you _____ _____ _____ the right ring?

W I'll help you. You have my word.

M You are a lifesaver. I'll buy you a big dinner!

이유 추론

16 대화를 듣고, 여자가 남자의 제안을 <u>거절한</u> 이유로 가장 적절한 것을 고르시오.

① 집안일이 많아서
② 시간이 맞지 않아서
③ 시계를 수리해야 해서
④ 영화를 좋아하지 않아서
⑤ 중간고사를 준비해야 해서

16

M Did you hear that the movie *Sisters* _____ _____ _____ this Saturday?

W Is that a fact? I have been waiting for the movie *Sisters*.

M Then let's go to see the movie _____ _____.

W I'd love to, but I have my _____ _____ on Monday. So I have to prepare for them.

M You can study _____ _____ _____ _____.

W That's impossible. There is so much for me to do.

그림 상황 파악

17 다음 그림의 상황에 가장 적절한 대화를 고르시오.

① ② ③ ④ ⑤

17

① W What are you _____ _____ _____?
　M One salmon pasta with cream sauce.

② W Honey, it's _____ _____ _____ _____.
　M Can I sleep five more minutes?

③ W Sorry. You are _____ _____ _____ enter here.
　M Can I ask you the reason?

④ W Charlie, _____ _____ _____ in the restaurant.
　M Okay, Mom. I'm sorry.

⑤ W Can I _____ this skirt _____?
　M Sure, the fitting room is right over there.

언급 유무 파악

18 다음을 듣고, 여자가 여행에 대해 언급하지 <u>않은</u> 것을 고르시오.

① 날씨
② 음식
③ 박물관
④ 전통 의상
⑤ 여행 간 나라

18

W Hello, everyone. I'd like to tell you about _____ _____ _____ _____. The weather was perfect for traveling. Almost every day was sunny and warm. I visited Gyeongbokgung Palace. Near the palace, I could wear a *hanbok*, _____ _____ _____. The *hanbok* was really pretty and _____ _____ _____. At a restaurant, I ate *bulgogi*. The most interesting thing was that I could get many side dishes _____ _____.

직절한 응답 찾기

[19~20] 대화를 듣고, 남자의 마지막 말에 이어질 여자의 말로 가장 적절한 것을 고르시오.

19 Woman: _____
① What about having lunch together?
② Don't worry. I can help you practice.
③ I think you have to prepare some material.
④ Hurry up. We should finish printing it.
⑤ It was nice talking to you. See you later.

I'm afraid (that) S + V
: 어떤 일에 대해서 두려움이나 걱정을 나타낼 때 쓰는 표현으로, '~할까 두렵다'라는 뜻이다.
= I'm worried (that) S + V
= I'm anxious (that) S + V

적절한 응답 찾기

20 Woman: _____
① I'll bring some balloons to your party.
② Don't forget to take a pill after dinner.
③ I'm so excited about my birthday party.
④ It's all right. I hope you get better.
⑤ That's okay. We are having Chinese food delivered.

19

W Aiden, _____ _____ _____ for the presentation?
M My material is fine. But I'm worried.
W About what?
M Actually, I am not good at _____ _____ _____.
W You're good enough. You just _____ _____ _____.
M But I'm afraid I might _____ _____ _____.
W Don't worry. I can help you practice.

20

[*Telephone rings.*]
M Hello. May I speak to Mihyun? This is Mike.
W Mike, it's me. Are you all right? You _____ _____.
M Actually, I _____ _____ _____.
W Oh, my! Maybe you should go to see a doctor.
M I already did. The doctor said I needed to _____ _____ _____.
W I agree. _____ _____ _____ and get some sleep.
M I'm sorry I can't *make it to your party tonight.
W It's all right. I hope you get better.

*make it [메이크] [잇] → [메킷]

1 다음을 듣고, 캘거리의 날씨로 가장 적절한 것을 고르시오.

① ② ③

④ ⑤

2 대화를 듣고, 남자가 입을 외출복으로 가장 적절한 것을 고르시오.

① ② ③

④ ⑤

3 대화를 듣고, 여자의 심정으로 가장 적절한 것을 고르시오.
① upset　　　　② lonely
③ excited　　　④ relieved
⑤ comfortable

4 대화를 듣고, 여자가 지난 금요일에 한 일로 가장 적절한 것을 고르시오.
① 극장에 가기　　② 저녁 사주기
③ 책 반납하기　　④ 대신 전화 받기
⑤ 휴대폰 수리하기

5 대화를 듣고, 두 사람이 대화하는 장소로 가장 적절한 곳을 고르시오.
① 은행　　　　② 인쇄소
③ 미술관　　　④ 경찰서
⑤ 문구점

6 대화를 듣고, 여자의 마지막 말의 의도로 가장 적절한 것을 고르시오.
① 조언　　　　② 칭찬
③ 동의　　　　④ 꾸중
⑤ 거절

7 대화를 듣고, 여자가 아프리카에서 하고 있는 일을 고르시오.
① 벽화 그리기
② 의료 활동하기
③ 아이들 가르치기
④ 여행지 안내하기
⑤ 집 짓는 거 돕기

8 대화를 듣고, 남자가 대화 직후에 할 일로 가장 적절한 것을 고르시오.
① 과일 깎기
② 피자 주문하기
③ 손 씻으러 가기
④ 치킨 샐러드 만들기
⑤ 냉장고에서 치즈 꺼내기

9 다음을 듣고, 여자가 사우나에 대해 언급하지 않은 것을 고르시오.
① 수천 년 전부터 사용되었다.
② 사람들을 편안하게 해 준다.
③ 건강상의 이점을 제공한다.
④ 술을 마시는 건 위험하다.
⑤ 임산부는 사우나를 할 수 없다.

10 다음을 듣고, 남자가 하는 말의 내용으로 가장 적절한 것을 고르시오.
① 음식 알레르기의 위험성
② 좋은 땅콩을 고르기
③ 편식을 없애는 방법
④ 심호흡이 주는 장점
⑤ 이번 주의 급식 메뉴

11 대화를 듣고, 여자가 언급한 내용과 일치하지 <u>않는</u> 것을 고르시오.
① 가족과 함께 캠핑하러 갔다.
② 1박 2일 동안 캠핑했다.
③ 오빠와 텐트를 쳤다.
④ 누워서 새 소리를 들었다.
⑤ 가족들과 노래를 불렀다.

12 대화를 듣고, 여자가 파리를 방문한 목적으로 가장 적절한 것을 고르시오.
① 와인을 마시기 위해
② 옷을 구입하기 위해
③ 친구를 만나기 위해
④ 역사를 연구하기 위해
⑤ 모나리자를 보기 위해

13 대화를 듣고, 여자가 지불해야 할 금액으로 가장 적절한 것을 고르시오.
① $25　　　② $30　　　③ $35
④ $40　　　⑤ $45

14 대화를 듣고, 두 사람의 관계로 가장 적절한 것을 고르시오.
① 유명 가수 ― 팬
② 선생님 ― 학생
③ 심사위원 ― 참가자
④ 건물주 ― 세입자
⑤ 운동선수 ― 감독

15 대화를 듣고, 남자가 여자에게 요청한 일로 가장 적절한 것을 고르시오.
① 청바지를 사 달라고
② 냄새의 원인을 찾아 달라고
③ 저녁을 같이 준비하자고
④ 에코 백을 만들어 달라고
⑤ 가방을 교환해 달라고

16 대화를 듣고, 여자가 쇼핑을 갈 수 <u>없는</u> 이유로 가장 적절한 것을 고르시오.
① 우산을 잃어버려서　　② 폭풍우가 몰아쳐서
③ 자동차가 고장나서　　④ 교통 체증이 심각해서
⑤ 백화점이 휴무일이라서

17 다음 그림의 상황에 가장 적절한 대화를 고르시오.

①　　　②　　　③　　　④　　　⑤

18 대화를 듣고, 두 사람이 원어민 과외에 관해 언급하지 <u>않은</u> 것을 고르시오.
① 수업 분야　　② 수업 장소　　③ 수업 횟수
④ 수업 시간대　　⑤ 수업료

[19-20] 대화를 듣고, 남자의 마지막 말에 이어질 여자의 말로 가장 적절한 것을 고르시오.

19 Woman: _____
① I was so lucky to find the money.
② It's not yours. Take it to the police.
③ Health is more important than money.
④ Never mind. I'll buy you some new jeans.
⑤ Don't walk with your hands in your pockets.

20 Woman: _____
① I learned how to fix computers.
② It will take a long time to upgrade it.
③ I'll let you know my email address.
④ Right. I think I should change mine.
⑤ She seems to have forgotten her password.

Listen and Check

정답 및 해설 p.073

🔊 대화를 다시 듣고, 알맞은 것을 고르시오.

1 How's the weather in Vancouver?
- ☐ warm and sunny
- ☐ cold and cloudy

2 The man is planning to visit his old teacher.
- ☐ True
- ☐ False

3 Did the woman have a car accident on the road?
- ☐ Yes
- ☐ No

4 The woman went to the theater last Friday.
- ☐ True
- ☐ False

5 How many copies did the woman need?
- ☐ 30 copies
- ☐ 40 copies

6 What does the man want to do tomorrow?
- ☐ stay home
- ☐ do something active

7 The man teaches children how to draw in Africa.
- ☐ True
- ☐ False

8 Does the woman want to eat fruit and salad?
- ☐ Yes
- ☐ No

9 Saunas are good for people with low blood pressure.
- ☐ True
- ☐ False

10 What does the man do for a living?
- ☐ school dietitian
- ☐ farmer

11 Did the man go camping last weekend?
- ☐ Yes
- ☐ No

12 Ashley visited Maxim, who lives in Paris.
- ☐ True
- ☐ False

13 How many tickets did the woman want to buy?
- ☐ four
- ☐ five

14 What does the man want to be in the future?
- ☐ a dance trainer
- ☐ an idol

15 The man made an eco bag out of his old jeans.
- ☐ True
- ☐ False

16 What's the weather like?
- ☐ rainy
- ☐ heavy snow

17 The woman covered her mouth when she sneezed.
- ☐ True
- ☐ False

18 The woman's friend wants to learn business English.
- ☐ True
- ☐ False

19 What did the man's mother find in his pocket?
- ☐ some money
- ☐ a letter

20 The man's computer got a virus.
- ☐ True
- ☐ False

그림 정보 파악

1 다음을 듣고, 캘거리의 날씨로 가장 적절한 것을 고르시오.

① ② ③

④ ⑤

1

M It's time for the weather report for some big cities in Canada. You can enjoy warm weather in Quebec since it's a perfect day _____ _____ _____. Vancouver is warm and sunny, too. However, you should _____ _____ _____ in Toronto. In Ottawa, you will experience cold and cloudy weather. Lastly, you can _____ _____ _____ _____ _____ in Calgary.

그림 정보 파악

2 대화를 듣고, 남자가 입을 외출복으로 가장 적절한 것을 고르시오.

① ② ③

④ ⑤

♥ **How do I look?**
: 상대방에게 자신의 모습에 대해서 괜찮은지 확인할 때 쓰는 표현으로, '나 어때 보여?'라는 뜻이다.

2

M Naomi, ♥how do I look?

W Do you _____ _____ _____ _____ your girlfriend?

M No. I'll _____ _____ _____ _____.

W Well, wearing shorts is not a good idea.

M Okay. I'll put on pants. How about this white shirt?

W It _____ _____ _____ _____.

심정 추론

3 대화를 듣고, 여자의 심정으로 가장 적절한 것을 고르시오.

① upset
② lonely
③ excited
④ relieved
⑤ comfortable

3

M Subin, why are you _____ _____ _____?

W I *took a bus, and it took more time _____ _____ _____ _____.

M A bus? What happened to your car?

W I found my car _____ _____ _____ _____ _____, so my car is at the repair shop now.

M I'm sorry to hear that.

W I'm so _____ _____ _____.

*took a [툭] [어] → [투커]

한 일 파악

4 대화를 듣고, 여자가 지난 금요일에 한 일로 가장 적절한 것을 고르시오.

① 극장에 가기
② 저녁 사주기
③ 책 반납하기
④ 대신 전화 받기
⑤ 휴대폰 수리하기

4

M   Esther, why didn't you answer my calls last Friday?

W   I didn't _____ _____ _____ _____. I left my phone at home.

M   Where did you go?

W   I went to the library to return some books.

M   You _____ _____ _____ _____ last Friday. I was waiting for you in front of the theater.

W   What? I thought we were meeting next Friday. I'm so sorry.

M   That's okay. You can _____ _____ _____ later.

W   Sure. I'll buy you a cup of coffee, too.

장소 추론

5 대화를 듣고, 두 사람이 대화하는 장소로 가장 적절한 곳을 고르시오.

① 은행   ② 인쇄소
③ 미술관   ④ 경찰서
⑤ 문구점

♥ **Is that all right?**
: 상대방에게 양해를 구하거나 동의를 확인할 때 쓰는 표현으로, '괜찮나요?'라는 뜻이다.
= Are you okay with it?

5

M   What can I do for you?

W   I'd like to _____ _____ _____ _____.

M   How many copies do you need?

W   30 copies. Please print them _____ _____.

M   Okay, but I've got _____ _____ _____ _____, so it will take 5 days.

W   5 days? Do you mean I can have them next Wednesday?

M   Yes. ♥ Is that all right?

W   All right. _____ _____ _____ next Wednesday.

의도 파악

6 대화를 듣고, 여자의 마지막 말의 의도로 가장 적절한 것을 고르시오.

① 조언   ② 칭찬
③ 동의   ④ 꾸중
⑤ 거절

6   🇬🇧

M   Tomorrow is my day off. Do you have _____ _____ _____?

W   Not yet. Why don't we just _____ _____ and watch some movies?

M   Actually, I'd rather _____ _____ _____.

W   What do you want to do?

M   Let's go to the park, play tennis, and _____ _____ _____.

W   I guess that's okay. Let's do it.

특정 정보 파악

7 대화를 듣고, 여자가 아프리카에서 하고 있는 일을 고르시오.

① 벽화 그리기
② 의료 활동하기
③ 아이들 가르치기
④ 여행지 안내하기
⑤ 집 짓는 거 돕기

7

M What brings you here to Africa?

W I came here to _____ _____ _____ _____.

M Same here. What exactly are you doing?

W I'm _____ _____ _____ _____ for the homeless. And you?

M I'm _____ _____ how to draw.

W It sounds great.

할 일 파악

8 대화를 듣고, 남자가 대화 직후에 할 일로 가장 적절한 것을 고르시오.

① 과일 깎기
② 피자 주문하기
③ 손 씻으러 가기
④ 치킨 샐러드 만들기
⑤ 냉장고에서 치즈 꺼내기

8

M Welcome home, sweetie. How was your _____ _____ _____ _____?

W I was _____ _____ _____. But the teachers were nice, and I think I have a friend.

M I'm glad to hear that.

W Dad, _____ _____ _____. Can you order a pepperoni pizza for me?

M Again? We ate a cheese pizza yesterday.

W Dad, pepperoni pizza and cheese pizza are not the same. I want pizza. Please.

M _____ _____. But this is the last time.

언급 유무 파악

9 다음을 듣고, 여자가 사우나에 대해 언급하지 <u>않은</u> 것을 고르시오.

① 수천 년 전부터 사용되었다.
② 사람들을 편안하게 해 준다.
③ 건강상의 이점을 제공한다.
④ 술을 마시는 건 위험하다.
⑤ 임산부는 사우나를 할 수 없다.

9

W Saunas have been used for thousands of years and are still popular today. A *sauna can _____ _____ _____ _____, and it may have other health benefits. However, drinking alcohol when using a sauna can be dangerous. Anyone who is pregnant or _____ _____ _____ _____ _____ should talk to their doctors to _____ _____ the sauna is safe.

*sauna [쏘나]

10 다음을 듣고, 남자가 하는 말의 내용으로 가장 적절한 것을 고르시오.

① 음식 알레르기의 위험성
② 좋은 땅콩을 고르기
③ 편식을 없애는 방법
④ 심호흡이 주는 장점
⑤ 이번 주의 급식 메뉴

10 🇬🇧

M   Hello, students. This is your school dietitian. Have you ever heard of food allergies? A food allergy is an _____ _____ _____ _____. For example, if you're allergic to peanuts, you may _____ _____ _____ after eating a peanut. It's very dangerous. If you have any food allergies, you _____ _____ _____ _____ _____.

내용 불일치 파악

11 대화를 듣고, 여자가 언급한 내용과 일치하지 <u>않는</u> 것을 고르시오.

① 가족과 함께 캠핑하러 갔다.
② 1박 2일 동안 캠핑했다.
③ 오빠와 텐트를 쳤다.
④ 누워서 새 소리를 들었다.
⑤ 가족들과 노래를 불렀다.

11

M   What did you do last weekend?

W   I went to a mountain with my family _____ _____ _____.

M   _____ _____ _____ _____ _____ there?

W   2 days and 1 night. It was not enough.

M   What did you do?

W   I *set up a tent with my brother. After that, we lay down on the ground and _____ _____ _____ _____.

M   It sounds peaceful.

*set up [쎗] [업] → [쎄럽]

목적 파악

12 대화를 듣고, 여자가 파리를 방문한 목적으로 가장 적절한 것을 고르시오.

① 와인을 마시기 위해
② 옷을 구입하기 위해
③ 친구를 만나기 위해
④ 역사를 연구하기 위해
⑤ 모나리자를 보기 위해

💜 **Make yourself at home.**

: 본인의 집에 있는 것처럼 편안하게 지내라고 말하고 싶을 때 쓰는 표현으로, '편하게 있어.'라는 뜻이다.

= Make yourself comfortable.

12 🇬🇧

M   _____ _____, _____ _____, Ashley. 💜Make yourself at home.

W   Thank you for _____ _____ _____, Maxim.

M   It's your first day in Paris. Do you have any plans for today?

W   I will visit the Louvre Museum to see the *Mona Lisa*.

M   That's _____ _____ _____ _____ _____ _____ in the world.

W   I really want to see it with my own eyes.

M   That's the real reason why you are visiting Paris.

숫자 정보 파악

13 대화를 듣고, 여자가 지불해야 할 금액으로 가장 적절한 것을 고르시오.

① $25   ② $30
③ $35   ④ $40
⑤ $45

13

W   Hello. I'd like to buy tickets for the dolphin show.

M   _____ _____ _____ do you want?

W   Three adults and two children, please.

M   It's ten dollars for adults and five dollars for children. So _____ _____ _____ 40 dollars.

W   Okay. Here's my credit card.

M   Oh, *with this credit card, _____ _____ _____ _____ _____.

W   That sounds great.

*with this [위드] [디스] → [윗디스]

관계 추론

14 대화를 듣고, 두 사람의 관계로 가장 적절한 것을 고르시오.

① 유명 가수 — 팬
② 선생님 — 학생
③ 심사위원 — 참가자
④ 건물주 — 세입자
⑤ 운동선수 — 감독

14

W   I enjoyed _____ _____ _____. Where did you practice?

M   I went to the practice room after work every day.

W   Every day? You must _____ _____ _____ _____ _____.

M   Yes, I do. These days, I'm making my own moves.

W   Interesting! Why do you _____ _____ _____?

M   Because someday I want to be a dance trainer for idols.

W   Okay! You _____ _____ _____. See you in the next round.

M   For real? Thank you very much.

요청한 일 파악

15 대화를 듣고, 남자가 여자에게 요청한 일로 가장 적절한 것을 고르시오.

① 청바지를 사 달라고
② 냄새의 원인을 찾아 달라고
③ 저녁을 같이 준비하자고
④ 에코 백을 만들어 달라고
⑤ 가방을 교환해 달라고

♥ **Just kidding.**
: 농담으로 던진 말이라고 설명할 때 쓰는 표현으로, '농담이야.'라는 뜻이다.
= I'm just joking.
= Only kidding.

15 🇬🇧

W   Surprise! I made this eco bag.

M   It's so cute. Did you really make it yourself?

W   Of course! I made it _____ _____ _____ _____ _____.

M   Your old jeans? I _____ _____ _____.

W   You are so mean.

M   ♥Just kidding. Well, can you make another one for me? I like it.

W   Sorry, but I'm busy. But I can _____ _____ _____ _____ _____ one.

이유 추론

16 대화를 듣고, 여자가 쇼핑을 갈 수 <u>없는</u> 이유로 가장 적절한 것을 고르시오.

① 우산을 잃어버려서
② 폭풍우가 몰아쳐서
③ 자동차가 고장나서
④ 교통 체증이 심각해서
⑤ 백화점이 휴무일이라서

16

M   Yeseo, where are you going? The weather forecast says that a
_____ _____ _____ _____.

W   Then I can drive from home to the department store.

M   I don't think so. It will be _____ _____ _____
_____ in the storm.

W   What about _____ _____ _____ _____?

M   The road conditions will be the same.

W   Oh, no. I promised Gahee that I would buy her a big doll today.

그림 상황 파악

17 다음 그림의 상황에 가장 적절한 대화를 고르시오.

①   ②   ③   ④   ⑤

17

① M   Do you have a cold? I'll _____ _____ _____.

W   It's kind of you to do that.

② M   [*Hiccupping sounds*] Please help me _____ _____
_____.

W   They'll stop if you drink some water.

③ M   You need to _____ _____ _____.

W   No, I don't. The weather is perfect.

④ M   _____ _____ _____ after meals.

W   Do you mean three times a day?

⑤ M   Don't forget to cover your mouth when you sneeze.

W   Sorry. I'll be careful _____ _____ _____.

언급 유무 파악

18 대화를 듣고, 두 사람이 원어민 과외에 관해 언급하지 <u>않은</u> 것을 고르시오.

① 수업 분야
② 수업 장소
③ 수업 횟수
④ 수업 시간대
⑤ 수업료

18 🇬🇧

W   Charlie, are you still looking for a tutoring job?

M   Sure. Do you _____ _____ _____ about one?

W   My friend wants to _____ _____ _____ at her
house.

M   _____ _____ _____ does she need a week?

W   Maybe _____ _____ _____ in the evening.

M   Hmm... Can you give me her phone number?

W   Sure. Wait a moment.

[19~20] 대화를 듣고, 남자의 마지막 말에 이어질 여자의 말로 가장 적절한 것을 고르시오.

19 Woman: _____
① I was so lucky to find the money.
② It's not yours. Take it to the police.
③ Health is more important than money.
④ Never mind. I'll buy you some new jeans.
⑤ Don't walk with your hands in your pockets.

19

M Mom, have you ever seen my black jeans?

W I washed them today. They were in the laundry basket.

M Did you _____ _____ _____?

W Absolutely. _____ _____ _____ _____ in one of your pockets.

M Maybe... a fifty-dollar bill?

W That's the correct answer. _____ _____ _____ _____ the money?

M I found it on the street on my way home.

W It's not yours. Take it to the police.

20 Woman: _____
① I learned how to fix computers.
② It will take a long time to upgrade it.
③ I'll let you know my email address.
④ Right. I think I should change mine.
⑤ She seems to have forgotten her password.

♥ **What should I do?**
: 본인이 무엇을 해야 할지 몰라서 물어볼 때 쓰는 표현으로, '난 무엇을 해야 하지?'라는 뜻이다.
= What do I need to do?

20

W What are you doing on the computer?

M I'm _____ _____ _____ _____.

W Why are you doing that all of a sudden?

M My friend's computer _____ _____ _____.

W That's so terrible. ♥What should I do to protect my computer?

M You should _____ _____ _____ _____.

W Right. I think I should change mine.

실전 모의고사 16회

1 다음을 듣고, 수요일 밤 날씨로 가장 적절한 것을 고르시오.

①   ②   ③

④   ⑤

2 대화를 듣고, 남자가 예약할 방을 고르시오.

①   ②   ③

④   ⑤

3 대화를 듣고, 남자의 심정으로 가장 적절한 것을 고르시오.
① upset
② envious
③ satisfied
④ surprised
⑤ embarrassed

4 대화를 듣고, 남자가 주말에 할 일로 가장 적절한 것을 고르시오.
① 차 세차하기
② 하이킹 가기
③ 방의 벽 칠하기
④ 새 집으로 이사하기
⑤ 엄마와 집 청소하기

5 대화를 듣고, 두 사람이 대화하는 장소로 가장 적절한 곳을 고르시오.
① 교회   ② 공원   ③ 미술관
④ 놀이 공원   ⑤ 어린이집

6 대화를 듣고, 남자의 마지막 말의 의도로 가장 적절한 것을 고르시오.
① 비난   ② 조언   ③ 사과
④ 동의   ⑤ 감사

7 대화를 듣고, 여자가 갖고 있는 증상이 아닌 것을 고르시오.
① 열   ② 기침   ③ 콧물
④ 두통   ⑤ 어지러움

8 대화를 듣고, 두 사람이 내일 할 일로 가장 적절한 것을 고르시오.
① 영화를 보러 가기   ② 하이킹 준비하기
③ 낚시를 하러 가기   ④ 비 피해를 대비하기
⑤ 날씨 정보를 검색하기

9 다음을 듣고, 남자가 미국에 대해 언급하지 않은 것을 고르시오.
① 넓은 크기   ② 다양한 기후
③ 나라의 수도   ④ 다양한 인종
⑤ 시간대의 변경

10 다음을 듣고, 여자가 하는 말의 내용으로 가장 적절한 것을 고르시오.
① 한국 미술의 역사
② 박물관의 위치 안내
③ 박물관의 투어 소개
④ 한국 전통 문화의 특징
⑤ 공공기관에서의 안전 준수

11 다음을 듣고, 남자의 오늘 일정과 일치하지 않는 것을 고르시오.
① 집에서 딸의 숙제를 도왔다.
② 부인을 기차역까지 데려다줬다.
③ 점심에 고객과 모임을 가졌다.
④ 저녁 식사 후에 설거지를 했다.
⑤ 아침에 딸을 도서관에 데려다 주었다.

12 대화를 듣고, 여자가 전화를 건 목적으로 가장 적절한 것을 고르시오.
① 비행기 시간을 바꾸기 위해서
② 출발 시간을 확인하기 위해서
③ 여행의 내용을 추가하기 위해서
④ 비행기 티켓을 예약하기 위해서
⑤ 여행의 일정을 문의하기 위해서

13 대화를 듣고, 여자가 서울역에 도착할 시간을 고르시오.
① 3시 ② 3시 20분
③ 3시 30분 ④ 4시
⑤ 4시 30분

14 대화를 듣고, 두 사람의 관계로 가장 적절한 것을 고르시오.
① 팬 — 운동선수
② 학생 — 선생님
③ 범인 — 경찰관
④ 배우 — 영화감독
⑤ 기자 — 영화배우

15 다음을 듣고, 남자가 여자에게 부탁한 일이 <u>아닌</u> 것을 고르시오.
① 문제가 발생하면 전화하기
② 매일 물고기에게 먹이 주기
③ 이틀에 한 번 식물에 물 주기
④ 신문지를 모아서 집 안에 넣기
⑤ 재활용 쓰레기를 분리수거하기

16 대화를 듣고, 남자가 여자와 함께 갈 수 <u>없는</u> 이유로 가장 적절한 것을 고르시오.
① 방학 중이기 때문에
② 다른 수업이 있어서
③ 노래를 잘 부르지 못해서
④ 연습을 하고 싶지 않아서
⑤ 축제에 가는 것을 싫어해서

17 다음 그림의 상황에 가장 적절한 대화를 고르시오.

① ② ③ ④ ⑤

18 다음을 듣고, 여자가 직업 체험의 날에 대해 언급하지 <u>않은</u> 것을 고르시오.
① 등록을 위해서는 참가비를 내야 한다.
② 학생은 행사 전에 경험할 직업을 결정해야 한다.
③ 양식은 이번 주 수요일까지 제출해야 한다.
④ 학생들은 행사장에 이름표를 가져와야 한다.
⑤ 기입한 양식은 학급 반장에게 제출해야 한다.

[19-20] 대화를 듣고, 여자의 마지막 말에 이어질 남자의 말로 가장 적절한 것을 고르시오.

19 Man: _____
① I can't wait to see the mountain.
② It is a great experience to go up there.
③ You know, the rainy season is in summer.
④ Before going, I need to get permission.
⑤ There are a lot of beaches by the East Sea.

20 Man: _____
① What an amazing coincidence!
② Don't worry. These things happen.
③ Let's go out to get some fresh air.
④ Cheer up. You can do it the next time.
⑤ Good for you. I think you deserve it.

Listen and Check

정답 및 해설 p.078

대화를 다시 듣고, 알맞은 것을 고르시오.

1 When will the rain stop?

☐ Wednesday ☐ Thursday

2 The man wants a room on the tenth floor because he wants to see the scenery.

☐ True ☐ False

3 Did the man buy a new shopping bag for his mother?

☐ Yes ☐ No

4 What will the woman do this weekend?

☐ clean the house ☐ go hiking

5 The picture looks relaxing thanks to its bright colors.

☐ True ☐ False

6 The man knows how to get to the store.

☐ True ☐ False

7 The woman has a runny nose but not a cough.

☐ True ☐ False

8 Did the woman know it would rain tomorrow because she saw clouds in the sky?

☐ Yes ☐ No

9 Each part of the U.S. has a different climate.

☐ True ☐ False

10 Which floor should people go to if people want to see Hongdo Kim's work?

☐ the first floor ☐ the second floor

11 When did the man meet a customer?

☐ early in the morning
☐ at lunchtime

12 The woman will be on a flight next Wednesday.

☐ True ☐ False

13 How much earlier does the woman want to get to the station before her train leaves?

☐ 30 minutes ☐ 40 minutes

14 Will the movie be released next week?

☐ Yes ☐ No

15 The woman should feed the fish every two days.

☐ True ☐ False

16 Where was the woman going?

☐ to school ☐ to her dance lesson

17 Does the man want to save money?

☐ Yes ☐ No

18 What should the students bring to the event?

☐ a form ☐ a name card

19 The woman has been to Jiri Mountain.

☐ True ☐ False

20 Did the woman fail the test because she made mistakes?

☐ Yes ☐ No

그림 정보 파악

1 다음을 듣고, 수요일 밤 날씨로 가장
적절한 것을 고르시오.

① ② ③

④ ⑤

1

M This is the weather forecast _____ _____ _____.
It will be a very bright day today. Tomorrow, dark clouds
are coming from the east. Cloudy weather will continue
until Wednesday, and we expect heavy showers that night.
_____ _____ _____ _____ _____ on
Thursday morning, and it will be sunny on Friday and throughout
the weekend. I hope you enjoy some nice outdoor activities
_____ _____ _____ this weekend.

그림 정보 파악

2 대화를 듣고, 남자가 예약할 방을
고르시오.

① ② ③

④ ⑤

2

W Hello. How may I help you?
M I want _____ _____ _____ _____ for two
nights.
W Okay. How many people will be staying in the room?
M There are _____ _____ _____ in our family. Two are
adults, and one is a kid.
W Then I recommend this room. It has a single bed and a king-
sized one.
M Okay. We'd like a room _____ _____ _____
_____, please. We want to look at the scenery outside.
W Sure.

심정 추론

3 대화를 듣고, 남자의 심정으로 가장
적절한 것을 고르시오.

① upset
② envious
③ satisfied
④ surprised
⑤ embarrassed

3

M Ta-da. Surprise!
W What is this, son?
M Mom, _____ _____ _____ _____. I made it with
your old jean jacket.
W That's very cute. How did you know that I needed a shopping
bag?
M You talked about it when we were having dinner the other day.
W How nice! I really like this bag. I will carry it _____ _____
_____ _____.
M _____ _____ _____ you like it.

할 일 파악

4 대화를 듣고, 남자가 주말에 할 일로 가장 적절한 것을 고르시오.

① 차 세차하기
② 하이킹 가기
③ 방의 벽 칠하기
④ 새 집으로 이사하기
⑤ 엄마와 집 청소하기

4

W   Do you have _____ _____ _____ for this weekend?

M   Not really. What are you going to do?

W   I'm going hiking with my friends. Would you like to go with us?

M   I'd like to, but I have to _____ _____ _____ _____ my room.

W   But you helped your mother clean the house last weekend, right?

M   Yes. But as you know, we moved to a new house recently. We _____ _____ _____ _____ _____ to do.

W   Oh, now I understand.

장소 추론

5 대화를 듣고, 두 사람이 대화하는 장소로 가장 적절한 곳을 고르시오.

① 교회
② 공원
③ 미술관
④ 놀이 공원
⑤ 어린이집

5

W   _____ _____ _____ _____ _____ that picture? I mean the one with the baby and his mom on it.

M   That picture looks peaceful and relaxing. But why is it painted in dark colors?

W   That's what I _____ _____ _____, too.

M   We need someone who can explain this.

W   I agree with you.

M   I've got an idea. We may get _____ _____ _____ with an audio tour.

W   That's a great idea.

의도 파악

6 대화를 듣고, 남자의 마지막 말의 의도로 가장 적절한 것을 고르시오.

① 비난
② 조언
③ 사과
④ 동의
⑤ 감사

6

[*Cellphone rings.*]

W   Hello, Jack.

M   Hi, Jill. Where are you? _____ _____ _____ there.

W   I'm at Evergreen Subway Station.

M   Are you going somewhere?

W   Yes. I have to _____ _____ _____ _____. You have been to the repair shop before, *haven't you?

M   Once. Why?

W   _____ _____ _____ _____ which subway I need to take. Do you know?

M   I don't remember. I think you had better call the store and ask.

*haven't you [해븐트] [유] → [해븐츄]

특정 정보 파악

7 대화를 듣고, 여자가 갖고 있는 증상이 <u>아닌</u> 것을 고르시오.

① 열
② 기침
③ 콧물
④ 두통
⑤ 어지러움

7

M Good morning. How may I help you?

W Yes, I have a terrible headache. And I feel dizzy.

M _____ _____ _____ on the forehead. You have a fever. Do you have a cough or a runny nose?

W I don't have a runny nose, but _____ _____ _____ _____.

M Okay. Try these pills. Take two pills thirty minutes after each meal for two days. If you feel better, visit me again _____ _____ _____ _____.

W Thank you.

할 일 파악

8 대화를 듣고, 두 사람이 내일 할 일로 가장 적절한 것을 고르시오.

① 영화를 보러 가기
② 하이킹 준비하기
③ 낚시를 하러 가기
④ 비 피해를 대비하기
⑤ 날씨 정보를 검색하기

8 🇬🇧

W What are you doing tomorrow, Neil?

M _____ _____ _____ going hiking or fishing.

W I don't think that's a good idea. I heard that it's going to rain heavily tomorrow.

M Are you sure? I don't see a cloud in the sky.

W Well, I just heard the weather forecast on the news.

M Then _____ _____ _____ _____? I don't want to stay at home.

W How about going to a movie _____ _____ _____?

M That's a good idea.

언급 유무 파악

9 다음을 듣고, 남자가 미국에 대해 언급하지 <u>않은</u> 것을 고르시오.

① 넓은 크기
② 다양한 기후
③ 나라의 수도
④ 다양한 인종
⑤ 시간대의 변경

9

M The United States is a really big country. The size of the U.S. is 43 times bigger than that of Korea. Its capital is Washington, D.C. Each part of the country has a different climate. In the south, it's usually hot. But in the middle and northern parts, _____ _____ _____ _____ _____ _____ _____. The country is so large that when people go to other states, they have to change their watches _____ _____ _____ different time zones.

화제·주제 파악

10 다음을 듣고, 여자가 하는 말의 내용으로 가장 적절한 것을 고르시오.

① 한국 미술의 역사
② 박물관의 위치 안내
③ 박물관의 투어 소개
④ 한국 전통 문화의 특징
⑤ 공공기관에서의 안전 준수

10

W Welcome to the National Museum of Korea. My name is Youngmi Kim, and I am the curator here. The museum opened in Yongsan in October 2005 and contains many works _____ _____ _____ _____. First, we will go to the Korean post-modern art room _____ _____ _____ _____. Then, works from masters such as Hongdo Kim and Yunbok Shin are waiting for you _____ _____ _____ _____. Please stay with me until the tour is over. Thank you for your attention.

내용 불일치 파악

11 다음을 듣고, 남자의 오늘 일정과 일치하지 <u>않는</u> 것을 고르시오.

① 집에서 딸의 숙제를 도왔다.
② 부인을 기차역까지 데려다줬다.
③ 점심에 고객과 모임을 가졌다.
④ 저녁 식사 후에 설거지를 했다.
⑤ 아침에 딸을 도서관에 데려다 주었다.

11

M I was very busy today. To begin with, I _____ _____ _____ to the library early in the morning. On my way to the office, I drove my wife to the railway station. She had a high school reunion in Busan, and she stayed there _____ _____ _____. At lunchtime, I *had a meeting with a customer. I went to pick up my daughter at 4:00 p.m. When I came back home, I cooked dinner and then _____ _____ _____ _____ _____.

*had a [해드] [어] → [해더]

목적 파악

12 대화를 듣고, 여자가 전화를 건 목적으로 가장 적절한 것을 고르시오.

① 비행기 시간을 바꾸기 위해서
② 출발 시간을 확인하기 위해서
③ 여행의 내용을 추가하기 위해서
④ 비행기 티켓을 예약하기 위해서
⑤ 여행의 일정을 문의하기 위해서

12

[*Telephone rings.*]

M Kitty Airlines. What can I do for you?

W This is Kelly Young, I'd like to ask _____ _____ _____ _____ to change my flight.

M _____ _____ _____ _____?

W It's this Wednesday at 10:00 a.m. I want to change it to next Wednesday.

M Next Wednesday. Okay, your flight _____ _____ _____.

W Thank you.

숫자 정보 파악

13 대화를 듣고, 여자가 서울역에 도착할 시간을 고르시오.

① 3시
② 3시 20분
③ 3시 30분
④ 4시
⑤ 4시 30분

13

W Excuse me, sir. How long will it take to get to Seoul Station from here?

M Let me think. There are _____ _____ _____. It will take around 40 minutes. What time is your train?

W It leaves at four thirty. But I'd like to _____ _____ _____ because I don't want to be in a hurry.

M Don't worry. You will get there _____ _____ _____ your train leaves.

W Thanks for your help.

관계 추론

14 대화를 듣고, 두 사람의 관계로 가장 적절한 것을 고르시오.

① 팬 – 운동선수
② 학생 – 선생님
③ 범인 – 경찰관
④ 배우 – 영화감독
⑤ 기자 – 영화배우

14

M Nice to meet you. _____ _____ _____ you a few questions?

W Sure. What do you want to know?

M When will your new film _____ _____?

W Next week. It's titled *The Suspect*.

M _____ _____ _____ _____ _____ in the film?

W I played a secret agent _____ _____ _____ and loves her country.

M Great. I look forward to seeing you on screen soon. Thank you for your time.

W My pleasure. Thank you.

부탁한 일 파악

15 다음을 듣고, 남자가 여자에게 부탁한 일이 아닌 것을 고르시오.

① 문제가 발생하면 전화하기
② 매일 물고기에게 먹이 주기
③ 이틀에 한 번 식물에 물 주기
④ 신문지를 모아서 집 안에 넣기
⑤ 재활용 쓰레기를 분리수거하기

15

W Hello. This is Michelle. I cannot pick up the phone right now. Please leave a message, and I will _____ _____ _____ as soon as possible. [*Beep*]

M Hi, Michelle. This is Jacob. Thank you so much for _____ _____ _____ my home during my business trip. I want to _____ _____ _____ _____ _____ once again. Please feed the fish every day and _____ _____ _____ every two days. Collect the newspapers and just put them inside the house. I have already separated the trash for recycling. If you have any problems, call my cellphone anytime. Thanks again.

16 대화를 듣고, 남자가 여자와 함께 갈 수 <u>없는</u> 이유로 가장 적절한 것을 고르시오.

① 방학 중이기 때문에
② 다른 수업이 있어서
③ 노래를 잘 부르지 못해서
④ 연습을 하고 싶지 않아서
⑤ 축제에 가는 것을 싫어해서

16

M Hi, Lily. Where are you going?

W Hello, Jason. I am going to school.

M But ＿＿＿＿＿ ＿＿＿＿＿ ＿＿＿＿＿. What's going on?

W There will be a singing festival next week, and Donna and I are ＿＿＿＿＿ ＿＿＿＿＿ ＿＿＿＿＿ ＿＿＿＿＿.

M That's cool.

W Do you want to ＿＿＿＿＿ ＿＿＿＿＿ ＿＿＿＿＿? Donna will be very happy to see you.

M I'd really love to, but I have to go to my dance lesson now. ＿＿＿＿＿ ＿＿＿＿＿ ＿＿＿＿＿.

W All right. See you.

17 다음 그림의 상황에 가장 적절한 대화를 고르시오.

① ② ③ ④ ⑤

17

① W May I speak to Jane?

   M Sorry, but ＿＿＿＿＿ ＿＿＿＿＿ ＿＿＿＿＿ ＿＿＿＿＿.

② W ＿＿＿＿＿ ＿＿＿＿＿! The truck is coming fast.

   M Thanks for warning me.

③ W What are your symptoms?

   M I can't walk because I ＿＿＿＿＿ ＿＿＿＿＿ ＿＿＿＿＿.

④ W *Come on. Hurry up!

   M Okay, okay. ＿＿＿＿＿ ＿＿＿＿＿ ＿＿＿＿＿ so hard!

⑤ W What can I do for you?

   M I am here ＿＿＿＿＿ ＿＿＿＿＿ some of my savings.

*come on [컴] [언] → [커먼]

18 다음을 듣고, 여자가 직업 체험의 날에 대해 언급하지 <u>않은</u> 것을 고르시오.

① 등록을 위해서는 참가비를 내야 한다.
② 학생은 행사 전에 경험할 직업을 결정해야 한다.
③ 양식은 이번 주 수요일까지 제출해야 한다.
④ 학생들은 행사장에 이름표를 가져와야 한다.
⑤ 기입한 양식은 학급 반장에게 제출해야 한다.

18

W Hello, students. As we told you the last time, we will have Job Experience Day in the student hall this Friday. There will be ＿＿＿＿＿ ＿＿＿＿＿ ＿＿＿＿＿ ＿＿＿＿＿ such as doctor, cook, and producer. The event will start at 9:00 a.m. Before you come here, please decide which job you want to experience. To *sign up, ＿＿＿＿＿ ＿＿＿＿＿ ＿＿＿＿＿ ＿＿＿＿＿ and give it to your class president by this Wednesday. Don't forget to ＿＿＿＿＿ ＿＿＿＿＿ ＿＿＿＿＿ to the event.

*sign up [싸인] [업] → [싸이넙]

적절한 응답 찾기

[19–20] 대화를 듣고, 여자의 마지막 말에 이어질 남자의 말로 가장 적절한 것을 고르시오.

19　Man: _____
　　① I can't wait to see the mountain.
　　② It is a great experience to go up there.
　　③ You know, the rainy season is in summer.
　　④ Before going, I need to get permission.
　　⑤ There are a lot of beaches by the East Sea.

19

W　_____ _____ _____ _____ _____ Jiri Mountain?

M　No, I haven't. How about you?

W　Me neither. I really want to go up to the top of that mountain. Shall we go there during summer vacation?

M　That's what I want to do.

W　What will _____ _____ _____ _____ in summer?

M　It is usually fine _____ _____ one thing.

W　What is that?

M　You know, the rainy season is in summer.

적절한 응답 찾기

20　Man: _____
　　① What an amazing coincidence!
　　② Don't worry. These things happen.
　　③ Let's go out to get some fresh air.
　　④ Cheer up. You can do it the next time.
　　⑤ Good for you. I think you deserve it.

💗 **I can't believe it.**
　: '난 믿을 수 없어.'라는 의미로 놀람, 기쁨, 실망 등을 표현할 때 사용된다.

20 🇬🇧

M　_____ _____ _____ _____, Mary?

W　Oh, 💗I can't believe it.

M　What is that paper?

W　It is my math test. I got it back this morning. I _____ _____ _____ to get a good grade.

M　And?

W　I thought I would fail, but _____ _____ _____ after all. In fact, I _____ _____ _____ because I made only two mistakes.

M　Good for you. I think you deserve it.

1 다음을 듣고, 내일 오후 날씨로 가장 적절한 것을 고르시오.

① 　② 　③

④ 　⑤

2 대화를 듣고, 남자가 구입할 시계로 가장 적절한 것을 고르시오.

① 　② 　③

④ 　⑤

3 대화를 듣고, 여자의 심정으로 가장 적절한 것을 고르시오.

① sad　② angry　③ thrilled
④ amazed　⑤ anxious

4 대화를 듣고, 남자가 오후에 한 일로 가장 적절한 것을 고르시오.
① 문화 공부하기
② 수업 신청하기
③ 작문 수업 듣기
④ 친구와 공부하기
⑤ 친구 집 방문하기

5 대화를 듣고, 두 사람이 대화하는 장소로 가장 적절한 곳을 고르시오.
① 교실　② 마트　③ 공원
④ 숙소　⑤ 거리

6 대화를 듣고, 남자의 마지막 말의 의도로 가장 적절한 것을 고르시오.
① 비난　② 제안
③ 칭찬　④ 응원
⑤ 위로

7 대화를 듣고, 여자가 살 옷을 고르시오.
① 코트　② 정장　③ 셔츠
④ 바지　⑤ 원피스

8 대화를 듣고, 여자가 대화 직후에 할 일로 가장 적절한 것을 고르시오.
① 전화 걸기
② 문서 작성하기
③ 고민 상담하기
④ 마감일 정하기
⑤ 이메일 확인하기

9 대화를 듣고, 두 사람이 텀블러에 대해 언급하지 <u>않은</u> 것을 고르시오.
① 재질　② 용량
③ 가격　④ 보온 가능 여부
⑤ 보온 최대 시간

10 다음을 듣고, 여자가 하는 말의 내용으로 가장 적절한 것을 고르시오.
① 스마트폰의 기능　② 스마트폰의 장점
③ 스마트폰 중독　④ 스마트폰 사용 시간
⑤ 스마트폰과 건강

11 대화를 듣고, 록 음악 축제에 대한 내용으로 일치하지 <u>않는</u> 것을 고르시오.
① 해운대 해변에서 열린다.
② 일반인도 공연을 할 수 있다.
③ 표 없이 무료로 볼 수 있다.
④ 푸드 트럭들이 많이 있다.
⑤ 금요일 저녁 7시에 열린다.

12 대화를 듣고, 여자가 이어폰을 산 목적으로 가장 적절한 것을 고르시오.
① 과제 준비에 필요해서
② 노래 연습을 하기 위해서
③ 동생에게 선물을 하기 위해서
④ 장거리 조깅할 때 쓰기 위해서
⑤ 강의실에서 하는 수업을 위해서

13 대화를 듣고, 여자가 지불해야 할 금액으로 가장 적절한 것을 고르시오.
① $6   ② $9   ③ $12
④ $18   ⑤ $21

14 대화를 듣고, 두 사람의 관계로 가장 적절한 것을 고르시오.
① 점원 — 고객
② 상사 — 직원
③ 강사 — 수강생
④ 시험 감독 — 학생
⑤ 안전 요원 — 주민

15 대화를 듣고, 남자가 여자에게 요청한 일로 가장 적절한 것을 고르시오.
① 책 빌려주기
② 등교 같이하기
③ 서점 같이 가기
④ 책 대신 사다 주기
⑤ 친구 집 방문하기

16 대화를 듣고, 여자가 반려동물을 키우지 <u>않는</u> 이유로 가장 적절한 것을 고르시오.
① 집이 넓지 않아서
② 아픈 추억이 있어서
③ 알레르기가 있어서
④ 해야 할 일이 많아져서
⑤ 동물을 좋아하지 않아서

17 다음 그림의 상황에 가장 적절한 대화를 고르시오.

①   ②   ③   ④   ⑤

18 대화를 듣고, 남자가 프러포즈에 관해 언급하지 <u>않은</u> 것을 고르시오.
① 준비한 선물
② 연주할 노래
③ 남자의 소망
④ 프러포즈할 장소
⑤ 장소를 고른 이유

[19-20] 대화를 듣고, 여자의 마지막 말에 이어질 남자의 말로 가장 적절한 것을 고르시오.

19 Man: _____
① I've studied it for three years.
② Painting is one of my hobbies.
③ You can relax with it.
④ I like the one with yellow flowers.
⑤ I'm sure you will like this book, too.

20 Man: _____
① You'd better explain the situation to him.
② I won't be around here by that time.
③ I can help you choose a gift.
④ Your child is very considerate.
⑤ It's a big day for both children and parents.

Listen and Check

정답 및 해설 p.082

● 대화를 다시 듣고, 알맞은 것을 고르시오.

1 How will the weather be tomorrow morning?

☐ sunny ☐ rainy

2 The man wants to buy a digital watch for his daughter.

☐ True ☐ False

3 What day is today?

☐ Wednesday ☐ Thursday

4 What does the man learn at the community center?

☐ how to speak English
☐ how to write essays

5 The man and the woman are planning to buy food first.

☐ True ☐ False

6 Does the woman agree with the man's opinion about her wasting money?

☐ Yes ☐ No

7 The woman's first day of work is next Monday.

☐ True ☐ False

8 What does the man suggest the woman do?

☐ wait for the papers ☐ set a deadline

9 About how many hours can the tumbler keep water warm?

☐ seven hours ☐ eight hours

10 The woman totally objects to teenagers using smartphones.

☐ True ☐ False

11 Do the man and the woman have to buy tickets to see the rock festival?

☐ Yes ☐ No

12 Does the man think that the Bluetooth earphones are great?

☐ Yes ☐ No

13 Will the woman buy a basket of carnations?

☐ Yes ☐ No

14 The man has gone surfing before.

☐ True ☐ False

15 How many books does the man ask the woman to buy for him?

☐ one book ☐ two books

16 Does the woman have a plan to own a pet?

☐ Yes ☐ No

17 The woman visited the place to buy a new phone.

☐ True ☐ False

18 What is the man going to do for his girlfriend on the playground?

☐ sing a song ☐ give a gift

19 Does the man feel relaxed by looking at paintings?

☐ Yes ☐ No

20 What is the woman worried about?

☐ buying a toy ☐ raising a pet

정답 및 해설 *p.078*

1 다음을 듣고, 내일 오후 날씨로 가장 적절한 것을 고르시오.

① ② ③

④ ⑤

1

M Good evening, everyone. This is _____ _____ _____ for tomorrow. It's been _____ _____ _____ all over the country for the whole week. But the weather will change tomorrow. There will be _____ _____ _____ in the morning. The rain will *stop in the afternoon, and you can _____ _____ _____. The weather will _____ _____ for the rest of the week.

*stop in [스탑] [인] → [스타삔]

---

2 대화를 듣고, 남자가 구입할 시계로 가장 적절한 것을 고르시오.

① ② ③

④   ⑤

2

W Hi. Welcome to Alice's Watches.

M I want to _____ _____ _____ for my young daughter.

W How about _____ _____ _____?

M They seem very good for kids.

W Which shape do you prefer, _____ _____ _____?

M I like circular ones with patterns on them.

W What about this one _____ _____ _____ _____?

M My daughter will love it. I'll take it.

---

3 대화를 듣고, 여자의 심정으로 가장 적절한 것을 고르시오.

① sad
② angry
③ thrilled
④ amazed
⑤ anxious

3

W _____ _____ _____ _____ _____ till Saturday. I _____ _____ _____ go to the amusement park.

M What do you want to ride the most?

W I want to _____ _____ _____ _____ first.

M Let's have a lot *of fun that day.

W Good!

M But _____ _____ _____ _____ before that.

*of fun [오브] [펀] → [오펀]

한 일 파악

4 대화를 듣고, 남자가 오후에 한 일로 가장 적절한 것을 고르시오.

① 문화 공부하기
② 수업 신청하기
③ 작문 수업 듣기
④ 친구와 공부하기
⑤ 친구 집 방문하기

4

W Where have you been? You were not home when I visited your house at 2:00 p.m.

M I was at the community center ＿＿＿＿＿ ＿＿＿＿＿ ＿＿＿＿＿.

W What lesson were you taking there?

M I was learning ＿＿＿＿＿ ＿＿＿＿＿ ＿＿＿＿＿ ＿＿＿＿＿.

W Sounds interesting. I love writing, too!

M ＿＿＿＿＿ ＿＿＿＿＿ ＿＿＿＿＿ ＿＿＿＿＿ next week?

W Can I? I'd love it!

장소 추론

5 대화를 듣고, 두 사람이 대화하는 장소로 가장 적절한 곳을 고르시오.

① 교실   ② 마트
③ 공원   ④ 숙소
⑤ 거리

5

M Judy, ＿＿＿＿＿ ＿＿＿＿＿ ＿＿＿＿＿ ＿＿＿＿＿ first?

W Let's get some tissue and towels.

M Okay. After we get the household items, let's get some food.

W Yes. We also need to ＿＿＿＿＿ ＿＿＿＿＿ ＿＿＿＿＿.

M They're over here.

W You're really ＿＿＿＿＿ ＿＿＿＿＿ ＿＿＿＿＿.

의도 파악

6 대화를 듣고, 남자의 마지막 말의 의도로 가장 적절한 것을 고르시오.

① 비난   ② 제안
③ 칭찬   ④ 응원
⑤ 위로

6

W This diary is so pretty. I'll buy it.

M You always ＿＿＿＿＿ ＿＿＿＿＿ ＿＿＿＿＿ ＿＿＿＿＿. Why do you do that?

W They are not the same. They are different in size and design.

M They are for ＿＿＿＿＿ ＿＿＿＿＿ ＿＿＿＿＿.

W I ＿＿＿＿＿ ＿＿＿＿＿ ＿＿＿＿＿. I just want to buy them.

M That's why you can ＿＿＿＿＿ ＿＿＿＿＿ ＿＿＿＿＿.

특정 정보 파악

7 대화를 듣고, 여자가 살 옷을 고르시오.

① 코트   ② 정장
③ 셔츠   ④ 바지
⑤ 원피스

7

W   I need to _____ _____ _____ for my first day of work.

M   Is it next Monday?

W   Yes. I should _____ _____ _____.

M   I recommend that you buy _____ _____ _____ _____.

W   Only shirts?

M   Yes. You can wear them with the pants you already have.

W   That's also a good idea.

할 일 파악

8 대화를 듣고, 여자가 대화 직후에 할 일로 가장 적절한 것을 고르시오.

① 전화 걸기
② 문서 작성하기
③ 고민 상담하기
④ 마감일 정하기
⑤ 이메일 확인하기

8

M   June, did you _____ _____ _____?

W   Yes, I did. I got your files.

M   What about _____ _____ _____?

W   Not yet. I'm waiting for them.

M   How about _____ _____ _____ now?

W   I think I have to.

M   _____ _____ _____ for the files first.

W   Okay.

언급 유무 파악

9 대화를 듣고, 두 사람이 텀블러에 대해 언급하지 <u>않은</u> 것을 고르시오.

① 재질
② 용량
③ 가격
④ 보온 가능 여부
⑤ 보온 최대 시간

9

M   Your tumbler looks cool. Does it _____ _____ _____?

W   Yes, it does. The warmth lasts for about eight hours.

M   That _____ _____ _____. It's *made of stainless steel, isn't it?

W   Yes. It's easy to use and wash.

M   _____ _____ _____ can you carry in there?

W   It can hold a maximum of 350 millilters.

*made of [메이드] [어브] → [메이더브]

10 다음을 듣고, 여자가 하는 말의 내용으로 가장 적절한 것을 고르시오.

① 스마트폰의 기능
② 스마트폰의 장점
③ 스마트폰 중독
④ 스마트폰 사용 시간
⑤ 스마트폰과 건강

10

W Do you have a smartphone? How many hours do you use it every day? It's true that it makes us more productive. We can work, study, and _____ _____ _____ _____ our friends with it. However, some teenagers spend too much time on their smartphones. If they _____ _____ _____ using them, their overall lives can become _____ _____ _____.

---

11 대화를 듣고, 록 음악 축제에 대한 내용으로 일치하지 <u>않는</u> 것을 고르시오.

① 해운대 해변에서 열린다.
② 일반인도 공연을 할 수 있다.
③ 표 없이 무료로 볼 수 있다.
④ 푸드 트럭들이 많이 있다.
⑤ 금요일 저녁 7시에 열린다.

11

M Are you going to _____ _____ _____ _____ _____ at Haeundae Beach?

W Is there a festival? I didn't know that.

M It _____ _____ _____ _____ at 7:00 p.m.

W Who's performing?

M Some singers and rock bands are performing.

W That sounds fun. Should I buy a ticket?

M The festival is free. There will be _____ _____ _____, too.

---

12 대화를 듣고, 여자가 이어폰을 산 목적으로 가장 적절한 것을 고르시오.

① 과제 준비에 필요해서
② 노래 연습을 하기 위해서
③ 동생에게 선물을 하기 위해서
④ 장거리 조깅할 때 쓰기 위해서
⑤ 강의실에서 하는 수업을 위해서

12

M Miyeon, what are those?

W _____ _____ _____ _____ Bluetooth earphones.

M I mean, why do you need them?

W I use them when I _____ _____ _____. They do not distract me because they are wireless.

M That sounds wonderful. I should _____ _____ _____ _____.

숫자 정보 파악

13 대화를 듣고, 여자가 지불해야 할 금액으로 가장 적절한 것을 고르시오.

① $6   ② $9
③ $12   ④ $18
⑤ $21

13

M   Hello. What flowers _____ _____ _____ _____ ?
W   I'm looking for some carnations.
M   Here, we sell them _____ _____ _____ or in a basket.
W   How much is it for _____ _____ _____ ?
M   Three dollars per flower and twelve dollars per basket.
W   I'll buy three individual flowers and _____ _____ _____ carnations.
M   Okay. Here you are.

관계 추론

14 대화를 듣고, 두 사람의 관계로 가장 적절한 것을 고르시오.

① 점원 — 고객
② 상사 — 직원
③ 강사 — 수강생
④ 시험 감독 — 학생
⑤ 안전 요원 — 주민

14 🇬🇧

W   Is this _____ _____ _____ for you to do this?
M   No, I did this once before.
W   I see. Do you have a surfboard?
M   No.
W   All participants are _____ _____ _____ _____ _____ here for free.
M   That's nice.
W   You can choose the board you like and _____ _____ _____ _____ _____ .

요청한 일 파악

15 대화를 듣고, 남자가 여자에게 요청한 일로 가장 적절한 것을 고르시오.

① 책 빌려주기
② 등교 같이하기
③ 서점 같이 가기
④ 책 대신 사다 주기
⑤ 친구 집 방문하기

🖤 **Can you do me a favor?**
: 상대방에게 무언가를 해줄 것을 부탁할 때 사용하는 표현으로, '부탁 좀 들어줄 수 있니?'라는 뜻이다. 정중하게 부탁을 하는 경우 can 대신 could를 쓸 수 있다.

15

M   Did you buy the book for history class?
W   I will _____ _____ _____ _____ after school.
M   🖤Can you do me a favor?
W   What is it?
M   _____ _____ _____ _____ one, too?
W   Okay. That's _____ _____ _____ _____ .
M   Thank you so much.

이유 추론

16 대화를 듣고, 여자가 애완동물을 키우지 않는 이유로 가장 적절한 것을 고르시오.

① 집이 넓지 않아서
② 아픈 추억이 있어서
③ 알레르기가 있어서
④ 해야 할 일이 많아져서
⑤ 동물을 좋아하지 않아서

♥ **used to + V**
: 과거에는 했지만 현재에는 더 이상 하지 않는 것을 말할 때 사용하는 표현으로, '~하곤 했었다'라는 뜻이다.

---

16 🇬🇧

W   That puppy _____ _____ _____.

M   Do you like animals?

W   I do, _____ _____.

M   Why don't you get one?

W   I ♥ used to have one, but it _____ _____ _____ _____.

M   I'm sorry for your dog.

W   I _____ _____ _____ _____ since then.

그림 상황 파악

17 다음 그림의 상황에 가장 적절한 대화를 고르시오.

① ② ③ ④ ⑤

17

① W   I would like to book a room for two.

  M   Sorry, but the rooms are _____ _____ today.

② W   What do you think about this curtain?

  M   I love it. But do you have _____ _____ _____?

③ W   How much is it to _____ _____?

  M   It will cost about fifty dollars.

④ W   When does your _____ _____ _____?

  M   It *starts on the fourteenth of July.

⑤ W   What are you going to play?

  M   I'm going to _____ _____.

*starts on [스탈츠] [언] → [스탈천]

언급 유무 파악

18 대화를 듣고, 남자가 프러포즈에 관해 언급하지 않은 것을 고르시오.

① 준비한 선물
② 연주할 노래
③ 남자의 소망
④ 프러포즈 할 장소
⑤ 장소를 고른 이유

18

W   Have you made plans for the proposal?

M   Yes, I'm _____ _____.

W   Where are you going to _____ _____ _____?

M   I want to do it on the playground near my house. She and I have many memories there.

W   That place _____ _____ _____.

M   I'm going to sing *Marry You* by Bruno Mars.

W   I think _____ _____ _____ _____ to propose to her.

M   I want to make this event unforgettable.

적절한 응답 찾기

[19-20] 대화를 듣고, 여자의 마지막 말에 이어질 남자의 말로 가장 적절한 것을 고르시오.

19 Man: _____
  ① I've studied it for three years.
  ② Painting is one of my hobbies.
  ③ You can relax with it.
  ④ I like the one with yellow flowers.
  ⑤ I'm sure you will like this book, too.

♥ **Definitely.**
: 상대방의 말에 당연하다고 대답할 때 사용하는 표현으로, '물론이야.', '확실히 그래.'라는 뜻이다.

19

W   What are you reading?

M   I'm actually just _____ _____ _____ _____.

W   That book has lots of pictures of paintings.

M   _____ _____ _____ by looking at them.

W   Are you sure?

M   ♥ Definitely. They _____ _____ _____.

W   Which painting here do you _____ _____ _____?

M   I like the one with yellow flowers.

적절한 응답 찾기

20 Man: _____
  ① You'd better explain the situation to him.
  ② I won't be around here by that time.
  ③ I can help you choose a gift.
  ④ Your child is very considerate.
  ⑤ It's a big day for both children and parents.

20

W   Do you know what?

M   What?

W   Children's Day _____ _____ _____.

M   I know that.

W   _____ _____ _____ _____ me to buy him a toy.

M   Raising a *child is never easy.

W   But I _____ _____ _____ _____ now.
    What should I do?

M   You'd better explain the situation to him.

*child is [촤일드] [이즈] → [촤일디즈]

1 다음을 듣고, 화요일의 날씨로 가장 적절한 것을 고르시오.

①   ②   ③

④   ⑤

2 대화를 듣고, 남자가 구입할 의자로 가장 적절한 것을 고르시오.

①   ②   ③

④   ⑤

3 대화를 듣고, 여자의 심정으로 가장 적절한 것을 고르시오.
① bored   ② lonely   ③ relieved
④ grateful   ⑤ upset

4 대화를 듣고, 여자가 양로원에서 한 일로 가장 적절한 것을 고르시오.
① 빨래하기
② 설거지하기
③ 방 청소하기
④ 저녁 식사 만들기
⑤ 아픈 사람 간호하기

5 대화를 듣고, 두 사람이 대화하는 장소로 가장 적절한 곳을 고르시오.
① 공항   ② 백화점   ③ 비행기
④ 산 정상   ⑤ 자동차 정비소

6 대화를 듣고, 남자의 마지막 말의 의도로 가장 적절한 것을 고르시오.
① 격려   ② 불평   ③ 거절
④ 조언   ⑤ 실망

7 대화를 듣고, 두 사람이 과일 가게에서 구입하지 않을 과일을 고르시오.
① 수박   ② 바나나   ③ 딸기
④ 포도   ⑤ 토마토

8 대화를 듣고, 여자가 대화 직후에 할 일로 가장 적절한 것을 고르시오.
① 침대로 가서 눕기   ② 우산 가지러 가기
③ 레몬차 만들기   ④ 집으로 걸어가기
⑤ 병원으로 가기

9 대화를 듣고, 여자가 외출 전에 해야 할 사항으로 언급하지 않은 것을 고르시오.
① 가스 끄기   ② 창문 잠그기
③ 쓰레기 버리기   ④ 짐 운반하기
⑤ 전등 끄기

10 다음을 듣고, 남자가 하는 말의 내용으로 가장 적절한 것을 고르시오.
① 자원 봉사   ② 규칙적인 식사
③ 운동의 중요성   ④ 독서의 장점
⑤ 신년 계획

11 다음을 듣고, 초콜릿 축제에 대한 내용과 일치하지 않는 것을 고르시오.
① 5월 11일부터 15일까지 열린다.
② 10개 이상의 회사가 참여한다.
③ 다양한 초콜릿을 맛볼 수 있다.
④ 아이스크림을 제공하는 행사도 있다.
⑤ 입장료는 5달러이다.

12 대화를 듣고, 여자가 전화를 건 목적으로 가장 적절한 것을 고르시오.
① 숙박을 예약하려고
② 청소를 부탁하려고
③ 편지를 부쳐달라고
④ 음식을 주문하려고
⑤ 호텔 방을 변경하려고

13 대화를 듣고, 두 사람이 만날 시각을 고르시오.
① 1:00 p.m.　　② 1:30 p.m.
③ 2:00 p.m.　　④ 2:30 p.m.
⑤ 3:00 p.m.

14 대화를 듣고, 두 사람의 관계로 가장 적절한 것을 고르시오.
① 경찰관 — 목격자
② 영화배우 — 매니저
③ 미용실 — 고객
④ 편의점 직원 — 손님
⑤ 택배 기사 — 수령인

15 대화를 듣고, 남자가 여자에게 부탁한 일로 가장 적절한 것을 고르시오.
① 차로 데리러 오기
② 식당으로 가기
③ 안전벨트 매기
④ 햄버거 구입하기
⑤ 대신 운전하기

16 대화를 듣고, 여자가 남자의 제안을 <u>거절한</u> 이유로 가장 적절한 것을 고르시오.
① 단풍을 보고 싶어서
② 사진 찍는 걸 싫어해서
③ 드럼 수업이 있어서
④ 등산을 좋아하지 않아서
⑤ 그림을 그리기로 약속해서

17 다음 그림의 상황에 가장 적절한 대화를 고르시오.

①　　②　　③　　④　　⑤

18 다음을 듣고, 여자가 수면 부족의 원인에 대해 언급하지 <u>않은</u> 것을 고르시오.
① 일어나는 시간
② 해야 할 숙제의 양
③ 친구와의 문제
④ 지나친 컴퓨터 게임
⑤ 자기 전의 스마트폰 사용

[19-20] 대화를 듣고, 남자의 마지막 말에 이어질 여자의 말로 가장 적절한 것을 고르시오.

19 Woman: _____
① You know, I'm a night person.
② What did your teacher say to you?
③ You're right. Going to school is exciting.
④ I finished my English homework last night.
⑤ You must have been very embarrassed.

20 Woman: _____
① I recommend this math workbook.
② Thank you for exchanging this book.
③ Then I'd like to get my money back.
④ Sorry, but I don't want to buy it anymore.
⑤ I want to improve my math skills.

Listen and Check

● 대화를 다시 듣고, 알맞은 것을 고르시오.

1 How will the weather be on Thursday?
☐ snowy   ☐ rainy

2 They are going to buy a chair online.
☐ True   ☐ False

3 Did the woman get a concert ticket?
☐ Yes   ☐ No

4 When did the woman go to the nursing home?
☐ last Wednesday   ☐ last weekend

5 Where are they flying?
☐ to Russia   ☐ to Hong Kong

6 The woman wants to be an interpreter for international meetings.
☐ True   ☐ False

7 Is Joanna allergic to strawberries?
☐ Yes   ☐ No

8 What will the woman make for the man?
☐ lemon tea   ☐ lemon cookies

9 What did the woman do before leaving the house?
☐ turned off the gas
☐ switched off the lights

10 What kind of dishes does the man want to learn?
☐ Korean dishes   ☐ Italian dishes

11 How long will the festival take place?
☐ for 3 days   ☐ for 5 days

12 The man works at the hotel as a member of the cleaning staff.
☐ True   ☐ False

13 What will the woman prepare for the picnic?
☐ sandwiches   ☐ fruit

14 Did the man see the face of the man with a gun?
☐ Yes   ☐ No

15 They will get some burgers.
☐ True   ☐ False

16 What does the woman do every Friday?
☐ take a drum lesson
☐ climb a mountain

17 Did the woman try to feed the giraffe?
☐ Yes   ☐ No

18 Teenagers in Korea are not having problems with their friends.
☐ True   ☐ False

19 On which day did Alex go to school?
☐ Saturday   ☐ Sunday

20 The woman exchanged her math workbook for a new one.
☐ True   ☐ False

정답 및 해설 *p.083*

그림 정보 파악

1 다음을 듣고, 화요일의 날씨로 가장 적절한 것을 고르시오.

①
②
③

④
⑤

1

W　Good morning. I'm Alex Gray with the weather report for this week. We are expecting a ＿＿＿＿＿ ＿＿＿＿＿ ＿＿＿＿＿ this country on Monday. You should stay inside. On Tuesday, the rain will stop, but it'll be foggy and cloudy all day. Starting on Wednesday, it will be ＿＿＿＿＿ ＿＿＿＿＿ ＿＿＿＿＿ ＿＿＿＿＿. And ＿＿＿＿＿ ＿＿＿＿＿ ＿＿＿＿＿ on Thursday and Friday.

그림 정보 파악

2 대화를 듣고, 남자가 구입할 의자로 가장 적절한 것을 고르시오.

①
②
③

④
⑤

♥ **Do you mean ~?**
: 다른 사람의 말의 의미를 재확인하기 위해 쓰는 표현으로, '~라는 의미니?'라는 뜻이다.
= I think you mean ~
= Did you say ~?

2

M　Catherine, look at this chair on this website.

W　Are you going to buy the chair online?

M　Of course. The ＿＿＿＿＿ ＿＿＿＿＿ ＿＿＿＿＿.

W　I agree. [*Pause*] Hmm... I like this chair.

M　♥Do you mean the wooden one *without a backrest?

W　No. The wooden chair ＿＿＿＿＿ ＿＿＿＿＿ ＿＿＿＿＿ ＿＿＿＿＿ ＿＿＿＿＿ ＿＿＿＿＿.

M　It ＿＿＿＿＿ ＿＿＿＿＿. I think I'll buy it.

*without a [위다웃] [어] → [위다우러]

심정 추론

3 대화를 듣고, 여자의 심정으로 가장 적절한 것을 고르시오.

① bored
② lonely
③ relieved
④ grateful
⑤ upset

3

M　You are looking at the ＿＿＿＿＿ ＿＿＿＿＿ ＿＿＿＿＿ ＿＿＿＿＿, right?

W　Right. Concert tickets are ＿＿＿＿＿ ＿＿＿＿＿ ＿＿＿＿＿ at 2 o'clock.

M　Then why do you ＿＿＿＿＿ ＿＿＿＿＿ ＿＿＿＿＿?

W　It's so popular that tickets will probably sell out in 10 minutes.

M　No way!

W　Wait! It's 2 o'clock. [*Keyboard typing sound*] Oh, no!

M　What's wrong?

W　My computer ＿＿＿＿＿ ＿＿＿＿＿ ＿＿＿＿＿! I think I can't get a ticket.

한 일 파악

4 대화를 듣고, 여자가 양로원에서 한 일로 가장 적절한 것을 고르시오.

① 빨래하기
② 설거지하기
③ 방 청소하기
④ 저녁 식사 만들기
⑤ 아픈 사람 간호하기

♥ **Be my guest.**

: 상대방의 부탁을 들어줄 때 쓰는 표현으로, '그렇게 해.'라는 뜻이다.
= Do what you want.
= Suit yourself.

4

M What did you do last weekend?
W I went to the _____ _____ near my school.
M A nursing home? What did you do there?
W I _____ _____ _____ and made lunch.
M You are so kind. Can I _____ _____ _____ _____ _____ _____ ?
W ♥ Be my guest.

장소 추론

5 대화를 듣고, 두 사람이 대화하는 장소로 가장 적절한 곳을 고르시오.

① 공항
② 백화점
③ 비행기
④ 산 정상
⑤ 자동차 정비소

5

W I can't believe that I'm _____ _____ _____ with you.
M Me neither. I'm so excited.
W I'm _____ _____ _____ . This is my *first time on a plane.
M I see. Yumi, look out the window.
W Wow! I can see many cars and buildings.
M They _____ _____ _____ . They are so small!
W Right. _____ _____ _____ _____ is so fun.

*first time [펄스트] [타임] → [펄스타임]

의도 파악

6 대화를 듣고, 남자의 마지막 말의 의도로 가장 적절한 것을 고르시오.

① 격려   ② 불평
③ 거절   ④ 조언
⑤ 실망

6

W Noah, how can I speak English fluently?
M What for?
W I want to be an interpreter for _____ _____ .
M Hmm... How about _____ _____ ?
W I was thinking about that. But I'm _____ _____ _____ _____ _____ .
M Don't worry. You are _____ _____ _____ I know.

특정 정보 파악

7 대화를 듣고, 두 사람이 과일 가게에서 구입하지 <u>않을</u> 과일을 고르시오.
① 수박 ② 바나나
③ 딸기 ④ 포도
⑤ 토마토

7 🇬🇧

M We'll have lots of visitors today.

W Why don't we _____ _____ _____?

M That's a great idea. Let's buy some apples.

W No. We already have an apple pie. A _____ _____

_____ _____.

M Okay. I also want bananas, strawberries, and grapes.

W Joanna is allergic to strawberries.

M Then _____ _____ _____ instead of strawberries?

W That's better.

할 일 파악

8 대화를 듣고, 여자가 대화 직후에 할 일로 가장 적절한 것을 고르시오.
① 침대로 가서 눕기
② 우산 가지러 가기
③ 레몬차 만들기
④ 집으로 걸어가기
⑤ 병원으로 가기

🖤 **It rains cats and dogs.**
: 비가 엄청나게 많이 내릴 때 쓰는 표현으로, '비가 억수같이 내린다.'라는 뜻이다.
= It rains heavily.

8

W What's wrong with you? You _____ _____.

M I _____ _____ _____. I had to walk home _____ _____ _____ yesterday.

W Why? 🖤 It rained cats and dogs yesterday.

M I _____ _____ _____.

W That's too bad. Let me *make you some lemon tea.

M Okay. Thanks a lot.

*make you [메이크] [유] → [메이큐]

언급 유무 파악

9 대화를 듣고, 여자가 외출 전에 해야 할 사항으로 언급하지 <u>않은</u> 것을 고르시오.
① 가스 끄기
② 창문 잠그기
③ 쓰레기 버리기
④ 짐 운반하기
⑤ 전등 끄기

🖤 **Let's hit the road!**
: 길을 떠나거나 어딘가를 향해 출발할 때 쓰는 표현으로, '이제 출발하자!'라는 뜻이다.
= Let's go.
= Let's head out.

9 🇬🇧

M Honey, we have to leave to _____ _____ _____.

W Please be sure to _____ _____ _____ _____.
I'll check that I've locked the windows.

M No problem. Anything else?

W Could you _____ _____ _____ _____? I'll switch off the lights.

M All done.

W 🖤 Let's hit the road!

화제·주제 파악

10 다음을 듣고, 남자가 하는 말의 내용으로 가장 적절한 것을 고르시오.

① 자원 봉사
② 규칙적인 식사
③ 운동의 중요성
④ 독서의 장점
⑤ 신년 계획

10 🇬🇧

M Hello, everyone. Did you make any _____ _____ _____? Let me tell you about my plans. I will get up early in the morning. I will also work out at least three times a week. I'm going to read more books _____ _____ _____ _____ _____. Lastly, I want to _____ _____ _____ _____ traditional Korean dishes. What's your new year's resolution?

내용 불일치 파악

11 다음을 듣고, 초콜릿 축제에 대한 내용과 일치하지 <u>않는</u> 것을 고르시오.

① 5월 11일부터 15일까지 열린다.
② 10개 이상의 회사가 참여한다.
③ 다양한 초콜릿을 맛볼 수 있다.
④ 아이스크림을 제공하는 행사도 있다.
⑤ 입장료는 5달러이다.

11 🇬🇧

W We'd like to invite you to the chocolate festival. It will _____ _____ for 5 days from May 11 to 15. More than 10 companies are _____ _____ _____. You can enjoy various real chocolate treats. There will also be _____ _____ _____ such as making chocolate bars. The entrance fee is 5 dollars. _____ _____ _____, please visit our website at www.chocolatefestival.com.

목적 파악

12 대화를 듣고, 여자가 전화를 건 목적으로 가장 적절한 것을 고르시오.

① 숙박을 예약하려고
② 청소를 부탁하려고
③ 편지를 부쳐달라고
④ 음식을 주문하려고
⑤ 호텔 방을 변경하려고

💜 **My pleasure.**

: 고마워하는 상대방에게 도움을 줄 수 있어서 기쁘다고 말할 때 쓰는 표현으로, '별 말씀을요.'라는 뜻이다.

= No problem.
= Don't mention it.

12

[*Telephone rings.*]

M This is the Imperial Hotel. How may I help you?

W Hello. This is Ashley in Room 715. Before I went out, I asked you to _____ _____ _____ _____.

M Yes.

W When I came back, I found that my room was _____ _____ _____.

M I'm sorry. I'll send you someone from the cleaning staff right away.

W Thank you _____ _____ _____ _____.

M 💜My pleasure. Is there _ _____ _____ you need?

W I don't think so. Thanks.

숫자 정보 파악

13 대화를 듣고, 두 사람이 만날 시각을 고르시오.

① 1:00 p.m.
② 1:30 p.m.
③ 2:00 p.m.
④ 2:30 p.m.
⑤ 3:00 p.m.

13

W How about going on a picnic in the afternoon?

M Good idea. We can _____ _____ _____ on the grass.

W And we can read books and eat something.

M Sounds like a _____ _____ _____. I'll make some sandwiches.

W Then I'll prepare _____ _____ _____ _____.

M Let's meet back here _____ _____ _____.

W As it's now 1:00 p.m., we can meet at 3 o'clock.

관계 추론

14 대화를 듣고, 두 사람의 관계로 가장 적절한 것을 고르시오.

① 경찰관 — 목격자
② 영화배우 — 매니저
③ 미용실 — 고객
④ 편의점 직원 — 손님
⑤ 택배 기사 — 수령인

> ♥ **Keep going.**
> : 하던 일을 계속 하라고 격려할 때 쓰는 표현으로, '계속하세요.'라는 뜻이다.
> = Go on.
> = Carry on.

14

M I'll tell you everything that I saw yesterday.

W Take your time and explain to me _____ _____.

M Um, I was in the convenience store at 10:00 p.m.

W ♥Keep going.

M A man with a gun _____ _____ and took some money.

W What did _____ _____ _____ _____?

M I couldn't see his face, but he was tall and thin _____ _____ _____ _____.

W That will be helpful. Thank you for your statement.

부탁한 일 파악

15 대화를 듣고, 남자가 여자에게 부탁한 일로 가장 적절한 것을 고르시오.

① 차로 데리러 오기
② 식당으로 가기
③ 안전벨트 매기
④ 햄버거 구입하기
⑤ 대신 운전하기

15

[*Car door closes.*]

W Dad, thank you for _____ _____ _____.

M Don't mention it. I love to _____ _____ _____.

W Can we go to a restaurant first? _____ _____.

M That's a good idea. What do you want to eat?

W Let's get some burgers.

M Okay! Honey, _____ _____ _____.

W I'm sorry. I forgot.

M It's important to buckle up when you're in a car.

16 대화를 듣고, 여자가 남자의 제안을 <u>거절한</u> 이유로 가장 적절한 것을 고르시오.

① 단풍을 보고 싶어서
② 사진 찍는 걸 싫어해서
③ 드럼 수업이 있어서
④ 등산을 좋아하지 않아서
⑤ 그림을 그리기로 약속해서

♥ **must have + 현재분사**
: 과거에 발생한 일에 대해서 확신을 나타낼 때 쓰는 표현으로, '~이었음에 틀림없다'라는 뜻이다.

16

M Look at those pictures. Cool, right?

W You took photos on the mountain. Where did you go?

M I went to Mt. Jiri. _____ _____ _____ _____ red, yellow, and orange leaves.

W It ♥ must have been wonderful. I _____ _____, too.

M Do you? Let's _____ _____ _____ _____ this Friday.

W I'm afraid I can't. I usually _____ _____ _____ _____ every Friday.

M I see. Maybe next time then.

17 다음 그림의 상황에 가장 적절한 대화를 고르시오.

① ② ③ ④ ⑤

17

① W Excuse me, but you should not feed the giraffe in the zoo.

M I'm sorry. I _____ _____ _____ _____.

② W When you touch the animal, please _____ _____.

M Okay. I will.

③ W Can you give me some cookies?

M Sure. _____ _____ _____.

④ W Look at the giraffe. Its neck is _____ _____.

M I agree. I've never *seen a neck this long before.

⑤ W You should not go _____ _____ _____.

M But I want to get a closer look at the animal.

*seen a [씬] [어] → [씨너]

18 다음을 듣고, 여자가 수면 부족의 원인에 대해 언급하지 <u>않은</u> 것을 고르시오.

① 일어나는 시간
② 해야 할 숙제의 양
③ 친구와의 문제
④ 지나친 컴퓨터 게임
⑤ 자기 전의 스마트폰 사용

18

W According to the survey, teenagers in Korea are _____ _____ a lack of sleep. How has this happened? First, they have to get up early because school starts at 9:00 a.m. They also _____ _____ _____ _____ _____ _____. They have to finish their assignments both from school and from private institutes. Sometimes they have problems with their friends, which _____ _____ _____. Lastly, they often _____ _____ _____ before going to bed.

[19~20] 대화를 듣고, 남자의 마지막 말에 이어질 여자의 말로 가장 적절한 것을 고르시오.

19 Woman: _____

① You know, I'm a night person.

② What did your teacher say to you?

③ You're right. Going to school is exciting.

④ I finished my English homework last night.

⑤ You must have been very embarrassed.

19

W Alex, how have you been?

M Hi, Hyeonji. A funny thing happened to me yesterday.

W I like funny stories. I'm _____ _____ _____

_____ .

M I _____ _____ _____ in the morning to go to school.

W What? I don't see what's funny.

M I'm _____ _____ _____ . When I was almost at school, I realized that _____ _____ _____ .

W You must have been very embarrassed.

---

20 Woman: _____

① I recommend this math workbook.

② Thank you for exchanging this book.

③ Then I'd like to get my money back.

④ Sorry, but I don't want to buy it anymore.

⑤ I want to improve my math skills.

20 🇬🇧

M Welcome to the Vanilla Bookstore. What can I do for you?

W I want to exchange this math workbook for a new copy.

M Is _____ _____ with it?

W I think so. This page is _____ _____ _____ .

M Ah, I'm sorry. But this book is sold out.

W Is there _____ _____ ?

M Not today. But we've already _____ _____ _____ _____ . You can _____ _____ _____ in five days.

W Then I'd like to get my money back.

1 다음을 듣고, 예상되는 마닐라의 날씨로 가장 적절한 것을 고르시오.

① 　② 　③

④ 　⑤

2 대화를 듣고, 화장대 위의 물건 배치로 가장 적절한 것을 고르시오.

① 　② 　③

④ 　⑤

3 대화를 듣고, 여자의 심정으로 가장 적절한 것을 고르시오.
① angry　② excited　③ amazed
④ worried　⑤ nervous

4 대화를 듣고, 여자가 어젯밤에 한 일로 가장 적절한 것을 고르시오.
① 휴식 취하기
② 친구 만나기
③ 시험 준비하기
④ 팀 과제 끝내기
⑤ 커피숍 아르바이트

5 대화를 듣고, 두 사람이 대화하는 장소로 가장 적절한 곳을 고르시오.
① 카페　② 교실　③ 병원
④ 공항　⑤ 공원

6 대화를 듣고, 여자의 마지막 말의 의도로 가장 적절한 것을 고르시오.
① 위로　② 사과　③ 격려
④ 비동의　⑤ 조언

7 대화를 듣고, 여자가 마켓에서 구입 할 물건을 고르시오.
① 빵　② 채소　③ 우유
④ 선풍기　⑤ 에어컨

8 대화를 듣고, 남자가 대화 직후에 할 일로 가장 적절한 것을 고르시오.
① 데이트하기　② 한옥 예약하기
③ 호텔 알아보기　④ 한복 대여하기
⑤ 한옥 마을 가기

9 다음을 듣고, 여자가 가방에 대해 언급하지 <u>않은</u> 것을 고르시오.
① 출시 년도　② 가방 크기
③ 할인 기간　④ 세척 방법
⑤ 구매 방법

10 다음을 듣고, 남자가 하는 말의 내용으로 가장 적절한 것을 고르시오.
① 세기의 인물들　② 메모의 중요성
③ 창의력의 원천　④ 좋은 펜의 기준
⑤ 건강한 인간관계

11 대화를 듣고, 여자가 언급한 내용과 일치하지 <u>않는</u> 것을 고르시오.
① 갈 곳을 미리 계획할 것이다.
② 하고 싶은 것들을 할 것이다.
③ 혼자 제주도 여행을 갈 것이다.
④ 일주일간 제주도에 머물 것이다.
⑤ 버스를 타거나 걸어 다닐 것이다.

12 대화를 듣고, 여자가 인형을 구입한 목적으로 가장 적절한 것을 고르시오.

① 친구에게 선물하기 위해서
② 여동생이 사달라고 부탁해서
③ 어릴 때부터 인형을 좋아해서
④ 잘 때 무서움을 떨치기 위해서
⑤ 우울한 자신을 위로하기 위해서

13 대화를 듣고, 여자가 지불해야 할 금액으로 가장 적절한 것을 고르시오.

① $12   ② $25   ③ $27
④ $30   ⑤ $34

14 대화를 듣고, 두 사람의 관계로 가장 적절한 것을 고르시오.

① 교수 — 학생
② 점원 — 고객
③ 코치 — 선수
④ 디자이너 — 의뢰인
⑤ 남자친구 — 여자친구

15 대화를 듣고, 남자가 여자에게 요청한 일로 가장 적절한 것을 고르시오.

① 영화 보기
② 책 읽어 주기
③ 물건 옮겨 주기
④ 고민 들어주기
⑤ 노트북 빌려주기

16 대화를 듣고, 여자가 휴대폰을 새로 구입한 이유로 가장 적절한 것을 고르시오.

① 휴대폰 속도가 느려져서
② 휴대폰을 물에 떨어뜨려서
③ 이전부터 기다리던 폰이어서
④ 통신사에 할인 혜택이 있어서
⑤ 쓰던 휴대폰에 싫증을 느껴서

17 다음 그림의 상황에 가장 적절한 대화를 고르시오.

①   ②   ③   ④   ⑤

18 대화를 듣고, 두 사람이 미용실에 관해 언급하지 <u>않은</u> 것을 고르시오.

① 미용실의 인기도
② 미용실 전화번호
③ 미용실 커트 가격
④ 미용실까지의 거리
⑤ 헤어 디자이너의 수

[19~20] 대화를 듣고, 남자의 마지막 말에 이어질 여자의 말로 가장 적절한 것을 고르시오.

19 Woman: _____

① Summer is my favorite season.
② I saw some campaigns for this.
③ I try to use public transportation.
④ I want to talk about this problem.
⑤ It has to do with where we live.

20 Woman: _____

① Exercise is good for your health.
② You really care a lot about your body.
③ Losing weight is not about eating less.
④ You need to avoid eating at night first.
⑤ I suggest that you do not skip breakfast.

Listen and Check

● 대화를 다시 듣고, 알맞은 것을 고르시오.

1 Will it be windy in Tokyo?

☐ Yes   ☐ No

2 The man will place his things in front of the jewelry box.

☐ True   ☐ False

3 What is the woman worried about her daughter?

☐ making friends   ☐ making noise

4 The woman didn't go to sleep last night due to her project.

☐ True   ☐ False

5 Is the woman about to take a picture of the man?

☐ Yes   ☐ No

6 The man is faster than the woman at memorizing words.

☐ True   ☐ False

7 What is the man going to buy at the market?

☐ an air conditioner   ☐ vegetables

8 Will the man and the woman stay at a *hanok* during the weekend?

☐ Yes   ☐ No

9 What is the way to wash the canvas bags?

☐ by dry cleaning them
☐ by washing them with water

10 What is one of the positive sides of taking notes?

☐ developing relationships
☐ being creative

11 The woman already planned where to go on Jeju Island.

☐ True   ☐ False

12 What makes the woman get scared?

☐ having no dolls   ☐ sleeping alone

13 The woman will buy a set of cans and a set of sticks.

☐ True   ☐ False

14 Why did the man go to the store?

☐ to buy a T-shirt   ☐ to exchange a T-shirt

15 The man wants to watch a movie on the woman's laptop.

☐ True   ☐ False

16 The woman used her old phone for only a few months.

☐ True   ☐ False

17 Who is supposed to sit in seat 17D?

☐ the woman   ☐ the man

18 Is the hair shop within walking distance?

☐ Yes   ☐ No

19 Which season does the woman think is disappearing fast?

☐ spring   ☐ summer

20 What does the woman think the cause of the man failing his diet is?

☐ exercising irregularly
☐ eating at night

그림 정보 파악

1 다음을 듣고, 예상되는 마닐라의 날씨로 가장 적절한 것을 고르시오.

① ② ③

④ ⑤

1

M Hello, everyone. I'm Harry Jackson with the weather report for tomorrow. In Seoul, the weather will be _____ _____ _____. In Beijing, it will be cloudy and a bit windy. The weather in Manila will be very _____ _____ _____. Don't forget to _____ _____ when you go out. Finally, in Tokyo, _____ _____ _____ _____ to hit the region.

그림 정보 파악

2 대화를 듣고, 화장대 위의 물건 배치로 가장 적절한 것을 고르시오.

① ② ③

④ ⑤

2

M Honey, we should _____ _____ _____ _____ _____.

W I'll do that.

M Please put my skincare products on the right side.

W I'll put mine there, too.

M What about _____ _____ _____?

W It would be better if I *put it in the back on the left-hand side.

M Good. Since you _____ _____ _____, you should put them in front of the jewelry box.

W That's a good idea.

*put it [풋] [잇] → [푸릿]

심정 추론

3 대화를 듣고, 여자의 심정으로 가장 적절한 것을 고르시오.

① angry
② excited
③ amazed
④ worried
⑤ nervous

3

M What are you thinking about?

W I'm _____ _____ _____ _____.

M Is there something wrong with her?

W She _____ _____ _____ for the first time today.

M She must be having fun.

W She gets shy when she's _____ _____ _____.

M She will make good friends. Don't worry.

한 일 파악

4 대화를 듣고, 여자가 어젯밤에 한 일로 가장 적절한 것을 고르시오.

① 휴식 취하기
② 친구 만나기
③ 시험 준비하기
④ 팀 과제 끝내기
⑤ 커피숍 아르바이트

4 🇬🇧

M   Maria, you look so tired.

W   I _____ _____ _____ _____.

M   Why?

W   I had to _____ _____ _____ _____.

M   You may *doze off in class.

W   I think I should _____ _____ _____ first.

M   Get some good rest when you go home after school.

*doze off [도즈] [어프] → [도저프]

장소 추론

5 대화를 듣고, 두 사람이 대화하는 장소로 가장 적절한 곳을 고르시오.

① 카페   ② 교실
③ 병원   ④ 공항
⑤ 공원

♥ **That's what I say.**
: 상대방의 말에 동의할 때 사용하는 표현으로, '그 말에 찬성이야.', '내 말이 그 말이야.'라는 뜻이다.

5

W   _____ _____ _____ _____ *around us. I can feel spring.

M   Do you want me to _____ _____ _____ _____ _____ over there?

W   I love it.

M   The trees *behind you and _____ _____ _____ are so beautiful.

W   Yeah. Let's come here sometime when the weather is fine.

M   ♥That's what I say.

*around us [어라운드] [어쓰] → [어라운더쓰]
*behind you [비하인드] [유]→ [비하인쥬]

의도 파악

6 대화를 듣고, 여자의 마지막 말의 의도로 가장 적절한 것을 고르시오.

① 위로   ② 사과
③ 격려   ④ 비동의
⑤ 조언

♥ **That's easier said than done.**
: 무언가를 실천하는 것이 어렵다고 얘기할 때 사용하는 표현으로, '실천하는 것보다 말하는 것이 더 쉽다.'라는 뜻이다.

6

M   We have so _____ _____ _____ _____ by tomorrow.

W   I wonder if it's possible.

M   _____ _____ _____ are there?

W   There are 400.

M   We can _____ _____ ____ _____ per hour. We just need four hours then.

W   ♥That's easier said than done.

특정 정보 파악

7 대화를 듣고, 여자가 마켓에서 구입할 물건을 고르시오.

① 빵
② 채소
③ 우유
④ 선풍기
⑤ 에어컨

7 🇬🇧

M   What are you going to buy?

W   The weather is _____ _____ _____ _____, and a fan's not enough.

M   So you _____ _____ _____ _____, don't you?

W   Yes, I do. What about you?

M   I need to get _____ _____ _____ _____.

W   Okay.

할 일 파악

8 대화를 듣고, 남자가 대화 직후에 할 일로 가장 적절한 것을 고르시오.

① 데이트하기
② 한옥 예약하기
③ 호텔 알아보기
④ 한복 대여하기
⑤ 한옥 마을 가기

8 🇬🇧

M   Is there anywhere you want to go this weekend?

W   I want to try the _____ _____ _____ called *hanbok*.

M   _____ _____ do you want to do?

W   I also want to experience a _____ _____ _____ called a *hanok*.

M   Okay. Then I'll reserve a room for a *hanok* in advance.

W   This weekend will be all about _____ _____ _____.

언급 유무 파악

9 다음을 듣고, 여자가 가방에 대해 언급하지 않은 것을 고르시오.

① 출시 년도
② 가방 크기
③ 할인 기간
④ 세척 방법
⑤ 구매 방법

9

W   Good afternoon. Let me _____ _____ _____ _____, the canvas bag. This bag was first *released in 1996 and has been one of our most popular bags. As you can see, it *comes in different sizes _____ _____ _____.
Like its name indicates, the bag is made of canvas cloth, so it's durable. You can easily _____ _____ _____ _____. It's available on our online shopping mall. Thank you.

*released in [릴리즈드] [인] → [릴리즈딘]
*comes in [컴즈] [인] → [컴진]

화제·주제 파악

10 다음을 듣고, 남자가 하는 말의 내용으로 가장 적절한 것을 고르시오.

① 세기의 인물들
② 메모의 중요성
③ 창의력의 원천
④ 좋은 펜의 기준
⑤ 건강한 인간관계

10

M Do you _____ _____? All the great people of the century _____ _____ _____ _____. They took notes. They simply wrote down their ideas. When we do that, we can come up with _____ _____ _____ for things. Taking notes *helps us become creative. For a successful life, pick up a pen and write down anything that _____ _____ _____ _____.

*helps us [헬쓰] [어쓰] → [헬써쓰]

내용 불일치 파악

11 대화를 듣고, 여자가 언급한 내용과 일치하지 <u>않는</u> 것을 고르시오.

① 갈 곳을 미리 계획할 것이다.
② 하고 싶은 것들을 할 것이다.
③ 혼자 제주도 여행을 갈 것이다.
④ 일주일간 제주도에 머물 것이다.
⑤ 버스를 타거나 걸어 다닐 것이다.

11 🇬🇧

W I'm going on a trip to Jeju Island by myself.
M _____ _____ _____ _____ _____ there?
W One week.
M How will you move from place to place?
W I'm going to take a bus or just walk.
M I see. Have you _____ _____ _____ _____?
W No. I'll do whatever I want at that moment.
M Great. _____ _____ _____ _____.

목적 파악

12 대화를 듣고, 여자가 인형을 구입한 목적으로 가장 적절한 것을 고르시오.

① 친구에게 선물하기 위해서
② 여동생이 사달라고 부탁해서
③ 어릴 때부터 인형을 좋아해서
④ 잘 때 무서움을 떨치기 위해서
⑤ 우울한 자신을 위로하기 위해서

12

M What are _____ _____ _____?
W They are lovely, right? I particularly love this big teddy bear.
M Did you buy them?
W Yes, I did.
M _____ _____ _____ _____ so many dolls?
W I feel scared when I *sleep in my room alone.
M You're _____ _____ _____ _____ _____.

*sleep in [슬립] [인] → [슬립삔]

수자 정보 파악

13 대화를 듣고, 여자가 지불해야 할 금액으로 가장 적절한 것을 고르시오.

① $12   ② $25

③ $27   ④ $30

⑤ $34

13

W   Hi. I'm looking for snacks for cats.

M   Which do you want, _____ _____ _____ _____ ?

W   How much is each?

M   It's _____ _____ for a can and _____ _____ for a set of ten sticks.

W   Do you also _____ _____ _____ _____ ?

M   Of course. A set of three cans is ten dollars.

W   Then I'll buy a set of cans and a set of sticks.

M   Okay. Here you are.

관계 추론

14 대화를 듣고, 두 사람의 관계로 가장 적절한 것을 고르시오.

① 교수 — 학생

② 점원 — 고객

③ 코치 — 선수

④ 디자이너 — 의뢰인

⑤ 남자친구 — 여자친구

14

W   Hello. What can I do for you?

M   I _____ _____ _____ here yesterday.

W   Is there a problem with it?

M   It is _____ _____ _____ _____ .

W   Do you want to exchange it for a _____ _____ ?

M   Yes, please. Can I _____ _____ _____ ?

W   Sure.

요청한 일 파악

15 대화를 듣고, 남자가 여자에게 요청한 일로 가장 적절한 것을 고르시오.

① 영화 보기

② 책 읽어 주기

③ 물건 옮겨 주기

④ 고민 들어주기

⑤ 노트북 빌려주기

15

W   _____ _____ _____ _____ now?

M   It still hurts. I can't move it.

W   That's too bad. Do you want to watch a movie on my laptop?

M   No. How about _____ _____ _____ _____ instead?

W   I'm happy to do that for you. What book do you _____ _____ _____ _____ ?

M   *The Little Prince.* The book's on the table.

W   Okay. _____ _____ .

이유 추론

16 대화를 듣고, 여자가 휴대폰을 새로 구입한 이유로 가장 적절한 것을 고르시오.

① 휴대폰 속도가 느려져서
② 휴대폰을 물에 떨어뜨려서
③ 이전부터 기다리던 폰이어서
④ 통신사에 할인 혜택이 있어서
⑤ 쓰던 휴대폰에 싫증을 느껴서

♥ **How come?**

: 상대방에게 이유나 원인을 물어볼 때 사용하는 표현으로, '어째서?', '왜?'라는 뜻이다.

16

M   Isn't that a new phone?

W   Yes, it is.

M   But you _____ _____ _____ _____ for only a few months.

W   _____ _____.

M   ♥ How come?

W   I _____ _____ it in the water.

M   Too bad. Be careful _____ _____ _____.

W   I know. I will.

그림 상황 파악

17 다음 그림의 상황에 가장 적절한 대화를 고르시오.

①   ②   ③   ④   ⑤

17 🇬🇧

① M   _____ _____ _____ do you need?

   W   Three tickets, please.

② M   Isn't _____ _____ _____?

   W   Not at all. It's very light.

③ M   How long does it take to go to city hall?

   W   It will take about ten minutes _____ _____.

④ M   Excuse me. Could you check your seat number again?

   W   Sorry. _____ _____ _____.

⑤ M   How do I look in this uniform?

   W   You _____ _____.

언급 유무 파악

18 대화를 듣고, 두 사람이 미용실에 관해 언급하지 <u>않은</u> 것을 고르시오.

① 미용실의 인기도
② 미용실 전화번호
③ 미용실 커트 가격
④ 미용실까지의 거리
⑤ 헤어 디자이너의 수

18

W   Is there a hair shop _____ _____ _____ _____ _____ in this neighborhood?

M   Yes, there is. It's a five-minute walk from here. It _____ _____.

W   Do many people go there?

M   It's _____ _____ _____.

W   How many hair designers are there?

M   I remember there were four.

W   Should I _____ _____ _____?

M   You have to. Here's the number. It's 1234-7777.

적절한 응답 찾기

[19~20] 대화를 듣고, 남자의 마지막 말에 이어질 여자의 말로 가장 적절한 것을 고르시오.

19 Woman: _____
① Summer is my favorite season.
② I saw some campaigns for this.
③ I try to use public transportation.
④ I want to talk about this problem.
⑤ It has to do with where we live.

19

M   It's _____ _____ _____.

W   It's still spring but feels like summer.

M   It's all _____ _____ _____ _____.

W   It seems like spring and fall are slowly disappearing.

M   We should do what we can do to reduce global warming.

W   You're right.

M   _____ _____ _____ _____ for that?

W   I try to use public transportation.

적절한 응답 찾기

20 Woman: _____
① Exercise is good for your health.
② You really care a lot about your body.
③ Losing weight is not about eating less.
④ You need to avoid eating at night first.
⑤ I suggest that you do not skip breakfast.

20

W   Are you still on a diet?

M   Yeah, but I _____ _____ _____ _____.

W   Have you changed your eating habits?

M   Well, I can't _____ _____ _____ _____.

W   That's why you aren't losing any weight.

M   _____ _____ _____ _____ ?

W   You need to avoid eating at night first.

1 다음을 듣고, 일요일의 날씨로 가장 적절한 것을 고르시오.

2 대화를 듣고, 남자가 찾고 있는 개로 가장 적절한 것을 고르시오.

3 대화를 듣고, 여자의 심정으로 가장 적절한 것을 고르시오.
① proud　　② excited　　③ nervous
④ satisfied　　⑤ surprised

4 대화를 듣고, 남자가 영화를 보기 위해서 할 일로 가장 적절한 것을 고르시오.
① 부모님께 외출 허락을 받기
② 식사를 하고 영화관에 가기
③ 영화관에 문의하여 항의하기
④ 내일 저녁 시간 영화를 예매하기
⑤ 아는 사람에게 영화표 예매를 부탁하기

5 대화를 듣고, 두 사람이 대화하는 장소로 가장 적절한 곳을 고르시오.
① 은행　　② 우체국　　③ 분실물 센터
④ 서비스 센터　　⑤ 가전 판매점

6 대화를 듣고, 여자의 마지막 말의 의도로 가장 적절한 것을 고르시오.
① 동의　　② 사과　　③ 충고
④ 격려　　⑤ 감사

7 대화를 듣고, 남자가 Chen에 대해 언급하지 않은 것을 고르시오.
① 부모님은 공무원이다.
② 테니스를 매우 좋아한다.
③ 피아노를 매우 잘 연주한다.
④ 베이징에서 태어나 자랐다.
⑤ 키가 크고 머리카락은 검은색이다.

8 대화를 듣고, 두 사람이 대화 직후에 할 일로 가장 적절한 것을 고르시오.
① 환전하기　　② 옷가게 가기
③ 점심 식사하기　　④ 몸무게 재기
⑤ 청바지 입어 보기

9 다음을 듣고, 여자가 새해 결심으로 언급하지 않은 것을 고르시오.
① 매일 영어 일기 쓰기　　② 수영 배우기
③ 스페인어 회화 배우기　　④ 날마다 건강 체크하기
⑤ 하루 100회 팔 굽혀 펴기 하기

10 다음을 듣고, 여자가 하는 말의 내용으로 가장 적절한 것을 고르시오.
① 분실물 습득 안내　　② 고객 서비스 소개
③ 엘리베이터 사용법　　④ 화장실의 위치 설명
⑤ 귀중품의 보관 요령

11 다음을 듣고, 남자가 언급한 내용과 일치하지 않는 것을 고르시오.
① 아침 5시에 일어난다.
② 직업은 동물 조련사이다.
③ Oriental 동물원 소속이다.
④ 매일 동물들의 수를 확인한다.
⑤ 동물 훈련에 매일 4시간을 보낸다.

12 대화를 듣고, 남자가 전화를 건 목적으로 가장 적절한 것을 고르시오.
① 계획을 수정하기 위해서
② 모임 약속에 갈 수가 없어서
③ 여자와 숙제를 상의하기 위해서
④ 모임의 목적을 설명하기 위해서
⑤ 여자의 메시지를 전달하기 위해서

13 대화를 듣고, 남자가 거스름돈으로 받을 금액을 고르시오.
① $17　　② $27　　③ $30
④ $37　　⑤ $47

14 대화를 듣고, 두 사람의 관계로 가장 적절한 것을 고르시오.
① 의사 — 환자
② 선생님 — 학생
③ 상사 — 부하 직원
④ 가게 점원 — 손님
⑤ 치료사 — 간호원

15 대화를 듣고 남자가 여자에게 부탁한 일로 가장 적절한 것을 고르시오.
① 식당 예약하기
② 식사 장소 찾기
③ 조사원 모집하기
④ 교통수단 선택하기
⑤ 전시 일정 알아보기

16 대화를 듣고, 남자가 역사 수업을 듣지 <u>않는</u> 이유로 가장 적절한 것을 고르시오.
① 한국에 관심이 없어서
② 이미 역사 수업을 들어서
③ 여름에 다른 계획이 있어서
④ 혼자 수업 듣는 것을 선호해서
⑤ 학교가 집에서부터 멀리 있어서

17 다음 그림 상황에 가장 적절한 대화를 고르시오.

①　　②　　③　　④　　⑤

18 다음을 듣고, 여자가 중앙 공공 도서관 이용에 대해 언급하지 <u>않은</u> 것을 고르시오.
① 매주 월요일에 도서관은 쉰다.
② 아침 9시부터 저녁 7시까지 개장한다.
③ 목요일 아침마다 요가 수업이 있다.
④ 휴일 도서 반납은 수거함을 이용한다.
⑤ 도서 대출 시 도서관 카드가 필요하다.

[19~20] 대화를 듣고, 여자의 마지막 말에 이어질 남자의 말로 가장 적절한 것을 고르시오.

19 Man: _____
① You can count on me.
② What brings you here?
③ Blue is my favorite color.
④ I would like to, but I can't.
⑤ Okay. I will follow your advice.

20 Man: _____
① I think you had better not tell me the truth.
② Don't worry. I believe you will do your best.
③ I really want to get along with my teacher.
④ I should, but I'm afraid he'll think I'm lying.
⑤ I know that the teacher is always kind to us.

Listen and Check

정답 및 해설 *p.096*

● 대화를 다시 듣고, 알맞은 것을 고르시오.

1 Will strong winds blow to the south on Saturday?

☐ Yes   ☐ No

2 The man's dog is a small brown dog.

☐ True   ☐ False

3 The woman will bring a camera to take pictures.

☐ True   ☐ False

4 The man and the woman will watch a movie after they have dinner today.

☐ True   ☐ False

5 The man should visit the service center to repair the cleaner.

☐ True   ☐ False

6 Did the woman expect her school team to win the game?

☐ Yes   ☐ No

7 Is the woman interested in the man's Chinese friend?

☐ Yes   ☐ No

8 What does the woman want to exchange?

☐ a pair of jeans   ☐ a skirt

9 Will the woman learn swimming for her health?

☐ Yes   ☐ No

10 Where is the customer service center?

☐ next to the elevator on the ninth floor

☐ next to the women's restroom on the fifth floor

11 Do the animals go to sleep at 6:00 p.m.?

☐ Yes   ☐ No

12 The man can't go to the meeting because of his homework.

☐ True   ☐ False

13 Does the man pay 30 dollars for the meals?

☐ Yes   ☐ No

14 The high heels caused the woman's waist to hurt.

☐ True   ☐ False

15 Where should the man and the woman have lunch?

☐ at the restaurant in the gallery

☐ at a restaurant near the gallery

16 Will the man and the woman take a Korean history class together?

☐ Yes   ☐ No

17 The woman can't feed the animals.

☐ True   ☐ False

18 There are free children's classes on Mondays.

☐ True   ☐ False

19 Is the man interested in buying the same T-shirt as the woman's?

☐ Yes   ☐ No

20 The man hasn't done his homework because he forgot about it.

☐ True   ☐ False

그림 정보 파악

1 다음을 듣고, 일요일의 날씨로 가장 적절한 것을 고르시오.

① ② ③

④ ⑤

1

M Hello. This is the Arirang weather forecast. On Friday, _____ _____ _____ _____ _____ in Korea. We will have a cloudy day on Saturday, and strong winds will _____ _____ _____ _____. You can see clear skies again on Sunday. The weather on Sunday _____ _____ _____ _____ outdoor activities all day long. See you next week.

그림 정보 파악

2 대화를 듣고, 남자가 찾고 있는 개로 가장 적절한 것을 고르시오.

① ② ③

④ ⑤

2

[*Telephone rings.*]

W Pet shelter. What can I do for you?

M I've lost my dog. Have you seen a dog around here?

W Oh, yes. We just found a little dog.

M It may be my dog. _____ _____ _____ _____ _____ about the dog?

W Yes. It's a small corgi _____ _____ _____.

M Would you check her forehead? She has two small marks on her forehead.

W Right. I can see two small marks on her forehead.

M It must be mine. _____ _____ _____ _____ _____ to check it out.

심정 추론

3 대화를 듣고, 여자의 심정으로 가장 적절한 것을 고르시오.

① proud
② excited
③ nervous
④ satisfied
⑤ surprised

3

W Dad, look! It's snowing! Can we go outside?

M Sure, Ariana. But, _____ _____ _____ _____ gloves and a heavy coat. It's very cold.

W All right, Dad. It's the first snow of the year. I've waited for this for so long.

M _____ _____ _____ _____. Why don't we bring a camera to take pictures?

W That's a good idea. I can't wait to make a snowman.

M Are you ready to _____ _____ _____ _____?

W Absolutely, yes.

할 일 파악

4 대화를 듣고, 남자가 영화를 보기 위해서 할 일로 가장 적절한 것을 고르시오.

① 부모님께 외출 허락을 받기
② 식사를 하고 영화관에 가기
③ 영화관에 문의하여 항의하기
④ 내일 저녁 시간 영화를 예매하기
⑤ 다른 사람에게 영화표 예매를 부탁하기

4

W   Did you get our tickets?

M   I didn't tell you. _____ _____ _____ _____.

W   What is it?

M   I tried to buy tickets. But they were all sold out.

W   Really? We promised _____ _____ _____ this movie.

M   That's right. We have been waiting for this movie to come out.

W   Why don't we reserve two tickets for tomorrow evening first and then _____ _____ _____ _____ _____?

M   Sounds good. I'll do that.

장소 추론

5 대화를 듣고, 두 사람이 대화하는 장소로 가장 적절한 곳을 고르시오.

① 은행
② 우체국
③ 분실물 센터
④ 서비스 센터
⑤ 가전 판매점

5

W   Hello. May I help you?

M   This wireless cleaner _____ _____ _____. When I got it home, it didn't work.

W   Sorry, but you need to go to the service center to fix any technical problems, not here.

M   But _____ _____ _____ _____.

W   All repairs are done at the service center. We only sell the products. I'm sorry for _____ _____.

M   All right. How do I get there?

W   Just cross the street. _____ _____ _____ the post office.

의도 파악

6 대화를 듣고, 여자의 마지막 말의 의도로 가장 적절한 것을 고르시오.

① 동의
② 사과
③ 충고
④ 격려
⑤ 감사

6

W   Did you see the soccer game yesterday?

M   Yes. _____ _____ _____ _____.

W   It really was. I didn't expect our school to beat Jaeil Middle School's team. I am very proud of our team.

M   I think they deserved to win. _____ _____ _____ _____ _____.

W   Yes. I saw them practicing very hard as well.

M   I was so excited when our team scored the winning goal right before the end of the game. _____ _____ _____ _____ that moment.

W   You can say that again.

언급 유무 파악

7 대화를 듣고, 남자가 Chen에 대해 언급하지 <u>않은</u> 것을 고르시오.

① 부모님은 공무원이다.
② 테니스를 매우 좋아한다.
③ 피아노를 매우 잘 연주한다.
④ 베이징에서 태어나 자랐다.
⑤ 키가 크고 머리카락은 검은색이다.

7

M My Chinese friend Chen _____ _____ _____ _____ _____ tomorrow. Maybe you will like him.

W Really? Tell me about him.

M He is tall and has short black hair. His parents are civil servants in Beijing.

W Great. When he comes, how about playing soccer with him?

M I don't think he will say yes. He _____ _____ _____, _____ _____ _____.

W Is there anything else you want to talk about him?

M He is _____ _____ _____ because he has played the piano for 8 years.

W Now I am really interested in him.

할 일 파악

8 대화를 듣고, 두 사람이 대화 직후에 할 일로 가장 적절한 것을 고르시오.

① 환전하기
② 옷가게 가기
③ 점심 식사하기
④ 몸무게 재기
⑤ 청바지 입어 보기

♥ **So am I.**
: '나도 역시 그래.'라는 의미로 앞 문장이 긍정을 나타내거나 앞 문장의 동사가 'be동사'일 때 쓰인다.

8 🇬🇧

W Do you want to go to the mall?

M Sure. I'd like to buy a pair of jeans. _____ _____ _____ _____ _____ _____?

W I need to exchange a skirt for one that's a bigger size. I think I have gained a little weight these days. _____ _____ _____, did you have lunch?

M No, I didn't. What about you? I'm getting hungry.

W ♥ So am I.

M Then _____ _____ _____ _____ _____? After that, we can go to the shop.

W Okay.

언급 유무 파악

9 다음을 듣고, 여자가 새해 결심으로 언급하지 <u>않은</u> 것을 고르시오.

① 매일 영어 일기 쓰기
② 수영 배우기
③ 스페인어 회화 배우기
④ 날마다 건강 체크하기
⑤ 하루 100회 팔 굽혀 펴기 하기

9

W Next year is just _____ _____ _____. Here are my New Year's resolutions. First, I hope to master basic Spanish. In order to do this, I am going to buy a book for Spanish conversation. Second, I've decided to do 100 push-ups a day. And I'll _____ _____ _____ _____ _____ _____. Lastly, I want to keep an English diary every day. I know all of these will be difficult for me. But I will do my best to keep _____ _____ _____ to myself.

10 다음을 듣고, 여자가 하는 말의 내용으로 가장 적절한 것을 고르시오.

① 분실물 습득 안내
② 고객 서비스 소개
③ 엘리베이터 사용법
④ 화장실의 위치 설명
⑤ 귀중품의 보관 요령

10 🇬🇧

W May I have your attention, please? This is an announcement for _____ _____ _____. We found a scarf in the women's restroom on the fifth floor. If anyone lost a silk scarf, please come to the customer service center. It is next to the elevator _____ _____ _____ _____. Again, we have an item that was found in the restroom on the fifth floor. It's a red silk scarf. Please come _____ _____ _____ _____ _____. Thank you.

---

11 다음을 듣고, 남자가 언급한 내용과 일치하지 <u>않는</u> 것을 고르시오.

① 아침 5시에 일어난다.
② 직업은 동물 조련사이다.
③ Oriental 동물원 소속이다.
④ 매일 동물들의 수를 확인한다.
⑤ 동물 훈련에 매일 4시간을 보낸다.

♥ **make sure ~**
: 뒤에 나오는 이야기를 확실히 하거나 다짐을 할 때 사용되며 '확실히 하다', '보장하다' 정도의 의미로 해석된다.

11

M Hello, animal lovers. I'm Harry Smith, and I'm an animal trainer. This is the Oriental Zoo, and I appreciate _____ _____ _____. My first job every day is to get up at five in the morning. I have to feed the animals their breakfast at around six o'clock. After that, I visit all of the animals and check whether they're _____ _____ _____ _____ _____. In the afternoon, I spend about four hours training the animals. The zoo closes at 6 in the evening, and I check up on the animals. Then, I ♥make sure they go into their cages for the night. Have a good time here and _____ _____ _____ _____.

---

12 대화를 듣고, 남자가 전화를 건 목적으로 가장 적절한 것을 고르시오.

① 계획을 수정하기 위해서
② 모임 약속에 갈 수가 없어서
③ 여자와 숙제를 상의하기 위해서
④ 모임의 목적을 설명하기 위해서
⑤ 여자의 메시지를 전달하기 위해서

12 🇬🇧

[*Telephone rings*.]

M Hello. May I speak to Soyoung?

W I'm sorry, but _____ _____ _____ _____. Who is speaking?

M This is Kiwoo. Can I *leave a message then?

W Sure.

M Please tell her that _____ _____ _____ _____ _____ _____.

W Oh, that's too bad. What is the reason?

M The reason is that I have lots of homework to do.

W Okay. I'll tell Soyoung _____ _____ _____.

*leave a [리브] [어] → [리버]

13 대화를 듣고, 남자가 거스름돈으로 받을 금액을 고르시오.

① $17
② $27
③ $30
④ $37
⑤ $47

13

W ＿＿＿＿＿ ＿＿＿＿＿ ＿＿＿＿＿ ＿＿＿＿＿ ＿＿＿＿＿, sir?

M No, thanks. Just bring me the check, please.

W *Wait a moment, please. Here you are.

M Wait. ＿＿＿＿＿ ＿＿＿＿＿ ＿＿＿＿＿ ＿＿＿＿＿ ＿＿＿＿＿ thirty-three dollars. I thought the price of my meal is thirty dollars. Am I wrong?

W You are right. But thirty dollars is for the meals, and we charge you ＿＿＿＿＿ ＿＿＿＿＿ ＿＿＿＿＿ ＿＿＿＿＿ ＿＿＿＿＿ of the meal for tax.

M Oh, I see. Here is a fifty-dollar bill.

*wait a [웨이트] [어] → [웨이러]

14 대화를 듣고, 두 사람의 관계로 가장 적절한 것을 고르시오.

① 의사 – 환자
② 선생님 – 학생
③ 상사 – 부하 직원
④ 가게 점원 – 손님
⑤ 치료사 – 간호원

14

M Please come in. ＿＿＿＿＿ ＿＿＿＿＿ ＿＿＿＿＿ ＿＿＿＿＿ the problem?

W My waist hurts. I can't sleep at night because of the pain.

M How long ＿＿＿＿＿ ＿＿＿＿＿ ＿＿＿＿＿ this problem?

W For five days. I have trouble walking now.

M Do you often wear high heels?

W Yes. I always wear them.

M That's the problem. I think ＿＿＿＿＿ ＿＿＿＿＿ ＿＿＿＿＿ ＿＿＿＿＿ ＿＿＿＿＿. And you need to get therapy on your waist for several days.

15 대화를 듣고 남자가 여자에게 부탁한 일로 가장 적절한 것을 고르시오.

① 식당 예약하기
② 식사 장소 찾기
③ 조사원 모집하기
④ 교통수단 선택하기
⑤ 전시 일정 알아보기

15 🇬🇧

W Andrew, ＿＿＿＿＿ ＿＿＿＿＿ ＿＿＿＿＿ go to the Modern Art Gallery for our field research?

M Good. How long does it take to get there from the school?

W It takes ＿＿＿＿＿ ＿＿＿＿＿ ＿＿＿＿＿ ＿＿＿＿＿ ＿＿＿＿＿.

M Can we have lunch there?

W Well, I don't think so. Maybe we need to find a place to eat.

M ＿＿＿＿＿ ＿＿＿＿＿ ＿＿＿＿＿ a good restaurant when we arrive there?

W Of course. Don't worry.

16 대화를 듣고, 남자가 역사 수업을
듣지 <u>않는</u> 이유로 가장 적절한 것을
고르시오.

① 한국에 관심이 없어서
② 이미 역사 수업을 들어서
③ 여름에 다른 계획이 있어서
④ 혼자 수업 듣는 것을 선호해서
⑤ 학교가 집에서부터 멀리 있어서

16

M Hi, Clara. Why are you looking at the notice so seriously?

W What do you think of this Korean history class?

M I heard that the history teacher is nice and _____ _____ _____.

W That's great. Why don't we take this class this summer?

M Sorry, but I don't need to take a history class _____ _____ _____ _____ last year.

W Well, then I'll take this one alone. Let's look for _____ _____ _____ _____ _____.

M Sounds great.

---

17 다음 그림 상황에 가장 적절한 대화를
고르시오.

①　②　③　④　⑤

17

① **W** What do you think of that sign?

  M It _____ _____ _____.

② **W** _____ _____ _____ _____ over there.

  M What a green field it is!

③ **W** Excuse me. Did I _____ _____ _____?

  M Yes. You can't feed the animals here.

④ **W** I am sorry to keep you _____ _____ _____.

  M That's okay. Can I ask a question?

⑤ **W** May I _____ _____ _____ _____ in the park?

  M Of course.

---

18 다음을 듣고, 여자가 중앙 공공 도서관
이용에 대해 언급하지 <u>않은</u> 것을
고르시오.

① 매주 월요일에 도서관은 쉰다.
② 아침 9시부터 저녁 7시까지 개장한
　다.
③ 목요일 아침마다 요가 수업이 있다.
④ 휴일 도서 반납은 수거함을 이용한
　다.
⑤ 도서 대출시 도서관 카드가 필요하
　다.

18

W Welcome to the Central Public Library. _____ _____ _____ from 9:00 a.m. to 7:00 p.m. We are closed every Monday. There are free children's classes from 10:00 to 11:00 a.m. on Thursdays. If _____ _____ _____ _____ _____, make sure to bring your library card. You can check out our books for two weeks. When you return books during a holiday, please _____ _____ _____ _____ _____ _____. It is *next to the front door. Thank you.

*next to [넥쓰트] [투] → [넥쓰투]

적절한 응답 찾기

[19–20] 대화를 듣고, 여자의 마지막 말에 이어질 남자의 말로 가장 적절한 것을 고르시오.

19 Man: _____

① You can count on me.
② What brings you here?
③ Blue is my favorite color.
④ I would like to, but I can't.
⑤ Okay. I will follow your advice.

19

W   Hi, Steve. _____ _____ _____ _____ today?

M   Wow. You look really different.

W   I just bought a brand-new T-shirt. It is very _____ _____ _____.

M   I know. I am thinking of buying one, too.

W   _____ _____. So we will be a fashionable couple.

M   Do you want me to do that? Okay. You got a red one, so I will buy _____ _____ _____ _____ _____.

W   Wait. Red is good. But I think you had better *get a different color.

M   <u>Okay. I will follow your advice.</u>

*get a [겟] [어] → [게러]

적절한 응답 찾기

20 Man: _____

① I think you had better not tell me the truth.
② Don't worry. I believe you will do your best.
③ I really want to get along with my teacher.
④ I should, but I'm afraid he'll think I'm lying.
⑤ I know that the teacher is always kind to us.

20

W   You look down. Did you do something wrong?

M   I haven't finished my homework. It's an important report, so I need to _____ _____ _____ _____ on it.

W   You mean the science report, right?

M   Yes. The problem is that _____ _____ _____.

W   So how come you haven't done that important homework?

M   Actually, I have been sick lately, so I have had to stay in bed.

W   I see. Why don't you tell your teacher _____ _____ _____?

M   <u>I should, but I'm afraid he'll think I'm lying.</u>

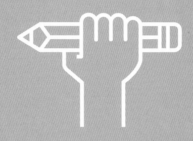

Vocabulary Test

A 들려주는 단어를 듣고 쓴 뒤, 괄호 안에 우리말 뜻을 쓰시오.

	영어	우리말			영어	우리말
1			6			
2			7			
3			8			
4			9			
5			10			

B 다음 문장을 잘 듣고 빈칸에 들어갈 단어를 채우시오.

1 I've learned it _____ _____ _____ little.

2 _____ _____ _____ the desserts there?

3 What hobby do you think is _____ _____ _____?

4 But please let me know even if it's _____ _____ _____.

5 Finally, please _____ _____ _____ _____ before you leave.

6 It's easy to _____ _____ _____ _____ on the Internet.

7 I left my bag when I _____ _____ _____ _____ last night.

8 They _____ _____ _____ and get ready for a debate.

9 Where are you _____ _____ _____ your experiment?

10 We _____ _____ _____ and had a birthday party for my little brother.

A   들려주는 단어를 듣고 쓴 뒤, 괄호 안에 우리말 뜻을 쓰시오.

	영어	우리말			영어	우리말
1				6		
2				7		
3				8		
4				9		
5				10		

B   다음 문장을 잘 듣고 빈칸에 들어갈 단어를 채우시오.

1   We can expect clear skies starting _____ ____ ____ _____ _____ _____.

2   You were _____ _____ _____ _____ in the snow.

3   So did you _____ _____ _____ _____ _____ to report it?

4   There were _____ _____ _____ _____ such as musicals and dance performances.

5   All the money we get from you will _____ _____ _____ the children in need.

6   _____ _____ _____ _____ the most famous doctors in the world.

7   Tell her that _____ _____ _____ _____ _____ in the morning.

8   Do you want _____ _____ _____ _____ _____ for you?

9   Please _____ _____ to _____ _____ our food and to see how it tastes.

10   At the time, _____ _____ _____ _____ _____ other places.

정답 및 해설 *p.097*

A 들려주는 단어를 듣고 쓴 뒤, 괄호 안에 우리말 뜻을 쓰시오.

	영어	우리말			영어	우리말
1				6		
2				7		
3				8		
4				9		
5				10		

B 다음 문장을 잘 듣고 빈칸에 들어갈 단어를 채우시오.

1 Okay. Let's _____ _____.

2 I'm a(n) _____ _____ _____ yours.

3 Look at me and do _____ _____ _____.

4 This plant grows well _____ _____.

5 I'm sorry. I thought _____ _____ _____.

6 It has a longer history _____ _____ _____.

7 How long do I _____ _____ _____ for the train?

8 His paintings are _____ _____ _____ and emotions.

9 There are so many people _____ _____ _____ _____.

10 I have to _____ and _____ _____ _____ on a leash every day.

A 들려주는 단어를 듣고 쓴 뒤, 괄호 안에 우리말 뜻을 쓰시오.

	영어	우리말			영어	우리말
1				6		
2				7		
3				8		
4				9		
5				10		

B 다음 문장을 잘 듣고 빈칸에 들어갈 단어를 채우시오.

1 I want to buy one that is _____ _____ _____.

2 I _____ _____ _____ _____ before the drugstore closes.

3 I think that _____ _____ is very important.

4 Someday, I want to be _____ _____ _____ like you.

5 You were supposed to return them _____ _____ _____.

6 How about _____ _____ _____ a field trip this semester?

7 I wrote them _____ _____ _____ _____ on the answer sheet.

8 I feel great today because _____ _____ _____ _____ _____.

9 I agree with you, but you must _____ _____ _____ _____.

10 Our regular meetings _____ _____ _____ every Thursday during lunchtime.

A 들려주는 단어를 듣고 쓴 뒤, 괄호 안에 우리말 뜻을 쓰시오.

	영어	우리말			영어	우리말
1				6		
2				7		
3				8		
4				9		
5				10		

B 다음 문장을 잘 듣고 빈칸에 들어갈 단어를 채우시오.

1 I _____ _____ _____ at school.

2 I will _____ _____ _____ _____ this time.

3 I should _____ _____ _____.

4 They are _____ _____ _____.

5 I need both _____ _____ _____ _____.

6 How long _____ _____ _____ your cellphone?

7 How should we _____ _____ _____ _____ people?

8 I like to _____ _____ _____ _____ _____.

9 How do you know _____ _____ _____ _____ _____ good for you?

10 If you _____ _____ _____, you can get fifty percent off.

A 들려주는 단어를 듣고 쓴 뒤, 괄호 안에 우리말 뜻을 쓰시오.

	영어	우리말		영어	우리말
1			6		
2			7		
3			8		
4			9		
5			10		

B 다음 문장을 잘 듣고 빈칸에 들어갈 단어를 채우시오.

1 You still have five days _____ _____ _____ _____.

2 I _____ _____ _____ _____ with my friends.

3 By the way, how about _____ _____ _____ _____?

4 It'll be _____ _____ _____ _____ at night.

5 I am sure we are _____ _____ _____ home.

6 It's _____ _____ _____ from here.

7 Let's meet _____ _____ _____ _____ _____ _____ at one thirty.

8 I think you'd better _____ _____ _____ relaxed about the contest.

9 If you have one, you can buy books _____ _____ _____.

10 You have to _____ _____ _____ your books and notebooks on your desk.

A 들려주는 단어를 듣고 쓴 뒤, 괄호 안에 우리말 뜻을 쓰시오.

	영어	우리말		영어	우리말
1			6		
2			7		
3			8		
4			9		
5			10		

B 다음 문장을 잘 듣고 빈칸에 들어갈 단어를 채우시오.

1 How much is it _____ _____?

2 I will _____ _____ _____ at five.

3 You _____ _____ _____ _____ today.

4 I'll _____ _____ your dog.

5 Hey, you _____ _____ _____ here.

6 It will _____ _____ _____ _____ the photos.

7 I just _____ _____ _____ on the ground.

8 I'm thinking of _____ _____ _____ a bit.

9 Do you _____ _____ _____ _____ some groceries?

10 But I _____ _____ _____ _____ in math this semester.

A 들려주는 단어를 듣고 쓴 뒤, 괄호 안에 우리말 뜻을 쓰시오.

	영어	우리말		영어	우리말
1			6		
2			7		
3			8		
4			9		
5			10		

B 다음 문장을 잘 듣고 빈칸에 들어갈 단어를 채우시오.

1 Don't ever _____ _____ in the bottles.

2 It takes only thirty minutes _____ _____ _____ _____ _____.

3 Do you think _____ _____ _____ _____ in twenty minutes?

4 I think he is _____ _____ _____ play with that.

5 They _____ _____ _____ _____ students at the end of the event.

6 The temperature _____ _____ _____ next week and get colder.

7 I am afraid I will _____ _____ _____ in front of the interviewers.

8 It helps _____ _____ _____ _____, and it is also good for digestion.

9 Advertisements can make people buy things _____ _____ _____ _____.

10 I never thought _____ _____ _____ _____ for me to work on a project with Cathy.

A 들려주는 단어를 듣고 쓴 뒤, 괄호 안에 우리말 뜻을 쓰시오.

	영어	우리말			영어	우리말
1				6		
2				7		
3				8		
4				9		
5				10		

B 다음 문장을 잘 듣고 빈칸에 들어갈 단어를 채우시오.

1 _____ _____ _____ guides in life.

2 I _____ _____ _____ _____ their cages.

3 Regular exercise _____ _____ _____.

4 I can draw and _____ _____ _____ anywhere I go.

5 It sounds like you _____ _____ _____ _____ to do.

6 That _____ _____ _____ _____ event in my life.

7 I'm going to miss my _____ _____ _____ so much.

8 _____ _____ _____ _____ a hand with the preparations for my bazaar?

9 Because _____ _____ _____ _____ full, we should wait for the next one.

10 You can get a stomachache if you take it _____ _____ _____ _____.

A 들려주는 단어를 듣고 쓴 뒤, 괄호 안에 우리말 뜻을 쓰시오.

	영어	우리말			영어	우리말
1			6			
2			7			
3			8			
4			9			
5			10			

B 다음 문장을 잘 듣고 빈칸에 들어갈 단어를 채우시오.

1 I can't believe _____ _____ _____ _____ in Japan.

2 They are trying to teach me _____ _____ _____ _____ .

3 How about this one _____ _____ _____ in the middle?

4 We often feel _____ _____ on our studies and jobs.

5 I have a(n) _____ _____ World War II tomorrow.

6 I will _____ _____ _____ _____ after dinner starting tomorrow.

7 We'll leave our school for the stadium _____ _____ one thirty.

8 I am not sure that we have _____ _____ _____ _____ at the shops.

9 I'll call your mother and tell her _____ _____ _____ _____ early today.

10 Some students _____ _____ _____ memorizing by using charts and flashcards.

A 들려주는 단어를 듣고 쓴 뒤, 괄호 안에 우리말 뜻을 쓰시오.

	영어	우리말		영어	우리말
1			6		
2			7		
3			8		
4			9		
5			10		

B 다음 문장을 잘 듣고 빈칸에 들어갈 단어를 채우시오.

1   I'm sure _____ _____ _____ _____.

2   I want to _____ _____ for 3 days.

3   Write down _____ _____ _____ _____ on the paper.

4   I'm going to _____ _____ _____ _____ for you.

5   Did you come back _____ _____ _____?

6   You are good at _____ _____, right?

7   It was the _____ _____ I've seen _____ _____.

8   All I want is that _____ _____ my name.

9   The baby is _____ _____ _____ _____ an object from the table.

10   Walking barefoot _____ _____ _____ through the body.

A 들려주는 단어를 듣고 쓴 뒤, 괄호 안에 우리말 뜻을 쓰시오.

	영어	우리말			영어	우리말
1				6		
2				7		
3				8		
4				9		
5				10		

B 다음 문장을 잘 듣고 빈칸에 들어갈 단어를 채우시오.

1 I will pick up _____ _____ _____ books.

2 I'll _____ _____ _____ in size 275.

3 When is _____ _____ _____ to go to see him?

4 Why don't you _____ _____ _____ _____ tomorrow's showing?

5 I was always careful not to _____ _____ _____ my friends.

6 I'd like to make a square _____ _____ _____ _____ in the middle of it.

7 The first is the city museum, where you can _____ _____ _____ _____.

8 _____ _____ _____ weather do you like?

9 Anyone _____ _____ _____ _____ the play will be admitted only during break time.

10 _____ _____ _____ moving over one seat so that my wife and I can sit together?

A 들려주는 단어를 듣고 쓴 뒤, 괄호 안에 우리말 뜻을 쓰시오.

	영어	우리말		영어	우리말
1			6		
2			7		
3			8		
4			9		
5			10		

B 다음 문장을 잘 듣고 빈칸에 들어갈 단어를 채우시오.

1 They both like _____ _____ _____.

2 How long _____ _____ _____ _____ my turn?

3 I wanted to _____ _____ _____ _____ myself.

4 I didn't _____ _____ _____ _____ so early.

5 I keep making _____ _____ _____ over again.

6 We can _____ _____ _____ _____ by a jazz band.

7 It's _____ _____ _____ for one week.

8 I see you _____ _____ _____ _____ work experience in this field.

9 _____ _____ _____ how the present society came to exist.

10 _____ _____ _____ from Paris are bestselling items.

A 들려주는 단어를 듣고 쓴 뒤, 괄호 안에 우리말 뜻을 쓰시오.

	영어	우리말		영어	우리말
1			6		
2			7		
3			8		
4			9		
5			10		

B 다음 문장을 잘 듣고 빈칸에 들어갈 단어를 채우시오.

1 You are _____ _____ _____ _____ here.

2 I can't even decide _____ _____ _____ _____.

3 Yeah, it was good _____ _____ _____ _____.

4 Because I lost my passport, I _____ _____ _____ _____.

5 I bought some _____ _____ _____ my room.

6 I'm sorry I can't _____ _____ _____ _____ _____ tonight.

7 You promised me that you'd _____ _____ _____.

8 Did you _____ _____ _____ _____ on your desk?

9 When you _____ _____ _____ _____, you should be careful.

10 _____ can have _____ _____ in different cultures.

A 들려주는 단어를 듣고 쓴 뒤, 괄호 안에 우리말 뜻을 쓰시오.

	영어	우리말			영어	우리말
1				6		
2				7		
3				8		
4				9		
5				10		

B 다음 문장을 잘 듣고 빈칸에 들어갈 단어를 채우시오.

1 Please _____ _____ in color.

2 With this credit card, _____ _____ _____ is free.

3 I made it _____ _____ _____ _____ _____.

4 I _____ _____ _____ _____ my brother.

5 A sauna can _____ _____ _____ _____.

6 Do you _____ _____ _____ _____?

7 _____ _____ _____ _____ in one of your pockets.

8 You should _____ _____ _____ regularly.

9 It will be _____ _____ _____ _____ in the storm.

10 I found my car damaged in _____ _____ _____ _____.

A 들려주는 단어를 듣고 쓴 뒤, 괄호 안에 우리말 뜻을 쓰시오.

	영어	우리말			영어	우리말
1			6			
2			7			
3			8			
4			9			
5			10			

B 다음 문장을 잘 듣고 빈칸에 들어갈 단어를 채우시오.

1 What will _____ _____ _____ _____ in summer?

2 Please stay with me _____ _____ _____ _____ _____ .

3 I think you _____ _____ _____ the store and ask.

4 I heard that it's _____ _____ _____ _____ tomorrow.

5 I _____ _____ _____ _____ you on screen soon.

6 I _____ _____ _____ the trash for recycling.

7 You talked about it when _____ _____ _____ _____ the other day.

8 Before you come here, please decide _____ _____ _____ _____ to experience.

9 Cloudy weather will continue until Wednesday, and we _____ _____ _____ that night.

10 She had a(n) _____ _____ _____ in Busan, and she stayed there for one night.

A 들려주는 단어를 듣고 쓴 뒤, 괄호 안에 우리말 뜻을 쓰시오.

	영어	우리말		영어	우리말
1			6		
2			7		
3			8		
4			9		
5			10		

B 다음 문장을 잘 듣고 빈칸에 들어갈 단어를 채우시오.

1 _____ _____ _____ _____ never easy.

2 _____ _____ _____ the fourteenth of July.

3 They are different _____ _____ _____ _____.

4 I like circular ones _____ _____ _____ _____.

5 It's true that _____ _____ _____ more productive.

6 That book has _____ _____ _____ of paintings.

7 I think _____ _____ _____ _____ to propose to her.

8 I was at _____ _____ _____ taking _____ _____.

9 I recommend that you buy _____ _____ _____ _____.

10 I'll buy three _____ _____ _____ one basket of carnations.

A 들려주는 단어를 듣고 쓴 뒤, 괄호 안에 우리말 뜻을 쓰시오.

	영어	우리말			영어	우리말
1				6		
2				7		
3				8		
4				9		
5				10		

B 다음 문장을 잘 듣고 빈칸에 들어갈 단어를 채우시오.

1   I'm _____ _____ _____.

2   But we've already _____ _____ _____ _____.

3   _____ _____ _____ _____ you need?

4   Sounds like a(n) _____ _____ _____.

5   We have to _____ _____ _____ _____ _____.

6   It will _____ _____ _____ _____ _____ from May 11 to 15.

7   Let me _____ _____ _____ _____ _____.

8   Take your time and _____ _____ _____ _____ _____.

9   I love to _____ _____ _____ _____.

10   Starting on Wednesday, it will be _____ _____ _____ _____.

A 들려주는 단어를 듣고 쓴 뒤, 괄호 안에 우리말 뜻을 쓰시오.

	영어	우리말			영어	우리말
1			6			
2			7			
3			8			
4			9			
5			10			

B 다음 문장을 잘 듣고 빈칸에 들어갈 단어를 채우시오.

1 I _____ _____ _____ _____.

2 I _____ _____ _____ _____.

3 You can easily _____ _____ _____ water.

4 I accidentally _____ _____ _____ the water.

5 Taking notes _____ _____ _____ creative.

6 So you _____ _____ _____ _____, don't you?

7 I feel scared when I _____ _____ _____ _____ alone.

8 Do you want to _____ _____ _____ _____ larger size?

9 Do you want me to _____ _____ _____ _____ you over there?

10 This weekend will be all about _____ _____ _____.

A 들려주는 단어를 듣고 쓴 뒤, 괄호 안에 우리말 뜻을 쓰시오.

	영어	우리말		영어	우리말
1			6		
2			7		
3			8		
4			9		
5			10		

B 다음 문장을 잘 듣고 빈칸에 들어갈 단어를 채우시오.

1 We _____ _____ _____ _____ this movie to come out.

2 I _____ _____ _____ _____ _____ their cages for the night.

3 I will _____ _____ _____ _____ _____ what I promise to myself.

4 How _____ _____ _____ _____ to get there from the school?

5 You need to get therapy on _____ _____ _____ _____ _____ .

6 I need to _____ _____ _____ for one that's a bigger size.

7 I didn't _____ _____ _____ _____ _____ Jaeil Middle School's team.

8 Actually, I have been sick lately, so I _____ _____ _____ _____ in bed.

9 The weather on Sunday will be perfect for _____ _____ _____ _____ _____ .

10 When you return books during a holiday, please _____ _____ _____ the drop box.

MEMO

MEMO

MEMO